The Best of Maine Railroads

by Ron Johnson

Printed by
Portland Litho

28 Smith Street
South Portland, ME 04106

Introduction

Maine railroading has been and continues to be as interesting and varied as any state in the country. It is the purpose of this book to provide a concise history plus the best pictures that could be located, many of which have never been published. The text is taken from a book long out of print called *Maine Railroads* by Edward E. Chase. Published in 1926 with a very limited press run, the book quickly became a collector's item. The original work had no pictures, maps or timetables, something this book seeks to remedy. Through the *Maine Railroad Time Line,* the last section in this book, rail history has been brought up to date. The focus of this book is on main line and connecting shortline rail service. The ocean and lake steamers, buses, hotels and airlines owned by the railroads plus street railways, industrial and logging lines are of too broad a scope to be included in this effort. It is hoped the reader will find this work a useful research reference, plus pleasing to the eye.

Ron Johnson September, 1985

Acknowledgements

I would like to thank Richard Dole, foremost historian on Maine railroads, who went over the original text from Edward Chase's book and made a number of additions and corrections along with photo contributions. Other persons who shared pictures and rail mementos include: Robert Baker, the Beverley Historical Society, Forest Bunker, C.B. Cobb, Carol Dinsmore, Francis Donahue, Preston Johnson, Howard Kirkpatrick, Jim McFarlane, Howard Moulton, Henry Preble, Edwin B. Robertson, Richard Sanborn, Sullivan Cameracraft, Ray Tobey, Richard White and the 470 Railroad Club.

[FRONT COVER:] **Maine Central Pacific 470 charges up the Waldoboro grade with a Westbound passenger train out of Rockland in September 1950.** *Ron Johnson collection*

[INSIDE FRONT COVER:] **On a frosty January 30, 1946 eastbound Maine Central Train 1 dashes across the Fairfield-Benton trestle spanning the Kennebec River.** *470 Railroad Club collection*

[PAGE 1:] **Maine Central 2-8-2 604 and 2-8-0 501 accelerate a freight train east out of Waterville over the Lower Road on October 29, 1949.** *Robert Baker*

[PAGE 3:] **Boston & Maine 2-8-2 3001 with a Maine Central freight extra west glides around a curve onto the Fore River bridge as seen from Tower 3 in Portland in the winter of 1945.** *Henry Preble*

[INSIDE BACK COVER:] **A westbound CP freight snakes around Boarstone Mountain at Onawa on August 22, 1959.** *Russell Monroe*

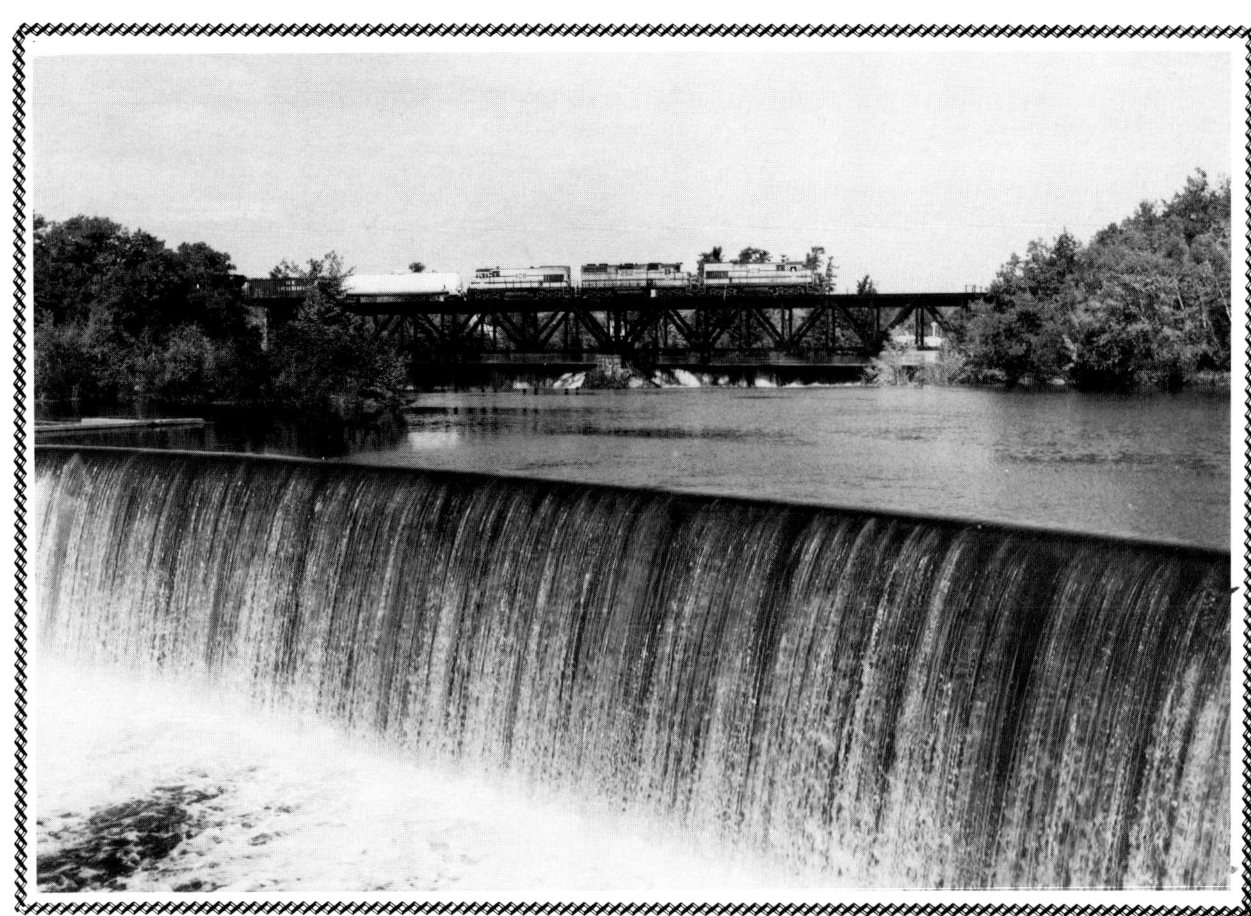

Train RB-1 (Rigby-Bangor) crosses the tumbling waters of the Androscoggin River into Lewiston on October 10, 1977 with two U18B's and a GP38 in the lead. *Ron Johnson*

Contents

Chapter		Page
One	General Veazie and the Early Lines	5
Two	John A. Poor and the Atlantic & St. Lawrence	9
Three	War of the Gauges	15
Four	John A. Poor and the European & North American More Power Plays	21
Five	Androscoggin Railroad's Broad Gauge Difficulties	25
Six	Maine Central Organized	29
Seven	European & North American Completed Building Out of Portland	31
Eight	Knox & Lincoln to Rockland Somerset Up the Kennebec Valley	41
Nine	Final Change to Standard Gauge Maine Central Dominated By the Eastern	51
Ten	Maine Central Grows to Largest Mileage in New England	55
Eleven	Bangor & Aroostook Begins Building Portland & Ogdensburg Leased to Maine Central	59
Twelve	Laying Rails Through Washington County Narrow Gauge Fever	67
Thirteen	Restoring the Maine Central to Maine People	89
Fourteen	Rails Fan Out Through Aroostook County	97
	Maine Railroad Time Line	111

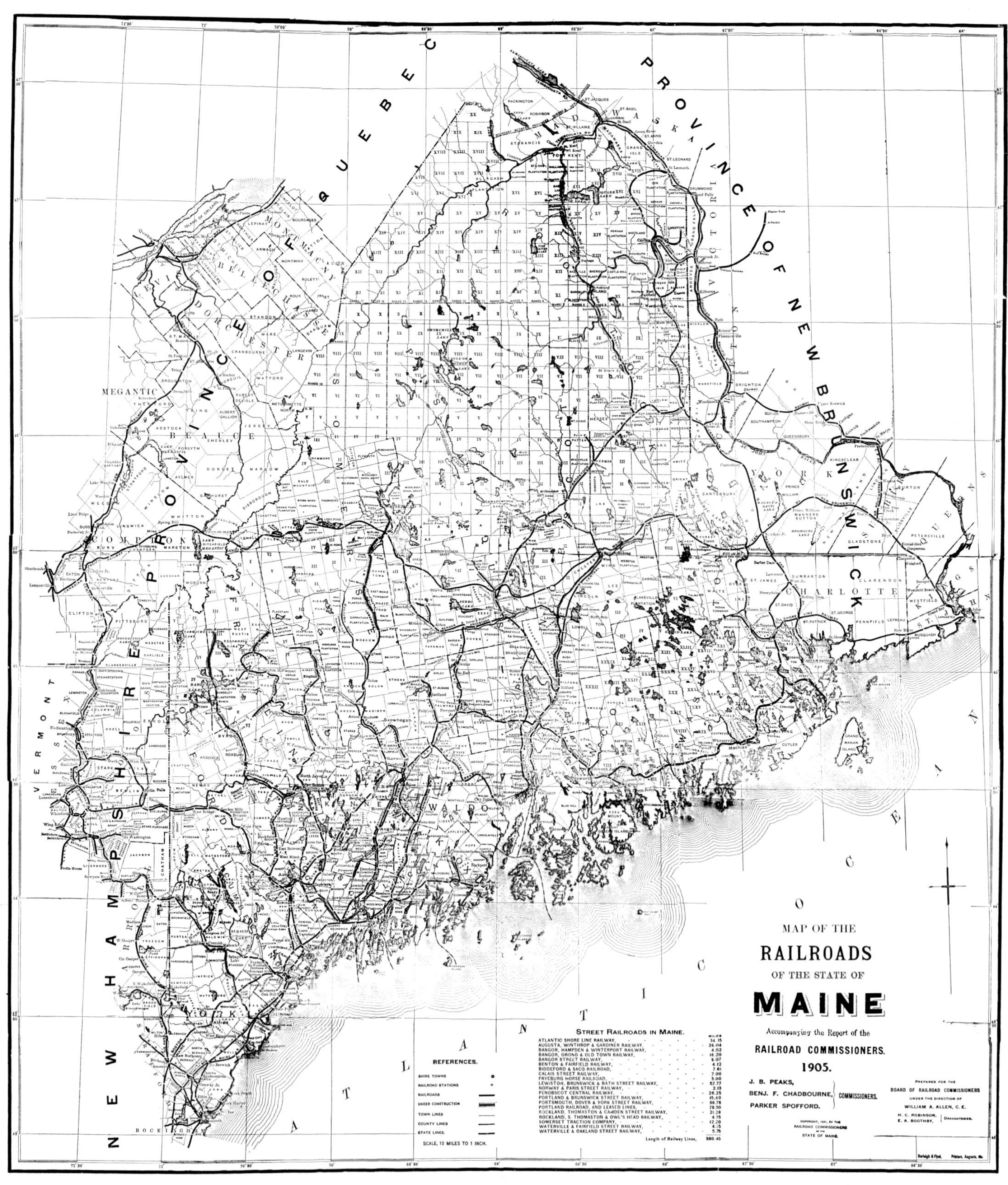

See map enlargements on pages 16, 17, 36, and 101.

Chapter One

General Veazie and the Early Lines

Railroad building came to Maine in 1832 when two railroad charters were granted. One was to the Calais Railway Company, chartered on February 17. It was superseded by the Calais Railroad Company on February 22, 1838. This two-mile long line operated with horses between Calais and Milltown. After being deemed unprofitable it was abandoned in 1841 and finally sold to the Calais & Baring Railroad Company in 1848. The other charter was granted to the Bangor & Old Town Railway Company on March 8, 1832 for the construction of the first steam railroad in Maine between Bangor and Old Town. The Bangor & Old Town Railway Company graded a portion of its right of way and built piers for bridges. In 1835 the franchise was sold to the Bangor & Piscataquis Canal and Railroad Company, which was a rival enterprise chartered in 1833 to build a road from Bangor via Old Town to the slate quarries around Williamsburg in Piscataquis County; and this company in 1836 completed the road from Bangor to Old Town. This enterprise was promoted by Edward and Samuel Smith of Bangor. Since the Smiths could not obtain enough funds to build, the local sawmill owners arranged to have the Boston & Worcester Railroad furnish funds and operate the line. The railroad ran by way of Upper Stillwater and came into Bangor along Harlow and Exchange Streets to the wharves. The track was laid with wooden rails with a three-eighths inch strap rail on top, later expanded to half-inch and finally replaced with No. 36 iron rails in 1849. The first engine, *Pioneer,* was bought secondhand from the Boston & Worcester in 1835. It was built by Stephenson in 1832. The second engine, *Bangor,* was bought new from Rothwell Works in England in 1836. Both locomotives were 2-2-0 type. In August 1853, General Samuel Veazie bought two-thirds of the stock and was elected president on August 3, 1854. He changed the name to the Bangor, Old Town & Milford Railroad in 1855. General Veazie was one of the largest lumber operators on Penobscot waters. He operated the road until his death in 1868. General Veazie built a railroad bridge at Milford and contemplated an extension of the road up the river. In 1870 the road was purchased from the Veazie heirs by the European & North American Railway, and was discontinued.

The superlatives affected by certain writers on Maine history have created the impression that Maine was a pioneer in railroad construction. As a

Maine's first steam locomotive "Pioneer" ran on the Bangor & Piscataquis Canal and Railroad Co. It was built by Robert Stephenson Co. in England in 1832. *Richard F. Dole collection*

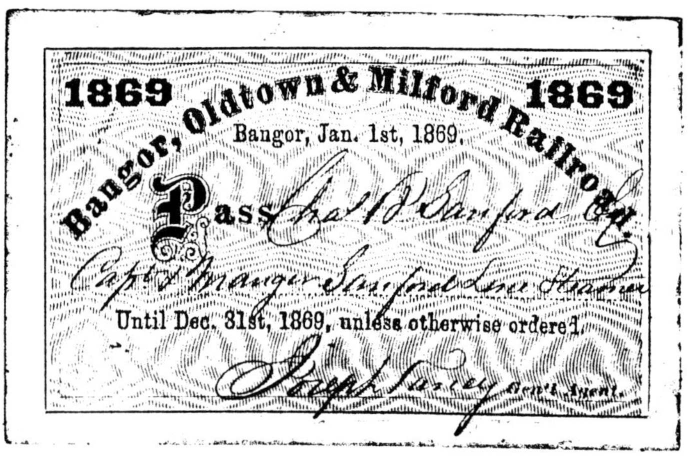

1869 Bangor, Oldtown & Milford Railroad 1869

Bangor, Jan. 1st, 1869,

Pass

Until Dec. 31st, 1869, unless otherwise ordered.

Gen'l. Agent.

Jim McFarlane collection

matter of fact, with the exception of the unimportant and isolated roads mentioned, there was no important railroad construction in Maine prior to 1840; and it was even five years later before Maine people were alive to the necessity of railroad transportation. There were a few leaders, however, who by their influence gradually persuaded the minds of many to the necessity of railroad transportation. This led to a rail building boom so that by 1870 there was a total of 772.63 rail miles. This increased to 1322.45 miles in 1889. The height of rail miles came in 1924 with a total of 2379.39. Afterwards it decreased until in 1981 rail miles amounted to 1681.64. The reduction came about due to mergers, abandonments, greater use of automobiles and depressions.

To explore the railroad potential in 1835 the State House of Representatives resolved that the governor be authorized to appoint and send two men to Quebec to start a survey of a railroad to the Maine border. This was done and a report was issued in August 1835 and printed January 7, 1836. As a result the legislature hired Lt. Col. S.H. Long to make a preliminary survey from Belfast, Maine to Quebec. This was dated on December 10, 1836 and printed January 9, 1837. The Belfast project actually attained some dignity and standing. In 1836 a Maine charter was granted to the Belfast & Quebec Railroad, and the Canadian Parliament granted a charter to a Canadian company to build a railroad from Quebec to the Maine state line. It was not organized because of the Depression of 1837. The promoters held several meetings in Maine and in Quebec, and the reports of their activities indicate that success was confidently expected. A survey was made in 1836, and the route was established through Unity to Skowhegan, up the Kennebec and Dead Rivers, across into the valley of the Moose River, and west in that valley to the state line where the route met the Quebec survey in the valley of the Chaudiere. In 1837 representatives of Belfast were at the legislature seeking state assistance in the construction of this railroad. By the terms of its constitution, however, Maine was prohibited from a direct loan of its credit for this purpose, and private initiative and capital were lacking. The charter was revived in 1845, but the enthusiasm of the citizens of Quebec had then disappeared.

About this time several other ambitious projects appeared on paper. The State Board of Internal Improvements had surveyed a railroad route from Portland to Bangor. The ambition of Belfast, not content with its Quebec railroad project, expanded in an attempt to establish that city as a railroad center, and charters were granted for a railroad from Belfast to Gardiner and from Belfast to Bangor. These proposed railroads, together with the projected Kennebec & Portland Railroad, would have formed a line from Portland to Bangor. Another plan proposed a railroad from Portland to Lake Champlain, and this route was surveyed in 1839. Many other charters were granted for railroad schemes of lesser magnitude. In 1836 Maine was enjoying one of those popular mental disorders familiarly known as "booms", attended by the usual features of extravagance, speculation in real estate, over-expansion of credit, and undue optimism. Under such conditions no project was too visionary to consider, and some railroad building might have been accomplished; but similar "boom" conditions in other sections of the country led to the inevitable collapse, and in 1837 the financial structure of the country fell into ruin.

The panic of 1837 was the culmination of a period of over-expansion in internal improvements. The tremendous investments in turnpikes and canals, and later in railroads, made on the credit of the states during the late twenties and early thirties, had resulted in an increase in state debts from about $13,000,000 in 1820 to about $200,000,000 in 1840. Under panic conditions many states were unable to pay interest on their debts, and several states, including Mississippi, Louisiana, Pennsylvania, Indiana and Michigan, repudiated their debts altogether. By the time Maine became definitely converted to the railroad idea the theory of state assistance was anathema to the people throughout the country; consequently, until 1861 no important assistance was given to Maine railroads by the State Government, and then only in one notable instance.

Another small, but nevertheless interesting, Maine railroad enterprise was the Palmer & Machiasport Railroad Corporation between Whitneyville and Machiasport. The Boston and Eastern Mill and Land Company, organized in 1833 for the purpose of doing a general lumber business at Whitneyville (then Middle Falls), started this road in 1841 and completed it in 1842, for the purpose of transporting its lumber from the mill to tidewater. Operation started in 1843, but did not run during the winter. It was renamed the Machiasport Railroad in 1845. The track was 4 feet 8½ inches gauge with 8 inch timbers

Palmer & Machiasport 0-4-0 "Lion" was built by Hinckley in 1846. It is now on display at the University of Maine at Machias. *Russell Monroe collection*

Portland, Saco & Portsmouth 21 "Scarborough" was built by the Portland Co. in 1871 and went to the Eastern as 94 in 1873. *Richard F. Dole collection*

laid on 8 inch ties, and 2 x 3 joist, covered on top with flat bars of iron, laid on top of timbers. The first engine was leased from Hinkley in Boston. The cars were four wheel affairs, eight feet long and six feet wide. The yearly traffic prior to 1866 was approximately ten million feet of long lumber, ten million laths, one million shingles, and other small lumber. After 1866 the business declined, and the railroad ceased operating in 1892. The Whitneyville Agency, successor to the Boston and Eastern Mill and Land Company, was dissolved in 1896, and the Sullivan family of Whitneyville succeeded to ownership in the entire property.

Another of these early lines was the Moosehead Lake Railway. The 3 foot 6 inch gauge line was chartered in 1847. It ran for several years for a couple of miles from Mud Pond to the Penobscot River hauling lumber products.

The first important railroad to be completed in Maine was the Portland, Saco & Portsmouth Railroad. This company was chartered in 1837 to build a road from Portland to Portsmouth and to connect there with a line to Boston. It was conceived by and always partially or wholly controlled by the Eastern Railroad during the active life of the latter company. The Eastern Railroad was incorporated in Massachusetts in 1836 to build a railroad from Boston to the New Hampshire state line. The original plan of the promoters was to build from Boston to Salem, but a charter could not be secured without undertaking the construction to New Hampshire. The available capital being insufficient for building the longer line, the Commonwealth of Massachusetts issued script in total amount of $590,000 to aid in construction. The Eastern Railroad of New Hampshire was incorporated in the same year to build from the Massachusetts line to Portsmouth. In 1839, during the process of construction of its road, the New Hampshire company leased its property to the Eastern Railroad of Massachusetts for 99 years. The road was opened from Boston to Portsmouth on December 31, 1840. The Great Falls & South

Eastern 75 was built in 1875 and became B&M 175 "John Thompson" in 1883. *Russell Monroe collection*

Berwick Branch Railroad Company was chartered in 1841 from the New Hampshire line to South Berwick to connect with the Portland, Saco & Portsmouth. It became a part of the Boston & Maine. The Portland, Saco, & Portsmouth Railroad was then under construction, and was opened to Portland in late 1842. The cost of this road was about $1,107,240.

During the time when the northern terminus was at Portsmouth the Eastern Railroad operated steamship lines from that city to Portland and to Kennebec River points. After the railroad was opened to Portland, the steamers connected with trains there, running to the Kennebec and Penobscot River points, and to Eastport, St. John and Halifax. For many years the Eastern Railroad had a large investment in steamers and wharf property in Maine. The Eastern and the Boston & Maine owned a substantial interest in the Penobscot Steam Navigation Company, which was organized in 1847 to operate steamers between Portland and Bangor. Railroad communication between Portland and Bangor was not established until 1855.

About two months after the completion of the Portland, Saco & Portsmouth road that company leased its property to the Eastern and to the Boston & Maine jointly at an annual rental of six per cent, with a penalty of $200,000 on either party for breach of contract. This joint lease was modified in 1847 so that the Eastern and the Boston & Maine shared equally in the profits of the Portland, Saco & Portsmouth over and above the guaranteed rental. Although the Eastern and the Boston & Maine had equal rights under the lease, the Eastern seems to have had the greater influence, and for several years the officials of the Eastern held the same offices in the Maine Company. The road was operated independently, but owned little equipment except locomotives. The trains were made up from Eastern and from Boston & Maine cars. The station in Portland was located near the wharves at the foot of State Street.

The Boston & Maine Railroad was opened to South Berwick early in 1843, but its line did not extend beyond that point in Maine until 1871, when the cancellation of its lease of the Portland, Saco & Portsmouth Railroad, under conditions to be mentioned later, made necessary the extension of its line to Portland. The Great Falls & Conway Railroad, organized in 1841, opened in 1849 from Somersworth to Rochester, New Hampshire with 3 miles in Maine.

A Portland, Saco & Portsmouth train ventures across the triple span through truss bridge at Biddeford. *Ron Johnson collection*

Chapter Two

John A. Poor and the Atlantic & St. Lawrence

The enthusiasm for railroad building, which had created in fifteen years 4633 miles of railroad in the United States, had aroused in Maine no important response. The only outstanding industries in Maine in 1840, outside of agriculture, were lumbering, fisheries, shipping and shipbuilding, all relying on water transportation; and the population was concentrated around the harbors and along navigable rivers. To the merchants of that day, trading in the markets of the world, there was little romance in the idea of building a few miles of railroad. Maine capital was largely invested in shipping and in lumbering and timberlands, and during the business depression in the late thirties no funds were available for a project large enough to arouse a general interest.

An interesting subject for speculation is how much Maine's tardiness in railroad development is reflected in the present condition of the State. It is certain that the increase in population after 1850 was at a much lower rate than in the first half of the century. In the early decades Maine had grown more rapidly than Massachusetts, in spite of a large and constant stream of emigration from Maine to the West. But in Massachusetts had taken place a gradual development of manufacturing establishments, fostered and protected by the "American System" of protective tariffs sponsored by Henry Clay, and later assisted by the development of railroad transportation facilities, whereas Maine had been slow in appreciating the advantages of manufacturing industry during the most favorable period for its development. It is more than a coincidence in dates that, as soon as a railroad was assured, the Franklin Company started operations in Lewiston in 1847 in developing water power for the cotton mills, which grew up immediately after the railroad was built.

The development of a railroad system tributary to Boston had diverted to that city a large part of the New Hampshire and Vermont trade that had formerly come to Portland, and the realization of this change in the channels of trade caused a more general appreciation of the economic necessity of a railroad system for Maine. It is certain that a tremendous change in sentiment toward railroads took place in Maine about 1844. The business depression, due to the panic of 1837 and subsequent deflation, had run its course, and money was again available for new projects. The enthusiasm of Maine's leading men was directed toward railroad building, the more ardently because so long repressed. And the High Priest of the new economic gospel was John A. Poor.

Atlantic & St. Lawrence 6 "Coos" was built in 1850 and eventually became GT 106. *Ron Johnson collection*

There is no place in economic history for extended biography, but it is impossible to understand the railroad history of Maine without a knowledge of the career of John Alfred Poor, and of his conceptions and ambitions. He was born in Andover, Maine in 1808. Having studied law and become admitted to the bar, he was practicing law in Bangor when the Bangor & Piscataquis Canal and Railroad Company opened its road in 1836. He had from the beginning of railroads an intense interest in their development, and had travelled from Bangor to Boston to witness the opening of the Boston & Worcester road on April 16, 1834. He believed in the development of Maine as the shipping center for the commerce of Canada and the Great Lakes district, and persuaded many persons to his opinion; but he and his friends could make little headway in combating the anti-railroad sentiment which existed in Maine until the early forties.

There was no important railroad built or building in Canada at this time. The total population of Canada was about 1,500,000. The commerce of the country moved on the Great Lakes and on the St. Lawrence River and its tributaries. The navigation of these waters had been made possible by the con-

Grand Trunk 4-4-0 126 hauls a cut of cars past the Mechanic Falls station around the turn of the century. *Robert Baker collection*

GT 0-6-0T 9 spent its lifetime in yard work around the system. *Ron Johnson collection*

struction of several important canals, of which the most vital was the Welland Canal around Niagara Falls. In 1845 the cheapest route from Ohio to England was by way of the St. Lawrence River. The only defect in this system was the impossibility of winter navigation. It was the plan of Poor to tap this artery of commerce and to divert the flow of trade to the open winter harbors on the Maine coast.

The conception of Maine harbors as the logical outlet for Canadian commerce was not originated by Mr. Poor. The same idea had actuated the promoters of the Belfast & Quebec Railroad several years earlier. But the basic conception of economic geography which supported the idea had been promulgated early in the seventeenth century by Champlain, the founder of the French colonization in America. The fulfillment of that destiny had been postponed by the interposing of a political barrier. John A. Poor was the first to prove that that barrier was not economic.

In pursuance of this program, Poor explored the country between the St. Lawrence and Maine in order to satisfy himself as to the practicability of a railroad. In 1844 he appeared in Portland, accompanied by a delegation of citizens from interior towns, and made public his plans for a railroad system for the State of Maine, urging upon the citizens of Portland and the wisdom of granting assistance to the enterprise.

Briefly stated, the original railroad program of John A. Poor contemplated the immediate construction of a railroad from the Atlantic Ocean at Portland to Montreal on the St. Lawrence River, for the purpose of diverting the commerce of Canada and the Great Lakes country, and the construction of another railroad line from a junction with the Portland to Montreal railroad through Lewiston to Gardiner, up the Kennebec River to Waterville, across to the Penobscot River at Bangor, and from Bangor east to St. John and Halifax. The railroad through Maine would be a trunk line from which branches would radiate, and thus connect the United States with the Maritime Provinces.

The plan for a railroad from Portland to Montreal was enthusiastically supported by the leading citizens of Portland, and, under the leadership of Mr. Poor, William Pitt Preble and Josiah S. Little, an organized movement was made for the accomplishment of this object. Montreal people were favorable to the idea of an Atlantic railroad. A preliminary survey was made, and in December, 1844, the engineer, James Hall, reported that a road through Dixville Notch was feasible and estimated the cost from Portland to the Canadian Boundary at $2,500,000. An application was made to the legislature which convened in January, 1845, for a charter to build a railroad from Portland to the Canadian boundary in the general direction of Sherbrooke and Montreal, to connect at the boundary with a Canadian railroad to be constructed from the boundary to Montreal. The charter was granted on February 10, 1845, in the name of the Atlantic & St. Lawrence Railroad, of 5 foot, 6 inch gauge.

The idea of a railroad from Montreal to the Atlantic was none the less captivating to the businessmen of Boston because it had originated in Maine, and there arose immediately a bitter controversy between Portland and Boston for the terminus of such a road. So much was said that was bitter, so much that was untrue, and so much plain mud slinging was indulged in that it is now difficult to determine the real comparative merit of the two projects. The people of Montreal were apparently indifferent to the question of the Atlantic terminus so long as the construction of the road to one port or the other was assured. Early in February, 1845, five days before the charter was granted by the Maine Legislature, John A. Poor learned that the Boston group had gained the advantage and that definite action would soon be taken committing Montreal to the Boston route. He started immediately from Portland toward Montreal, driving in a sleigh in the worst blizzard of the winter. By frequent changes of horses and by almost super-human exertion, he broke his way through the snow-blocked passes of the White Mountains, and by constant and almost sleepless travel arrived in Montreal on February tenth in time to appear before the Board of Trade at the meeting called for the purpose of action on the Boston proposition. He was successful in having the decision deferred; and about a week later Mr. Preble arrived with the charter granted by the Maine legislature. The Portland railroad thereafter steadily grew in favor, and was soon definitely started.

Grand Trunk, a subsidiary of Canadian National, Train 393 with three GP38-2's and a GP9 dust off the bridge over the Presumpscot River at West Falmouth in December 1977.
Ron Johnson

Subscriptions for stock in the Atlantic & St. Lawrence Railroad were received during 1845; and the result was so encouraging that organization was effected in September, 1845. In the meantime the leaders had decided against the Dixville Notch route, and had ordered a second survey which resulted in the location of the present line. The estimate of cost on the new location was higher, but since the people of Portland were now committed to the enterprise, cost was a minor consideration. In April, 1846, a convention was agreed upon by the American and Canadian Companies, and on July 4, 1846, actual construction was begun. The ceremony of breaking ground for the Atlantic & St. Lawrence Railroad was one of the most important events in the history of Portland, and that its importance was fully appreciated at the time is proved by the accounts of the tremendous celebration held in Portland on that day.

A Grand Trunk passenger train with Pacific 5283 prepares to depart the India Street station on June 17, 1949. *Beverley Historical Society from the collection of Russell Monroe*

A short Train 393 with four CN M420's, two cars and a caboose departs Portland in the Fall of 1984 with harbor and Fort Gorges in the background. *Ron Johnson*

[RIGHT:] **CN Train 393 with three GP9's is about to clatter across the diamond with the Maine Central at Yarmouth Jct. during 1962.** *Russell Monroe*
[BELOW:] **A CN passenger train with two FPA4's departs Portland in the early 1960's.** *Frank Difalco from the collection of Russell Monroe*

[BELOW:] **Grand Trunk Mogul 713 pauses with its combine to let off passengers at Danville Jct. on December 1, 1945.** *Robert Baker*

[ABOVE:] **Four CN M420's put on a smokey show as they lift Train 393 up the grade out of Danville Jct.** *Ron Johnson* [BELOW:] **GT4-8-2 6029 with Train 17 also lays down a nice smoke plume leaving Danville Jct. on July 18, 1953.** *Gerald Boothby from the collection of the 470 Railroad Club*

There was considerable difficulty in financing the construction of the road. The ill feeling in Boston helped to undermine public faith in the undertaking, and stock could not be sold readily. It was December 4, 1848, before the road was opened to Danville Junction, where it connected with the Androscoggin & Kennebec Railroad, already in the process of construction. On February 4, 1849, the road was opened to Mechanic Falls, and in October to Oxford. During 1849 the project received a tremendous impetus from the repeal of the "Corn Laws" in England, and the consequent opening of the English market to American and Canadian breadstuffs. The road then built had already cost nearly as much as the estimate for the entire line. The company had neither funds nor credit, but faith in the enterprise was still abundant in its promoters. A contract was made with Wood, Black & Company for the construction of the railroad from South Paris to the Canadian boundary at $26,200 per mile, payable half in cash, a quarter in bonds, and a quarter in stock. The City of Portland had been authorized to loan its credit to the extent of $1,000,000, of which about $400,000 had been advanced to the company before the contract was made with Wood, Black & Company. Legislation was secured permitting the grant of additional financial assistance by the City of Portland. Construction under the contractors went forward rapidly. The road opened to Bethel in March, 1851; to the state line in July of that year; and to the Canadian boundary in February, 1853. The Canadian company soon completed its road; and the whole line was opened from Portland to Montreal in July, 1853.

On August 5, 1853, the Atlantic & St. Lawrence Railroad was leased to the Grand Trunk Railway of Canada for 999 years. The Atlantic & St. Lawrence corporate name was dissolved in 1959. It passed to the control of the Dominion of Canada when the Canadian Government took over the Grand Trunk System in 1920, and it is now a part of the Canadian National Railway system. The capitalization at that time was $3,494,000 in funded debt and $2,494,900 par value stock, the total cost being nearly $6,000,000. By the terms of the lease the Grand Trunk Railway assumed all the debts, and guaranteed six per cent dividends on the stock.

The City of Portland had loaned its credit to the Atlantic & St. Lawrence Railroad to the extent of $2,000,000, and this amount was repaid in full after the successful conclusion of the undertaking. The railroad had made Portland a port of first importance. A line of winter steamers to Liverpool was established as soon as the road was opened, and large expenditures were made in the creation of terminal facilities. The Marginal Way, a new street now known as Commercial Street, was built along the waterfront across the heads of the wharves.

Another branch line off the Grand Trunk was the 5.4 mile Lewiston & Auburn Railroad opened in July 1874. Because the main line of the Grand Trunk missed the two cities they decided to build the branch line to connect with the Grand Trunk 7 miles west of Danville Junction. It was leased to the Grand Trunk. One other twig was the Norway Branch Railroad which opened in December 1879 off the main line at South Paris. It too was leased to the Grand Trunk in May 1880.

Chapter Three

War of the Gauges

Androscoggin & Kennebec 6 "Bangor" was built in 1849 by Kirk. *Russell Monroe collection*

The railroad program of John A. Poor had been well received in most sections of the State. The same legislature which granted the charter to the Atlantic & St. Lawrence later granted two other charters for the construction of the two roads which, with a portion of the Atlantic & St. Lawrence, would form a trunk line between Portland and Bangor, following closely the line recommended by Mr. Poor. The Androscoggin & Kennebec Railroad was chartered to construct and operate a railroad from some point of intersection with the Atlantic & St. Lawrence easterly through Lewiston to some point on the Kennebec River between the north line of Waterville and the south line of Hallowell. The Penobscot & Kennebec Railroad was chartered to build and operate a railroad from Bangor to some point on the Kennebec River between the north line of Waterville and the south line of Gardiner. Both charters were sponsored by the same group, and from the charter description of the termini, it is obvious that both projects were part of the same plan.

In 1836 a charter had been granted, and subsequently several times renewed, by the legislature to the Kennebec & Portland Railroad to build a railroad from Portland to Augusta through the towns of Yarmouth, Freeport, Brunswick, Topsham and Gardiner. The promoters were citizens of Gardiner, including George Evans and Robert Hallowell Gardiner; and their original plan was to build a railroad from Portland to Gardiner and a railroad or a canal from Gardiner to Winthrop. The influence of Augusta was used in opposition to the proposed charter, and it became necessary to make Augusta the terminus of the proposed route. The project was in a fair way to die altogether when it suddenly became enlivened by the proposals of Mr. Poor and of the friends of the Androscoggin & Kennebec project. Reuel Williams of Augusta then became the active head of the Kennebec & Portland Railroad. The Augusta group came into conflict with the Portland, Lewiston and Waterville groups and started a railroad war which lasted for twenty-five years. This long and bitter quarrel is generally described as the "War of the Gauges", but its causes were deeper than a mere matter of gauge.

The partisan nature of the testimony afforded in the arguments of the period furnishes so many direct contradictions that it is difficult to find any reliable statements of the real motives of the contending parties. The Portland group, heavily interested in the Atlantic & St. Lawrence project, naturally wanted the main line through Maine to connect with the Montreal road and bring it traffic. The promoters of the Androscoggin & Kennebec originally contemplated a line from Lewiston to Gardiner, Hallowell or Augusta. The Waterville group wanted the terminus in their city. The Augusta group wanted a railroad terminus in Augusta, and favored the Kennebec Valley route as surveyed for the Kennebec & Portland Railroad. They also wanted a railroad connecting with the Boston road, which involved the question of gauge, as the proposed gauge of the Montreal road was different from the Boston road. But the question of gauge was not a vital matter at that time.

The impossibility of amicable adjustment of the differences of the contending factions led to a decision by the promoters of the Androscoggin & Kennebec Railroad to ignore Augusta altogether and to locate their railroad from Danville through Lewiston and Winthrop to Waterville on what is now known as the "Back Route". Subscriptions for

WHITTON
SPAULDING
STATE LINE 144.8 MILES FROM MATTA'G
LAKE
DITCHFIELD
MEGANTIC
Lowell
Boundary
DENNIS TOWN PLANTATION
PLANTATION
FORSYTHE
Jackman
Holeb
ATTEAN
JACKMAN TOWN PLANTATION
LONG POND
SANDWICH ACADEMY GRANT
LOWELL
HOLEB
Attean Pond
NORTH LINE OF BINGHAM'S KENNEBEC PURCHASE
PARLIN POND
MISERY TOWNSHIP
Marr's Camp
Somerset Jct.
Brassua Lake
MOOSEHEAD LAKE
Rockwood
Kineo
Lower Roach Pond
A.2
BOWDOIN COLLEGE GRANT
CHASE STREAM TOWNSHIP
Indian Pond
Greenville
GREENVILLE
CLINTON
WOBURN
HOBBSTOWN
SPENCER POND
Katahdin Iron Works
SQUARETOWN
Lake Moxie
Shirley
SHIRLEY
Ship Pond
PACIFIC
BARNARD
WILLIAMSBURG
BOWERBANK
Onawa
WILLIMANTIC
Dead River
WEST FORKS PLANTATION
FORKS PLANTATION
EAST MOXIE TOWNSHIP
MOXIE POND
MONSON
Monson
SEBEC LAKE
Blanchard
BLANCHARD
SEBEC
FOXCROFT
GUILFORD
FLAGSTAFF PLANTATION
PIERCE POND
CARRATUNK PLANTATION
BALD MOUNTAIN
CARRYING PLACE
Monson Jc.
Abbot
ABBOT
BANGOR & AROOSTOOK
Dover & Foxcroft
Dover
E. Dover
DOVER
ATKINSON
EUSTIS
WEST EUSTIS
Little Kennebago Lake
PARMACHENEE LAKE
Stratton
BIGELOW PLANTATION
DEAD RIVER PLANTATION
Dead Water
KINGSBURY PLANTATION
MAYFIELD
MOSCOW
Guilford
Sangerville
SANGERVILLE
PARKMAN
KENNEBAGO LAKE
Coplin
COPLIN PLANTATION
Bigelow
JERUSALEM
HIGHLAND PLANTATION
PLEASANT RIDGE
Bingham
BINGHAM
BRIGHTON
WELLINGTON
LYNCH TOWN
Berlin Mills Camp
Carrabasset
LEXINGTON
CONCORD
CAMBRIDGE
DEXTER
Dexter
GARLAND
CHARLESTON
Dead River
Redington Mill
MOUNT ABRAM TOWNSHIP
The Bluff
KINGFIELD PLANTATION
Kingfield
RANGELEY
Oquossoc
PHILLIPS PLANT'N
RIPLEY
So. End
LINCOLN PLANTATION
RANGELEY LAKES
Rangeley
GREENVALE & SANDY RIVER PLANTATION
MADRID
Sanders
SALEM
North Freeman
NEW PORTLAND
EMBDEN
Embden
Solon
SOLON
ATHENS
HARMONY
Mainstream
MOOSE POND
ST. ALBANS
CORINNA
Corinna
EXETER
S. Rangeley
RANGELEY PLANTATION
Bemis
Salem
Reeds
Madrid
FREEMAN
W. Freeman
Hartland
HARTLAND
CORNVILLE
PALMYRA
Palmyra
Camp Benson
NEWPORT
STETSON
Newport Pond
MAGALLOWAY PLANTATION
RICHARDSON TOWN
Summit
Phillips
SANDY
STRONG
Strong
NEW VINEYARD
No. Anson
ANSON
Anson
MADISON
Madison
Skowhegan
CANAAN
Newport
Etna
ETNA
Carmel
Pittsfield
PITTSFIELD
DETROIT
Detroit
PLYMOUTH
UPTON
Houghton
Byron
BYRON
AVON
INDUSTRY
STARKS
FARMINGTON
SKOWHEGAN
Norridgewock
NORRIDGEWOCK
ANDOVER NORTH SURPLUS
TEMPLE
W. Farmington
Farmington
NEW SHARON
MERCER
Good Will Farm
SMITHFIELD
Hinckley
CLINTON
Clinton
Burnham Jc.
BURNHAM
Burnham
TROY
DIXMONT
NEWBURGH
Roxbury
ROXBURY
ANDOVER
WILTON
Wilton
East Wilton
Sandy
SHARON
FAIRFIELD
Shawmut
UNITY POND
Unity
UNITY
GRAFTON
CARTHAGE
CHESTERVILLE
VIENNA
Fairfield
BENTON
Benton
Waterville
Thorndike
JACKSON
MONROE
Hale
MEXICO
RUMFORD
Androscoggin R.
DIXFIELD
North Jay
JAY
Oakland
WINSLOW
Winslow
ALBION
Albion
Brooks
BROOKS
Knox
KNOX
RILEY PLANTATION
NEWRY
Rumford Falls
Dixfield
Peru
PERU
CANTON
Riley
Jay Bridge
Chisholm's Mills
Livermore Falls
Parker Pond
MOUNT VERNON
Belgrade
So. Belgrade
Lakeside
Yassalboro
China
China Pond
FREEDOM
MONTVILLE
WALDO
City Point
BETHEL
MILTON PLANT'N
FRANKLIN PLANTATION
Gilbertville
E. Livermore
Canton
FAYETTE
SIDNEY
Vassalboro
GILEAD
Gilead
Bethel
West Bethel
Lockes Mills
WOODSTOCK
Bryants Pond
GREENWOOD
FRYEBURG ACADEMY GRANT
LIVERMORE
Strickland
KENNEBEC
Readfield
READFIELD
Riverside
Palermo
PALERMO
BELFAST
BELMONT
SUMNER
Hartford
HARTFORD
East Sumner
North Leeds
Maranacook
WAYNE
Lake Maranacook
AUGUSTA
Augusta
Hallowell
Weeks Mills
LIBERTY
SEARSMONT
NORTHPORT
BATCHELDERS GRANT
MASON
ALBANY
WOOD
West Paris
Leeds Centre
LEEDS
Winthrop
WINTHROP
MANCHESTER
Togus
Windsor
WINDSOR
SOMERVILLE
APPLETON
LINCOLNVILLE
STONEHAM
PARIS
Buckfield
BUCKFIELD
Paris
TURNER
Curtis Cor.
Annabessacook
Cobbosseecontee Pond
Farmingdale
FARMINGDALE
Chelsea
CHELSEA
WHITEFIELD
Coopers Mills
WASHINGTON
HOPE
NORWAY
East Hebron
HEBRON
GREENE
Leeds Jc.
Monmouth
MONMOUTH
WEST GARDINER
Randolph
RANDOLPH
No. Whitefield
Union
UNION
Simontons Corner
CAMDEN
Camden
LOVELL
WATERFORD
Norway
So. Paris
West Minot
LITCHFIELD
Gardiner
So. Gardiner
PITTSTON
Whitefield
JEFFERSON
WALDOBORO
KNOX
ROCKPORT
Rockport
North Bridgton
Harrison
SWEDEN
Oxford
OTISFIELD
MINOT
Auburn
Lewiston
Sabattus
Pleasant Pond
Dresden
RICHMOND
Iceboro
Head Tide
LINCOLN
ROCKLAND
CASCO
Mechanic Falls
Poland
Poland Spring
Danville Jc.
Lisbon
LISBON
WEBSTER
Crowleys Jc.
BOWDOIN
Richmond
Bowdoin
Bowdoinham
DRESDEN
Alna
ALNA
NEW CASTLE
Newcastle & Damariscotta
Waldoboro
Warren
Thomaston
Rockland
Fryeburg Centre
BRIDGTON
Bridgton
Sandy Cr.
Fryeburg
S. Bridgton
DENMARK
Perley Mills
Brownfield
BROWNFIELD
W. Sebago
SEBAGO
Lisbon Falls
Rowes
NEW GLOUCESTER
New Gloucester
DURHAM
TOPSHAM
Pejepscot Mills
WOOLWICH
Westport
Sheepscot
WISCASSET
Damariscotta Mills
DAMARISCOTTA
So. Newcastle
EDGECOMB
BREMEN
FRIENDSHIP
CUSHING
SOUTH THOMASTON
ST. GEORGE
BRISTOL
RAYMOND
SEBAGO LAKE
Little Sebago Lake
GRAY
Gray
POWNAL
Pownal
Freeport
North Yarmouth
Brunswick
Hillside
CENTRAL
BRUNSWICK
Harding
Bath
BOOTHBAY
PORTER
Hiram
Bridgton Jc.
BALDWIN
W. Baldwin
Cornish
Mattocks
Steep Falls
Kezar Falls
White Rock
WINDHAM
Cumberland Jc.
FREEPORT
HARPSWELL
Yarmouth
Cumberland
CUMBERLAND
PHIPPSBURG
GEORGETOWN
MONHEGAN ISLAND
CORNISH
LIMINGTON
Sebago Lake
STANDISH
Newhall
So. Windham
GORHAM
Cumberland Mills
Gorham
FALMOUTH
Portland
PARSONSFIELD
LIMERICK
BUXTON
Buxton
NEWFIELD
Saco
SEGUIN ISLAND
OXFORD
FRANKLIN
ANDROSCOGGIN
SAGADAHOC
CUMBERLAND
SOMERSET
PISCATAQUIS

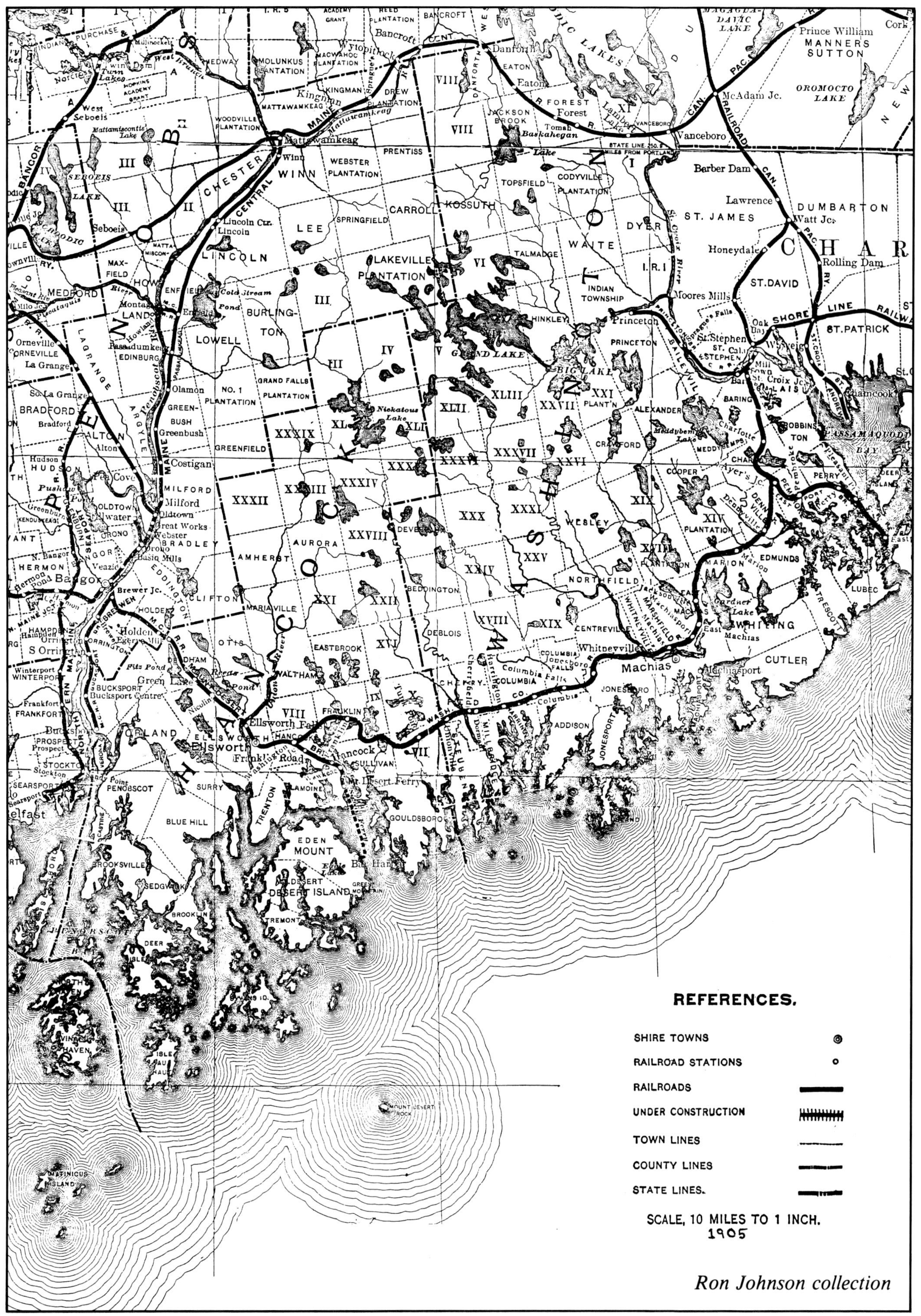

Ron Johnson collection

The last Portland & Kennebec locomotive built was the 20 "H.N. Jose" by the Portland Co. in 1870.
Russell Monroe collection

stock having been secured in the necessary amount, the Androscoggin & Kennebec Railroad was organized early in 1847, and construction was started the same year. The railroad was put under construction in three sections, all to be completed by July 1849. The original estimate of $1,000,000 as the probable cost of the road was less than half the actual cost, and the difficulty of securing additional funds delayed the construction program, while the expensive methods of financing materially increased the cost. It was necessary to mortgage two sections of the road in order to pay for the rails. The road was opened to Lewiston in December, 1848; to Winthrop in July, 1849; and to Waterville on December 5, 1849. The Kennebec & Portland Railroad, the rival project backed by Augusta interests, had at this time built its line only as far as Brunswick and Bath, and the completion of the Androscoggin & Kennebec road to Waterville was celebrated by its friends as a great victory.

The stock of the Androscoggin & Kennebec, 5 feet 6 inch gauge, was practically all owned by Maine people, and was at one time distributed among 1854 holders in eighty-seven towns in Maine, with only four stockholders outside of Maine. The earnings were disappointing, and for several years the stock had only a nominal value. When the road was completed to Waterville, there was no connection with the Boston road to Portland. The Atlantic & St. Lawrence had agreed to furnish this connection and did so in 1850, but the difference in gauge made through traffic impossible, and all freight and passengers had to be transferred. There was considerable difficulty at first in securing a satisfactory division of rates with the Atlantic & St. Lawrence, and it was not until 1855, after the lease of the Atlantic & St. Lawrence to the Grand Trunk Railway, that a definite and satisfactory contract was made.

The controversy regarding the route of the railroad to Waterville and Bangor stimulated interest in the Kennebec & Portland Railroad, 4 feet 8½ inch gauge, and aroused its promoters to action. The company was organized late in 1846, the original subscription for stock totalling about $625,000. The line from Yarmouth to Augusta and the branch to Bath were located early in 1847, and construction was started on the Bath branch in June, 1847. The estimate of cost for the entire road was about $1,635,000. The road was opened from Bath to Yarmouth Junction on July 4, 1848, connecting at Yarmouth with the Atlantic & St. Lawrence. This arrangement was naturally very unsatisfactory on account of the difference in gauge, and plans were made for extending the road to a connection with the Boston road in Portland. In 1850 this extension was made to a connection with the York & Cumberland Railroad at Deering Junction, funds being secured by mortgaging that part of the road, and soon after, with the assistance of the Portland, Saco & Portsmouth Railroad which purchased $100,000 par value of stock, the road was extended from the York & Cumberland station in Portland to a junction with the Boston road in Cape Elizabeth (now South Portland). In 1859 the legislature passed an act authorizing the cities and towns along the route to grant financial assistance, and about $750,000 was secured in this manner. In January, 1851, the road was opened from Brunswick to Richmond, and the entire line from Portland to Augusta was opened in 1852. Like most of the early railroads the cost was largely in excess of the estimates. The geographical position of the towns along the route seems to have been considered of greater importance than the possible location of easy gradients in the determination of the location.

In the late forties the question of gauge became a

[ABOVE:] **A Portland & Kennebec passenger train crosses the bridge at Augusta with locomotive 11 "J.D. Lang" built by Amoskeag in 1854.** *Richard Dole collection* [BELOW:] **In the same location in a different era, BR-4 with three Maine Central GP-38's cross the Kennebec River. Note the old stone pilings from the first bridge in the foreground.** *Ron Johnson*

Portland & Kennebec 7 "Reuel Williams" was built by Hinkley in 1852 and rebuilt by the Portland Co. in 1875. *Ron Johnson collection*

vital matter in Maine. The gauge of 4 feet 8½ inches, now known as standard gauge, had been copied from early English railroads. The dimension was said to have been an accident in the first place; and it had certainly not been determined by any scientific demonstration. It had been adopted by the Massachusetts railroads and by many other roads, but its merit was questioned by many able engineers. Mr. A.C. Morton, the engineer in charge of the Atlantic & St. Lawrence Railroad, had persuaded the Canadian authorities to revoke their original decision in favor of the 4 feet 8½ inches gauge and to adopt a broad gauge of 5 feet 6 inches. At that time there were only fifteen miles of railroad in all Canada. The Portland,Saco & Portsmouth had the narrow gauge, but no connection was planned between the Montreal and the Boston road. The construction of the Atlantic & St. Lawrence with the broad gauge was the cause of the existence of the broad gauge on the major portion of the Maine railroad system for many years. In 1847 the Androscoggin & Kennebec had adopted the broad gauge to connect with the Atlantic & St. Lawrence, and the Kennebec & Portland had elected to connect with the Boston road on the narrow gauge.

Soon after the organization of the Kennebec & Portland Railroad Company its active head, Mr. Reuel Williams, had tried to secure a charter authorizing the extension of the narrow gauge system up the Kennebec Valley and to Bangor; but, in the face of the active opposition of the broad gauge roads, he had not been successful. The Penobscot & Kennebec Railroad had the right of location in the Kennebec Valley as far south as Gardiner, and this right was maintained until 1852. The Somerset & Kennebec Railroad had been chartered in 1848 to build a railroad from some point near Carratunk down the Kennebec Valley to connect with the Androscoggin & Kennebec or with the Penobscot & Kennebec at or near Waterville, and to connect with the Kennebec & Portland at Augusta, provided the Penobscot & Kennebec had not built to Augusta within the time limit of its charter, which limit was originally December 31, 1850, but was extended to December 31, 1852.

The Penobscot & Kennebec Railroad, 5 feet 6 inch gauge, from the Kennebec River to Bangor was an essential part of the original plan of Mr. Poor; and this company had been chartered in the same year with the Atlantic & St. Lawrence and the Androscoggin & Kennebec. In 1850, shortly after the Androscoggin & Kennebec was opened to Waterville, organization was effected by the choice of George W. Pickering, Samuel P. Strickland, Moses L. Appleton and Wyman B.S. Moor of Bangor, and Francis O.J. Smith, John M. Wood and John A. Poor of Portland as directors. The original subscription for stock totalled 4066 shares, of which 2000 shares were subscribed by Francis O.J. Smith and 2000 shares by John M. Wood. The early construction of the Bangor road was then expected.

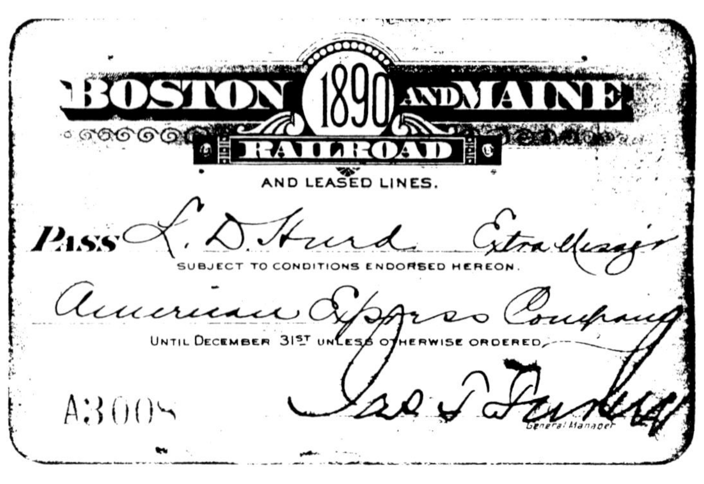

Edwin B. Robertson collection

Chapter Four

John A. Poor and the European & North American More Power Plays

European & North American locomotive 12 "Prince of Wales" is pictured at St. John, N.B. on the occasion of the visit of the Prince of Wales in June 1860. *Russell Monroe collection*

In following the history of the railroad enterprises which eventually came through consolidation to compose the present Maine Central Railroad system, it is easy to lose sight of contemporary events and of the influence of one undertaking upon another. In all the phases of the early railroad quarrels, the only outstanding figure whose activities give the appearance of continuity and of adherence to a definite plan is John A. Poor. While most of the men active in Maine railroads were content to consider local advantages, the scope of his conception of Maine railroads was international. He saw, perhaps more clearly than any man of his time, the opportunity afforded by Maine's geographical position on the American continent, and he believed that the community of business interests between the United States and Canada would require the solution of all the problems involved in international commerce. Poor was a railroad builder, not an operator. As soon as the completion of the Atlantic & St. Lawrence was assured, his activities were directed to the undertaking proposed in his original railroad plan, the railroad through Maine to St. John and Halifax. In December, 1849, the Androscoggin & Kennebec opened to Waterville; and it was expected that construction would start promptly on the Penobscot & Kennebec road. In 1850 a charter was granted to the European & North American Railroad to build a railroad from Bangor to the eastern boundary of Maine, connecting there with a railroad to be built from St. John. The tremendous influence of this project upon contemporary enterprises entitles the European & North American Railroad to a place in Maine railroad history for nearly twenty years before the road was actually built.

The European & North American Railroad project was formally presented at a convention organized by Mr. Poor and his associates and held in Portland in 1850. This convention was largely attended, and an intense public interest in the plan was aroused. The active men in New Brunswick and Nova Scotia were enthusiastically interested, and undertook the arrangements for the construction of the Canadian portion of the line. The State of Maine was asked to grant two million acres of the public lands to the railroad, on the ground that transportation facilities afforded by the road would largely increase the value of the remaining public lands. Massachusetts was also asked for assistance by a grant of part of her Maine lands. Although this request was denied, a committee of the Massachusetts legislature did recommend a loan of the state's credit to the company, and a bill providing for such assistance was defeated by a narrow margin through the influence of Boston merchants and the Cunard line. The National House of Representatives actually passed a bill granting 1,350,000 acres of land to the Company, but this bill was defeated in the Senate.

In the meantime an interesting situation had arisen in the Provinces. It appears that New Brunswick was prepared to carry her full share of the burden of construction; but that Nova Scotia authorities started a correspondence with the British Government in the hope of securing the guarantee of Great Britain on the bonds to be sold by the railroad company. This interesting correspondence discloses the primary interest of the British Government in the construction of a railroad from Halifax to Quebec through British territory; and a considerable pressure was put upon the Provinces to support the Halifax-Quebec project. Nova Scotia authorities were advised that the guarantee of the British Government would be available for the European & North American, provided arrangements should first be made assuring the construction of the Quebec road. The building of a railroad from Halifax to Quebec was a military measure, pure and simple, as there was no chance that such a railroad could pay, and the Province authorities were not pleased that military measures should be considered in priority to the economic advantages of the Provinces. In 1851 the New Brunswick authorities definitely advised Earl Grey that the provincial credit would not be pledged as assistance for the Halifax-Quebec road.

It seems apparent that in the beginning of the European & North American Railroad project there was unanimity of purpose among its promoters. But it is no less clear that the enterprise was retarded by the necessity of reconciling two conflicting ideas which were diametrically opposed. The people of Bangor, especially the lumbermen, had been in trouble with the Canadians along the border for many years. The public passions had been inflamed by the timber depredations which had caused the Aroostook War, and the settlement of the Northeastern Boundary controversy by the Webster-Ashburton Treaty in 1843 had aroused bitter resentment. Bangor could not be indifferent to the European & North American project, but no enthusiasm was generated there by the vision of international conciliation and good will, which was the basis for arguments advanced by Mr. Poor and others in favor of the proposed railroad to Halifax. The railroad desired by the people of Bangor was a railroad with a military purpose, running from Bangor to the St. John River in the Aroostook region, and capable of providing a means of communication for the defense of the Northeastern boundary. The promoters of the European & North American came eventually to a partial adoption of this idea.

In 1851 the construction of the European & North American seemed assured. But the road from Waterville to Bangor had not been put under construction, and this was an essential feature of the plan. Efforts were made without success to hasten the building of the Penobscot & Kennebec road, and in 1853 the legislature authorized the European & North American to lease the Penobscot & Kennebec. It was said at the time that British capital was available to build the road from Waterville to Halifax. The Bangor group declined to grasp this opportunity, and the outbreak of the Crimean War later in 1853 caused the withdrawal of the offer of British capital for the railroad.

From the time of the organization meeting of the Penobscot & Kennebec Railroad Company until July, 1852, nothing was done about building the road or raising more money. This delay was irksome to the three Portland directors who were all interested in the European & North American project and, therefore, especially eager for the completion of the railroad to Bangor. The company was at war with the Somerset & Kennebec Railroad Company which was associated with the Kennebec & Portland Railroad group and which was considered a part of the plan of the narrow gauge interests for an extension of the narrow gauge to Bangor; and the delay of the Penobscot & Kennebec in finally locating its line made the construction of the Somerset & Kennebec road practically impossible. The preliminary plans of the Penobscot & Kennebec contemplated crossing the Kennebec River at Waterville, but after the Somerset & Kennebec had filed its location between Fairfield and Waterville, the Penobscot & Kennebec, by virtue of its prior right of location, changed its plans and located on the exact ground selected by the Somerset & Kennebec, and during 1852 and 1853 built a broad gauge road between Waterville and Fairfield (then Kendall's Mills). The section of broad gauge road between Waterville and Fairfield was known as Moor's Battery on account of a remark made by W.B.S. Moor that "they would plant a battery at Kendall's Mills that would blow the Somerset road to the devil."

In 1852 the Portland directors of the Penobscot & Kennebec, Messrs. Smith, Wood and Poor, attempted to force definite action for construction of the road to Bangor, and the proposal of John M. Wood to build the road for $26,200 a mile was submitted to the directors. The Bangor directors were unable to agree to this proposition, and thereupon Mr. Smith and Mr. Wood, each holding 2000 shares of the total original subscription of 4066 shares, proceeded to elect a new board of directors, composed of George W. Stanley of Augusta, Thomas Pickard of Lewiston (probably Samuel Pickard, as there was no one in Lewiston named Thomas Pickard), and Ira Crocker, Nathan Cummings, James C. Churchill, John M. Wood and William Kimball of Portland.

There was consternation in Bangor on account of

Skowhegan was at the end of the 37 mile Somerset & Kennebec line from Augusta. The station boasted an impressive clock tower. *Richard Sanborn from the collection of Russell Monroe.*

this action, as it was believed that Bangor would lose control of the road. The Bangor group claimed that the proceedings were illegal, and the old board — minus the Portland members — continued to act and refused to turn over the records to the new board. Upon legal action being taken to compel delivery of the records, the Court ruled that the new board was ineligible. Messrs. Smith, Wood and Poor afterwards severed their connection with the company.

While the control of the management of the Penobscot & Kennebec was still in doubt, Mr. Poor, who apparently feared that the bitter quarrels of the day would prevent any railroad building, issued a call for a railroad convention to all the active railroad men in Maine, in the hope that by conference some compromise might be reached which would solve the most serious problems and make possible a renewal of construction. The convention was attended by representatives of all the contending factions, and resolutions were adopted by which it was agreed that the Somerset & Kennebec should be free to proceed with the extension of the narrow gauge line up the Kennebec River, and that the narrow gauge interests would abandon their plan for the extension of the narrow gauge to Bangor. In 1853 the Legislature confirmed the right of the Somerset & Kennebec to build to Augusta.

In 1852, shortly after the Bangor directors had decided to refuse to retire in favor of the board chosen by Mr. Smith and Mr. Wood, the Bangor directors made a contract with Moor and Dunning of Bangor for the construction of the railroad to Bangor at a price of $1,000,000, part in stock, plus the excess cost of the iron over $50 a ton, the contractors assuming the contract already made for the construction from Waterville to Fairfield. At the annual meeting in July, 1853, the Bangor ticket for directors, composed of George W. Pickering, Moses L. Appleton, Samuel Farrar, William Cutter and Rufus Dwinel of Bangor, William Connor of Fairfield, and George W. Chamberlain of Carmel, was elected by a narrow margin.

The cost of the road overran all estimates by several hundred thousand dollars. To aid in construction the City of Bangor issued $800,000 in script, receiving as security a first mortgage on the entire road. Second and third mortgage bonds were issued and other loans were required. On one occasion the company gave a note for $15,000 at fifteen per cent interest secured by $19,000 City of Bangor bonds as collateral. The road was opened to Bangor in August, 1855, and in 1856 the company leased the road to the Androscoggin & Kennebec. By the terms of this lease the Androscoggin & Kennebec received four-sevenths of the net earnings. The remainder of the net earnings were not sufficient to pay interest charges, and the company defaulted interest on its third mortgage and later on its second mortgage. The road was operated by the Androscoggin & Kennebec until 1862 when both roads were consolidated in the Maine Central.

The Somerset & Kennebec Railroad, although it maintained a separate corporate existence which enabled it to have its share in the quarrels of the day, was during practically all of its existence operated by the Kennebec & Portland (later the Portland & Kennebec), and its history is practically identified with the history of the latter road. It was chartered in 1848 and organized in 1852. The first directors were Abner Coburn of Bloomfield, Edward McLellan of Skowhegan, William Connor and Ezra Totman of

Maine Central 29 "J.S. Cushing", ex-Portland & Kennebec 13, is viewed at Hallowell in 1872. *Richard Dole collection*

Fairfield, Samuel P. Shaw of Waterville, Joseph Morrill of Augusta and David Bronson of Bath. Financial assistance by towns enabled the company to make a contract, and construction was started in 1853. While under construction the road was leased to the Kennebec & Portland under an operating contract. The road was opened from Augusta to Fairfield in 1855 and to Skowhegan in December, 1856.

The operation of the Kennebec & Portland Railroad was not profitable. Interest having been defaulted on its second mortgage bonds, in 1857 the trustees for the bondholders took over the road, and in 1859 gave notice of foreclosure. In 1860 the same trustees took over the road in the interest of the holders of the first mortgage bonds. The road was operated by the trustees from 1857 to January, 1864, when the Portland & Kennebec Railroad, a company organized by the second mortgage bondholders, finally took possession. Under the management of the trustees, the net earnings had increased from $8,000 in 1858 to about $103,000 in 1863. The contract with the Somerset & Kennebec had not been binding on the trustees, and during the period of trustee operation the relations between the two roads had been unsatisfactory and indefinite. As soon as the Portland & Kennebec took over the property, the new company leased the Somerset & Kennebec road for twenty years at a definite annual rental of $36,000.

The proceedings which led to the disappearance of the Kennebec & Portland Railroad Company and the subsequent appearance of the Portland & Kennebec Railroad Company as owners of the same property were the subject of a long and bitter controversy, and the rights of the parties remained unsettled until 1870. It was claimed that Richard D. Rice and associates had conspired with some of the directors of the Kennebec & Portland and with some of the trustees of the mortgage in order to force a default on the second mortgage bonds for the purpose of bringing the road into their possession. Through an agent, Rice had purchased from Reuel Williams for $113,000 all of the securities of the

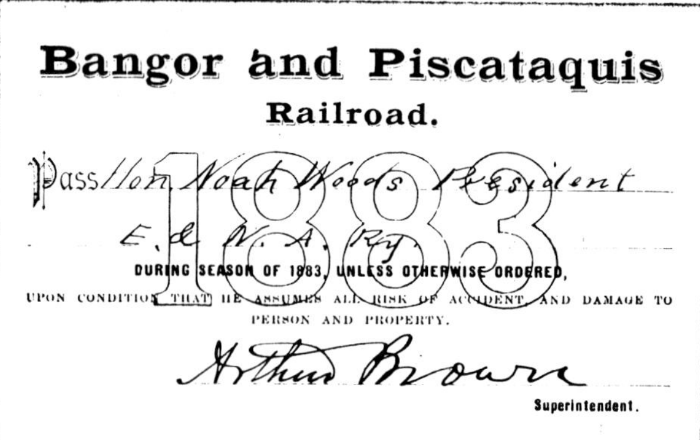

Bangor and Piscataquis
Railroad.

Pass Hon. Noah Woods President
E. & N. A. Ry.

1883

DURING SEASON OF 1883, UNLESS OTHERWISE ORDERED,
UPON CONDITION THAT HE ASSUMES ALL RISK OF ACCIDENT, AND DAMAGE TO PERSON AND PROPERTY.

Arthur Brown
Superintendent.

Richard Dole collection

Kennebec & Portland owned by Williams, including a majority of the second mortgage bonds. It was said that Mr. Williams made this sale with the belief that he was selling to assist the railroad out of its financial difficulties, and that he had been deceived as to the intent of the purchaser. The charges were made that, in pursuance of the alleged conspiracy, the trustees had used funds of the railroad to assist in the purchase of these securities, for the benefit of Rice and his associates and not for the benefit of the railroad. The merits of the controversy cannot now be accurately analyzed. It was natural that the restoration of the road to a prosperous condition should have been irritating to the Kennebec & Portland stockholders whose investment had been wiped out in the reorganization; but there is no evidence to prove that these stockholders had been willing to assist the old company before or during the period of trustee operation. Some of the actions of members of the Rice group had undoubtedly been injudicious, but no wrongdoing or conspiracy was ever proved. The result was that the second mortgage bondholders, Mr. Rice and his associates, came into possession of the railroad, and their title to the property was later confirmed by the Supreme Court. The old Kennebec & Portland stockholders were wiped out, and Mr. Rice and his friends presently emerged with a large profit on the transaction and with the control of the Maine Central Railroad.

Chapter Five

Androscoggin Railroad's Broad Gauge Difficulties

The Androscoggin Railroad, 5 feet 6 inch gauge, was chartered in 1848 to build a railroad from some point on the Androscoggin & Kennebec Railroad in Greene or Monmouth northerly through intervening towns to Jay Bridge. In 1849 the charter was amended to grant the right to build as far north as Phillips. The members of the first board of directors were William Kilbourne, President, Ensign Otis, Giddings Lane, David Benjamin, Ezekiel Treat, Elisha Keyes and William Glidden. Alonzo Garcelon soon succeeded Mr. Kilbourne as President.

In the early days of railroad planning one of the proposed routes for a railroad to Quebec was through Franklin County; and the idea of a Canadian connection and an extension to Moosehead Lake seems to have been in the minds of the promoters of the Androscoggin; but this plan was abandoned when the Atlantic & St. Lawrence was started. In 1847 the location of a railroad in this section was again proposed, and a charter was secured in the name of the Franklin & Kennebec Railroad to build a road from Farmington to some point on the Kennebec River near Gardiner. Other efforts had as an objective the construction of a railroad from Bath into Franklin County. Capital was not available for either project.

When the Androscoggin Railroad was organized in 1848, the subscriptions for stock were secured with difficulty on account of a competing project to build from Lewiston to Rumford Falls, but the rival enterprise never received a charter. The route from Jay to Leeds Junction was surveyed by an engineer loaned by the Androscoggin & Kennebec, and the original estimate of cost was $330,000. Contracts were let in October, 1849, construction to be completed by August, 1851. More stock was offered, but could not be sold, and in 1850 it was necessary to mortgage the property to secure funds to pay for the rails. The road was originally built broad gauge.

While the problem of financing the construction under contract was still unsolved, efforts were made to secure the building of the road to Farmington, and, the management having failed to raise sufficient funds, it was voted to sell the whole property, provided the purchaser would guarantee to build to Livermore Falls within two years. No purchaser appeared, and efforts made to secure assistance from towns along the line ended in failure. Many of the stockholders were dissatisfied with the progress of the road; and finally the board of directors agreed to resign if funds could be raised for building the extension to Livermore Falls. A sufficient amount having been raised, the board of directors did resign, and a new board was elected consisting of the men most active on the old board, with the addition of Benjamin H. Cushman, who became Superintendent. Construction went forward rapidly during 1852, and the road was opened to Livermore Falls in November of that year. In 1854 it was voted to extend to Farmington when funds were available. The money required having been raised in 1856, a contract was made in 1857 for iron on the new division; but again serious financial difficulties caused delay, and the road was not completed until June, 1859. The section from Livermore Falls to Farmington

The "Wood Job" out of Waterville pauses to pick up more cars at Leeds Jct. before heading up the wye on the left to Rileys (Jay) and a paper mill in the Fall of 1977. *Ron Johnson*

[ABOVE:] **Maine Central Class 0 4-6-0 381 emerges from the through truss bridge at West Farmington in February 1941.** *Eugene Ellis from the 470 Railroad Club* [BELOW:] **Crowleys Jct., as seen in the 1930's, was where the Lewiston Lower branch and the line to Leeds Jct. and Farmington met, originally operated by the Androscoggin Railroad.** *Lawrence Breed Walker from the collection of Russell Monroe*

was cheaply built and there were many defects in the engineering work which were partially corrected later.

The division of rates between the Androscoggin and the Androscoggin & Kennebec Railroads had been a source of dissatisfaction to the management of the former company, and after negotiations had secured no relief and an appeal to the Railroad Commissioners had produced no definite result, the Androscoggin management decided upon a new construction program, which would make the company more independent by creating another outlet for its traffic. In 1860 the legislature authorized the Androscoggin to build a line to Gardiner or to Brunswick. The Brunswick route, which was of the two apparently more favored, was surveyed, and an attempt was made to buy the branch of the Kennebec & Portland road between Brunswick and Bath. The City of Bath was authorized to loan its credit to the Androscoggin Railroad to the extent of $200,000, which amount was later increased to $425,000. In April, 1860, President John B. Jones resigned, and there were added to the board of directors Oliver Moses, who became President, Samuel I. Robinson and David Patten, all of Bath. Washington Gilbert, also of Bath, soon became a director, and these men were the dominating influence in the later affairs of the company.

Immediately after the advent of the Bath directors the road to Brunswick with a branch to Lewiston was put under contract; and in 1861 the road was completed from Leeds Junction to Brunswick, narrow gauge. It was the intention of the directors to change the gauge of the line between Leeds and Farmington as soon as connection was made with

the narrow gauge road at Brunswick, but this decision had been secret, and the plan was not discovered until several months later by the Androscoggin & Kennebec officials. The credit of the company had been improved somewhat by the prospect of business on the proposed extension and by the assurance of assistance from the City of Bath, but its financial condition was nevertheless serious. The road between Leeds and Farmington had cost about $800,000, while the net earnings were about two per cent on the cost. The existing property was heavily mortgaged, some of the bonds were in default, and the floating debt was about $175,000.

In September, 1861, the Supreme Court, acting upon a petition of the Androscoggin & Kennebec officials, granted an injunction to restrain the Androscoggin management from changing the gauge of its road between Leeds and Farmington. The Androscoggin officials avoided actual service of the injunction, and on the next day, Sunday, proceeded to change the gauge, for which action some of the directors were held to be in contempt of court. The right of the company to change the gauge was in litigation for several years; and in 1864 a final decree sustained the right to change the gauge. During the period of litigation the Androscoggin was doing most of its business with the narrow gauge road at Brunswick.

In 1865 the holders of the mortgage on the road between Leeds and Farmington obtained title to the property by foreclosure, and organized a new corporation named the Leeds & Farmington Railroad Company. In 1867 this company leased its property to the Androscoggin Railroad for fifty years, and the road was operated by the latter company until 1871, when both railroads were leased to the Maine Central Railroad, and subsequently were merged in the Maine Central.

[ABOVE:] **Maine Central GP7 578 passes by the West Farmington station and church on October 29, 1977.** *Ron Johnson* [BELOW LEFT:] **1894 was the occasion of the 100th anniversary of Bowdoin College and the train shed at Bath got plastered with posters. MEC steamers 14 on left, built by the Portland Co., and 21, built in Rhode Island, go about their duties.** *Robert Baker collection* [BELOW RIGHT:] **Train 394 with consolidation 526 spewing coal dust over the white snow blasts by the Wilton depot in February 1941.** *Eugene Ellis from the 470 Railroad Club collection*

[LEFT:] **Note the two-foot gauge Sandy River & Rangeley Lakes track crossing Maine Central tracks twice plus the ball signal.** *Richard White collection* [BELOW:] **MEC Ten-Wheeler 284 dwarfs the tiny SR&RL engine at Farmington in the teens.** *Ron Johnson collection*

Boston & Maine E7 3813 heads up MEC Train 24 at Farmington on October 6, 1956. *Preston Johnson*

Chapter Six

Maine Central Organized

The Androscoggin & Kennebec and the Penobscot & Kennebec Railroads had been originally received as part of the same plan; and as soon as the latter company had completed its road from Waterville to Bangor, it was agreed that the two should be consolidated. In 1856 the legislature authorized this consolidation, but the narrow gauge interests, the Kennebec & Portland and the Somerset & Kennebec railroad groups, managed to insert in the law authorizing consolidation the famous "Ninth section", which provided that passengers between Fairfield and Portland were entitled to travel over either route at the same rate of fare. The broad gauge roads refused to consolidate under this law, and the Penobscot & Kennebec road was leased to the Androscoggin & Kennebec, which action placed both roads under one operating management.

The intersection of the roads at Fairfield caused keen competition for the passenger business. The narrow gauge line had an advantage because of its direct connection with the Boston road, while the passengers on the broad gauge road entered Portland on the Grand Trunk and were obliged to transfer across the city. In the legislature of 1857 an unsuccessful effort was made to repeal the "Ninth section". The Androscoggin & Kennebec, in order to

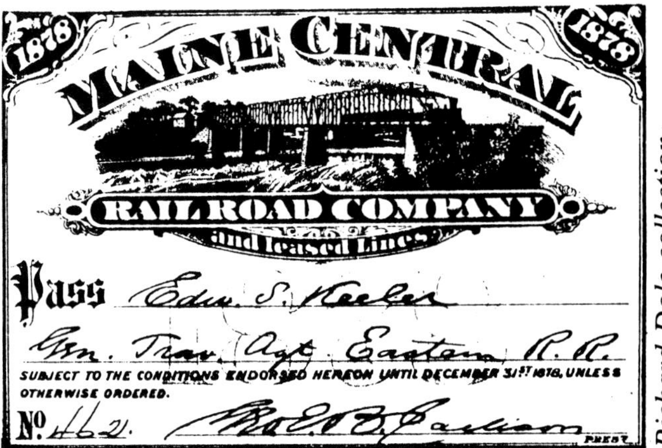
1878 MAINE CENTRAL 1878
RAIL ROAD COMPANY
and leased lines
Pass Edw. S. Keeler
Gen. Trav. Agt. Eastern R.R.
SUBJECT TO THE CONDITIONS ENDORSED HEREON UNTIL DECEMBER 31ST 1878, UNLESS OTHERWISE ORDERED.
No. 462.
PREST.

Richard Dole collection

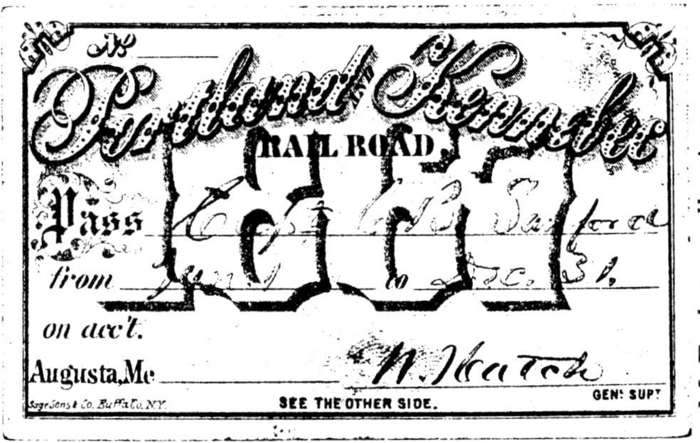
Portland & Kennebec
RAIL ROAD
Pass
from
to
on acc't.
Augusta, Me.
SEE THE OTHER SIDE.
GEN. SUPT.

Jim McFarlane collection

A Maine Central passenger train pulls through Lewiston with locomotive 34, "L. Strickland", towing four coaches and a baggage car in the late 1880's. *Richard Sanborn from the collection of Russell Monroe*

secure the passenger business from the west to points east of Fairfield, ran their passenger trains at a high rate of speed, and by this method were usually able to leave Fairfield before the arrival of the train over the narrow gauge route. They also operated a stage line between Augusta and Belgrade connecting with their trains, selling tickets from all stations east of Fairfield to Augusta at a lower price than the all-rail rate.

In 1858 the narrow gauge interests secured the passage of an act intended to compel connection between trains at Fairfield, and established a board of railroad commissioners with power to establish terms, times and rates for connecting railroads when the parties in interest were unable to agree. This was the beginning of the Board of Railroad Commissioners which was in existence from 1858 to 1915 when the Public Utilities Commission was established. The Androscoggin & Kennebec refused to comply with the provisions of this law, claiming that it was in conflict with the original charters. The railroad commissioners were called upon to fix terms and times, and the superintendent of the Androscoggin & Kennebec was arrested for violating the law. The question was argued before the Maine Law Court, which rendered a decision to the effect that the charters were contracts, the obligations of which the legislature had no power to impair. The decision led to the repeal of the "Ninth section" in 1862.

In August, 1862, the directors of the Androscoggin & Kennebec and the Penobscot & Kennebec Railroads agreed upon Articles of Consolidation, subsequently ratified by the stockholders, consolidating the two companies under the name of Maine Central Railroad Company. The Maine Central acquired all the properties, rights, privileges and franchises and assumed all obligations and liabilities of the former companies. The Maine Central Railroad Company was organized in October, 1862. Maine Central stock was issued share for share for stocks of the consolidating companies. The first balance sheet issued June, 1863, shows the total debt as $3,208,000 and capital stock $1,050,860, and the construction account $4,211,877.

The Maine Central Railroad as originally constituted was by no means the dominating influence in Maine railroading. Its gross earnings were about $350,000 in 1863 and about $600,000 in 1870. The annual net earnings during that period were never more than $250,000, barely covering the fixed charges. The combined traffic of the Androscoggin & Kennebec and Penobscot & Kennebec Railroads in 1860 was about 111,000 passengers and about 73,000 tons of merchandise. The stock was selling around $3.00 to $5.00 a share between 1865 and 1868. The railroad had no connection and no joint facilities with the Boston road, and all the westbound freight had to be hauled across Portland with no assurance that it would be received by the Boston road when delivered. The rival Portland & Kennebec was of the two roads the more prosperous and better managed, and although its relations with the Boston road were the subject of complaint on account of unfair rates and inadequate terminal facilities, its position in this respect seems to have been much more favorable than that of the Maine Central. The narrow gauge line had been directly connected with the Boston road for many years, and in 1865 the connection was improved by an arrangement for the joint use with the Portland, Saco & Portsmouth of the Portland station of the latter company.

Maine Central 0-4-0T 54 "Atlas" was built by the Portland Company in 1872, and rebuilt in 1884. Nicknamed "Ladybug" the faithful switcher is shown at South Gardiner about 1899. It was scrapped in 1906. *Richard Dole collection*

Maine Central 58 "Lewis Pearce" is under the train shed at Bangor in 1880. It was built by Taunton in 1873. *Ron Johnson collection*

Chapter Seven

European & North American Completed Building out of Portland

During the Civil War little attention was given to railroad building in the East, but the prosperity of railroads during the war led to an era of railroad building in the late sixties, and several important roads were built in Maine about that time. Railroad financing was especially easy, as European capital was available in large amounts; while in Maine the cities and towns, reflecting in their actions the prevailing sentiment of the people, were very generous in their assistance to railroad projects. This wholesale aid by municipalities was made possible by a law enacted by the legislature in 1867, which permitted cities and towns to raise by tax or loan any amount up to five per cent of the assessed valuation and to appropriate the funds to aid in construction of any railroad in Maine, provided two-thirds of the voters should so vote. Advantage was taken of this method to assure the construction of several railroads; and a substantial portion of the present debt of several Maine cities and towns is the result of unfortunate railroad investments made during the late sixties and early seventies.

The most important project of the time, which unfortunately never had any existence except on paper, was the plan of the Portland, Rutland, Oswego & Chicago Railway. This company was incorporated in 1868 as the Portland & Rutland Railroad by John A. Poor, John B. Brown, A.W.H. Clapp, William Deering, Charles Fobes, H.S. Libby, Israel Washburn, Jr., A.K. Shurtleff, Frederick Robie and other prominent men. The plan was to create a trunk line between Chicago and Portland, and the ultimate design seems to have been a Transcontinental Railway connecting, as far as possible by land, the commercial centres of North America, Europe and Asia. The plan was presented to an international convention held in Portland in 1868 and attended by more than three hundred men prominent in the affairs of the United States and Canada. The Chicago Board of Trade adopted resolutions favorable to the project. The consummation of the railroad to Chicago was confidently expected, as this required only the assent of seven railroads, six of which had agreed to the main features of the plan. The delay of one company prevented a definite agreement, and during this period of delay Mr. Poor died. The plan had been his conception, and its success required his vision and enthusiasm, so that the project virtually died with him.

The European & North American Railroad had not been forgotten by its promoters, in spite of the

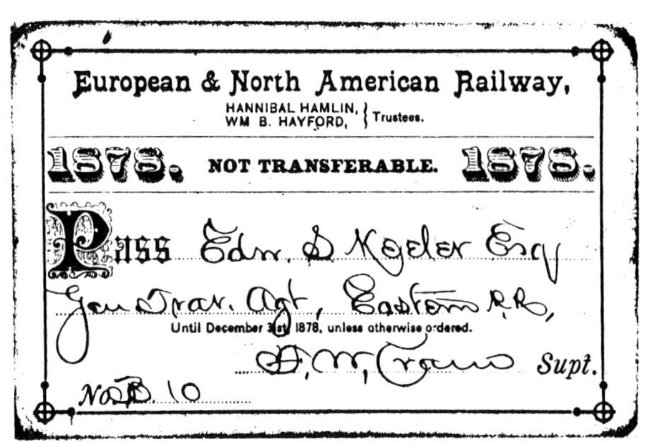
European & North American Railway,
HANNIBAL HAMLIN, WM B. HAYFORD, } Trustees.
1878. NOT TRANSFERABLE. 1878.
Pass
Until December 31st, 1878, unless otherwise ordered.
Supt.

Richard Dole collection

keen disappointment caused by the withdrawal of the British capitalists who had been expected to assist in building the road. The charter was kept alive by legislative enactment, and Mr. Poor left unturned no stone which might conceal a means for forwarding the enterprise. The first of a series of events which eventually restored active life to the European & North American was the incorporation of the Aroostook Railroad Company. It was the plan of the promoters of this company to secure railroad communication with Aroostook County, either by connection with the European & North American near Mattawamkeag or, in the event of the abandonment of that project, by construction from the terminus of the existing railroad at Milford. In 1859 the legislature passed "An Act to aid the Aroostook Railroad Company, increase the value and promote the sale and settlement of the public lands", subject, however, to approval by popular vote. The election was held in that year, and the Act was defeated by a vote of 18,795 against 14,922. In 1861 the legislature passed a similar Act, allocating a portion of the proceeds of sale of all remaining public lands in Penobscot and Aroostook Counties to be paid to the Aroostook Railroad Company, conditional upon the completion of the railroad to Mattawamkeag within four years, and further conditional upon the vote of the City of Bangor to loan its credit to the company. The funds received from the state could be paid only against actual construction on the road between Mattawamkeag and the eastern boundary and on the branch to Houlton. Terms were fixed by which the European & North American could purchase the Aroostook Railroad practically at cost. The City of Bangor voted not to loan its credit upon the specified terms, and the project failed again.

[ABOVE:] **Brand new Maine Central RS-3's 557 and 556 are ready to haul what seems like an endless string of passenger and mail cars west out of Vanceboro in 1953.** *Richard Dole collection* [BELOW:] **Eastbound VIA "Atlantic Limited" hurtles through Mattawamkeag in June 1985 at 6:30 A.M. shortly after startup of passenger service across Maine after an absence of several years. Train consist included an FP4 A and B and nine cars, including a dome car pictured on the opposite page in a going away shot at the same location.** *Ron Johnson*

This late 1800's view at Vanceboro show the complete facilities with enginehouse and turntable on the left and station on the right. Canadian Pacific locomotive 4-4-0 45 and train are on the left while Maine Central 4-4-0 63 "William G. Davis" has just arrived with an eastbound passenger train. *Robert Baker collection*

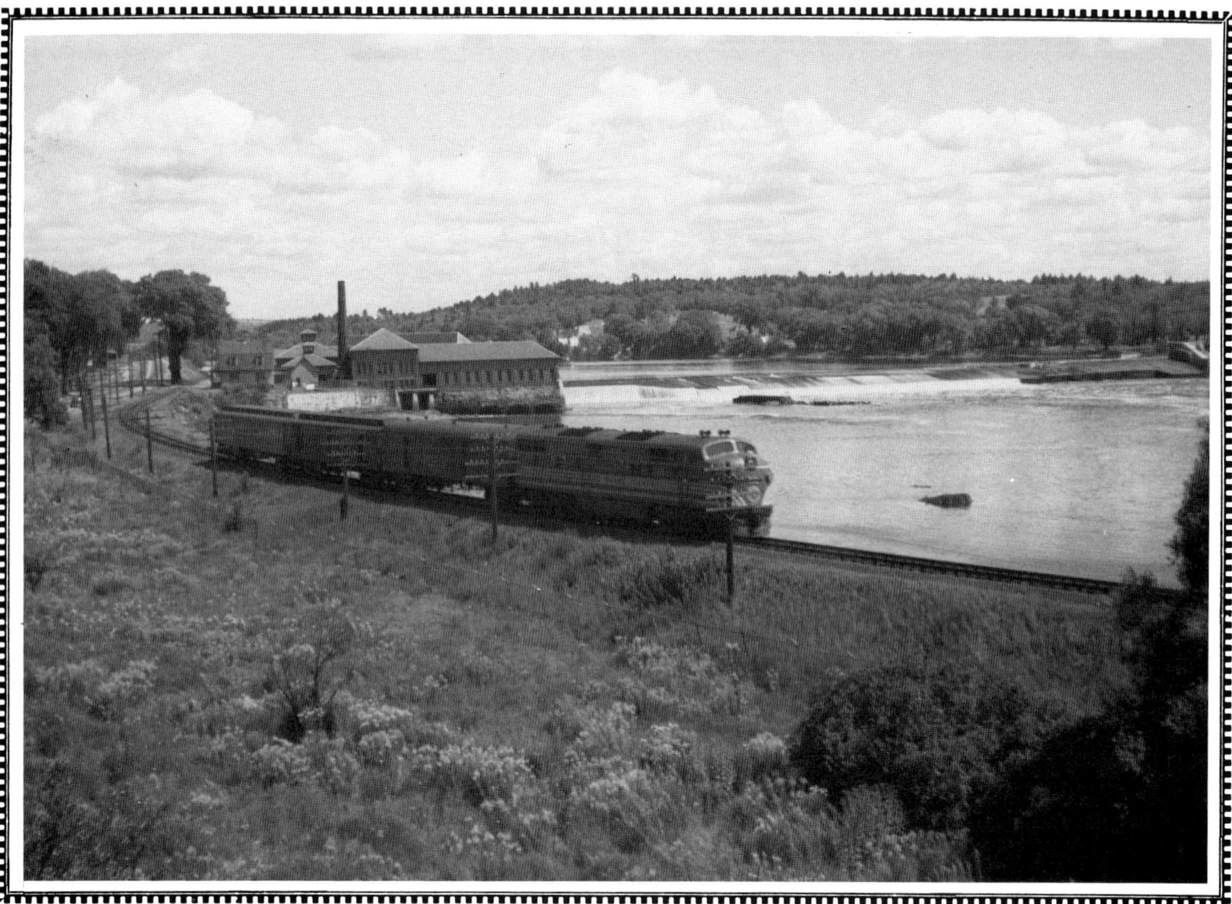

The reader is treated to latter day views along the former European & North American line from Bangor to Vanceboro. [ABOVE:] **Westbound Train 92 with a MEC E7 cruises past Bangor Hydro and the Penobscot River in April 1949.** *470 Railroad Club collection* [BELOW:] **MEC RS-11 802 is eastbound across the Penobscot River at Old Town with local freight for Mattawamkeag in August 1982.** *Ron Johnson*

Maine Central diesel railcar 901 hauls westbound Train 92 through Orono in the Fall of 1946. The 600 HP unit had space for passengers as well as RPO-baggage. Built in 1933, 901 still exists today as a shell in Belfast. *Howard Moulton from the collection of Russell Monroe*

In the meantime Mr. Poor and his associates had been busily seeking the means by which to build the European & North American road. The Maine representatives in Congress continued to urge the national government to lend assistance. The old claims of Maine and Massachusetts against the United States were revived by Mr. Poor, and probably because the claims had been practically repudiated for thirty years and were generally regarded as of small value, he succeeded in persuading the two states to assign their rights to his company, which ultimately collected about $800,000 in settlement. He secured the repeal of a law passed in 1860, which forbade the extension of the broad gauge by laying a third rail west of Portland, in order to appease the Massachusetts authorities who refused assistance to the European & North American on account of this unfriendly act. And during the Civil War, when the relations of the United States with England became strained and war appeared probable, the pronounced purpose of the European and North American Railroad group became the defense of the frontier, and to assist in that purpose the state granted to that company in somewhat modified form the public lands formerly granted conditionally to the Aroostook Railroad. The lands granted contained about 734,942 acres, of which about 70,000 acres in Piscataquis were later assigned to the Bangor & Piscataquis Railroad Company. The lands granted to the European & North American were for the most part located in Aroostook County, and their value when granted was about $1.50 an acre. There is some humor in a situation where a military exigency is assigned as a reason for granting assistance to a railroad which had been so highly commended by its promoters as a means for promoting international good will with the only country against which there was color of excuse for defending the northeastern frontier. But in 1864 there was a real possibility of war with England, and English troops had marched in the valley of the St. John within the memory of many men then living. The opinion once held by many that this land grant was an organized steal of the public lands does not appear to be sustained by the actual facts.

In 1863 the company had bought out the Penobscot Railroad, which had partially graded a line between Bangor and Milford; and this portion of the road was completed and opened in 1868. In 1864 the City of Bangor was authorized to aid in construction, and in 1869 the city loaned the railroad company $1,000,000, which loan was secured by mortgage on the road between Bangor and Winn. In 1869, after obtaining title to the public lands, a second bond issue was sold in the principal amount of $2,000,000 secured by first mortgage on the lands and on the portion of the road between Winn and Vanceboro, and by second mortgage on the road between Bangor and Winn. The road was opened to Mattawamkeag in 1869, and in 1870 the net earnings of this portion of the road were substantially in excess of interest charges on the City of Bangor mortgage. In 1870 a survey was made of a route from Moluncus north into Aroostook county. In 1871 the road was completed to Vanceboro. During the same year the European and North American Railway of New Brunswick was completed, making the road continuous between Bangor and St. John. President Grant and the Governor General of Canada and many other notables were present at the ceremony of formal opening of the railroad. John A. Poor had died six weeks before.

The history of the Portland & Rochester Railroad covers a period of about thirty years; but the influence of this enterprise on contemporary events was so slight and its part in the railroad quarrels so small that its story can here be fully written. The company was originally chartered in 1846 as the York & Cumberland Railroad with the right to build from Portland through Westbrook, Gorham, Buxton, Hollis, Sanford and other towns to South Berwick or Berwick, to connect there with a road to Boston, presumably the Boston & Maine which had its eastern terminus at South Berwick. One of the advantages claimed for a railroad over this route was the military importance of a means of interior communication. Construction started in 1850. John A. Poor became president in 1851, and by reconciling the factions then struggling for control, he was able to secure the construction of the road from Portland to the Saco River. The company maintained a precarious existence during fourteen years of almost constant litigation which prevented the further extension of the road. The bondholders eventually foreclosed and in 1865 organized a new company called the Portland & Rochester Railroad which took over the property, then consisting of eighteen miles of railroad in bad condition and having an estimated value of $200,000, as compared with a book value of over $560,000.

The management of the former company is credited with the suggestion that the western terminus should be changed from South Berwick to Rochester, New Hampshire, to connect with a proposed road between Rochester and Nashua which would connect with the Nashua & Worcester Railroad and form a continuous line from Portland to New York and to the West. This plan was approved by the new company, and in 1866 the legislature granted authority to change the route. The City of Portland was authorized to aid in construction to the extent of $300,000 on the condition that $150,000 should first be raised by sale of stock. This condition was never fulfilled.

In 1867 the general law authorizing cities and towns to aid in construction of railroads without specific legislative action was passed by the legislature. Under the provisions of this act the City of Portland voted to loan $700,000 to the Portland & Rochester Railroad, and in 1867 the city issued

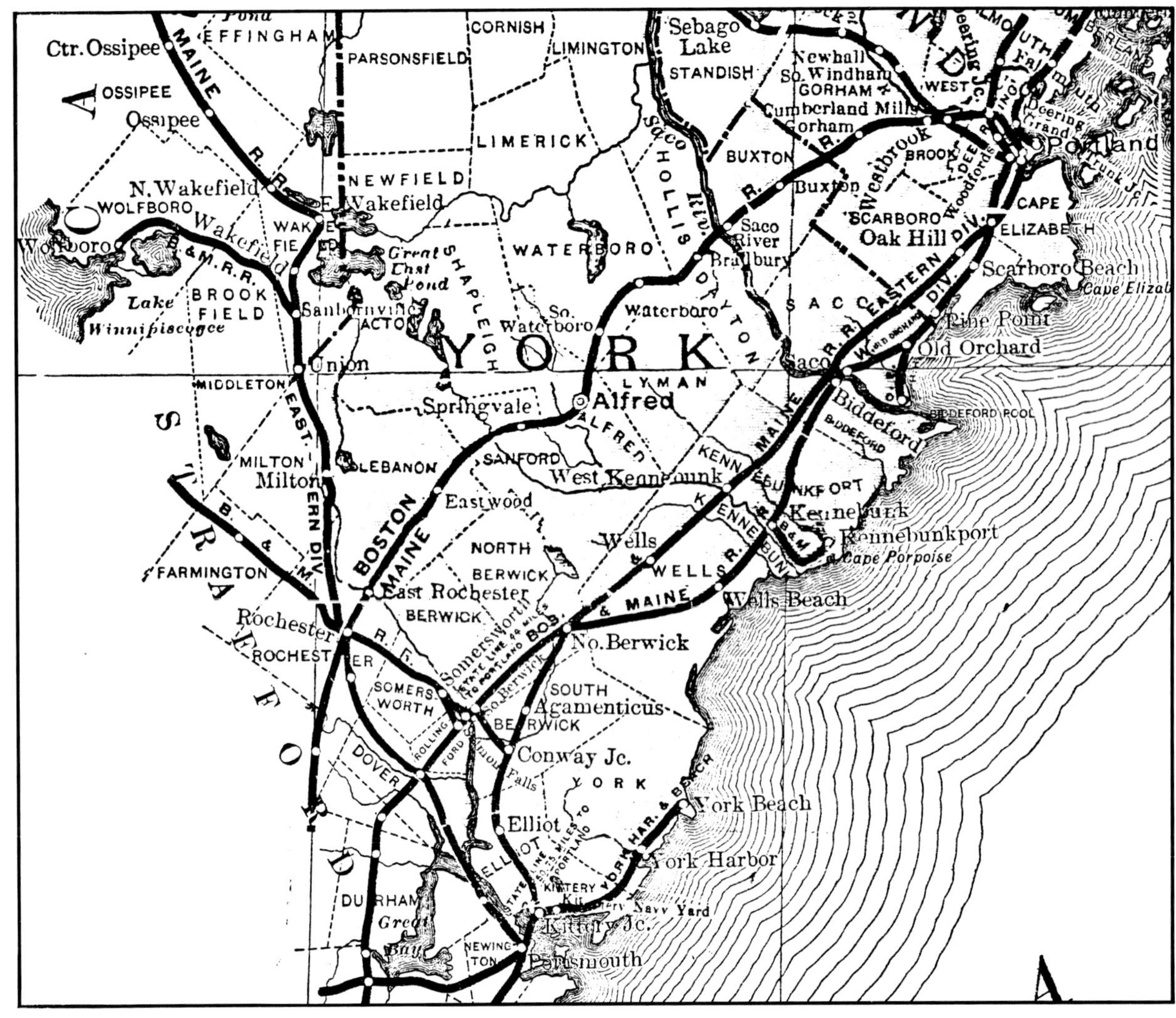

Portland & Rochester 3 "Rochester" was built by the Portland Co. in 1867. *Richard Dole collection*

[ABOVE:] **Sanford & Eastern 44 tonner 14 pulls a string of cars over former Portland & Rochester tracks past the boarded up Gorham station on November 25, 1960. The station has outlived the railroad as it has been converted to a restaurant while the shortline gave up the ghost in the early 60's.** *Russell Monroe* [LEFT:] **In a rare turn of the century action shot P&R 7 handles two coaches, a combine and baggage car.** *Russell Monroe collection*

bonds to that amount, receiving as security for the loan a mortgage on the railroad. With the proceeds of sale of the City of Portland bonds and about $68,000 additional raised by subscription in towns along the line the road was completed nearly to Springvale late in 1870. Additional funds being required, the City of Portland was persuaded to waive its rights as holder of a first mortgage and to permit the sale of $350,000 par value seven per cent bonds secured equally with the former mortgage. In 1871 more money was needed, and a new mortgage for $450,000 was created, but the bonds secured by this mortgage could not be sold. Ordinary methods having failed to effect a sale of these bonds, the company obtained a special act at the legislature in 1872, authorizing the City of Portland to grant additional aid, and by diligent effort secured the necessary two-thirds vote at the city election held the following summer. In this manner the new bond issue was sold to the City of Portland.

The road had been opened to Rochester but was by no means completed. Its earnings were very disappointing when compared with the estimates of the promoters. The railroad panic of 1873 injured its business and destroyed the small remaining vestige of its credit, and in 1874 the management advised the City of Portland that the company would be unable to pay interest on its loans. The city promptly issued bonds to secure funds to pay to the city the interest on the mortgages held by the city, virtually lending more money to the Portland & Rochester to enable the railroad to meet its fixed charges. By this arrangement the company's existence was prolonged until 1876 when it finally and conclusively defaulted. The Trustees of the mortgage securing the $350,000 bond issue were requested to foreclose, and in February, 1877, George P. Wescott, former president of the company, was appointed receiver. The company was reorganized in 1881, and the holders of the bonds received stock in the new company, which was capitalized at $600,000. The stock held by the City of Portland was sold and passed into the hands of the Boston & Maine, which by this purchase secured control of the railroad. The management was retained, and the road was operated as a separate company. In 1885 the Boston & Maine leased the Worcester, Nashua & Rochester Railroad, and it was then expected that the Portland & Rochester would also be leased and operated as part of the Boston & Maine system, but this lease was not executed. The affairs of the company were directed by a Maine board of directors until 1900, when the railroad was merged in the Boston & Maine. By this purchase and lease the Boston & Maine came into possession of the entire line of road, originally destined for a direct line from Portland to New York and for connection with western roads. It is hardly necessary to add that this destiny has never been achieved under Boston & Maine management.

The plan of the promoters of the Portland & Og-

Portland & Ogdensburg 2-6-0 7 "Carrigain" was built in 1872 by the Portland Co. *Ron Johnson collection*

[ABOVE:] **YR-1 (St. Johnsbury-Rigby) nears the end of its run in the early morning sun in the late 1970's. Three U18B's pull the train from Mountain Jct. onto the main line and into Rigby Yard. Note the General Office building in the background.** [OPPOSITE PAGE:] **A snowplow extra with GP7 567 hustles through Hiram on its way west to do battle with snow drifts in Crawford Notch during the winter of 1977.** *Both photos Ron Johnson*

densburg Railroad was of the same pattern as the Atlantic & St. Lawrence Railroad in its conception. The design was to secure the commerce of the Great Lakes district by a line of railroad from Portland to the Lakes at Ogdensburg, New York. A similar route for a railroad to Lake Champlain connecting with the Canadian canal system had been surveyed about 1839. The idea of Ogdensburg as a terminus attained great popularity on account of the recommendation of Charles Francis Adams that a road be built from Boston to the Lakes at that point. The distance from Ogdensburg to Portland was 42 miles less than to Boston, and many prominent Portland men hastened to seize the great opportunity which bore so strong an endorsement as the approval of Mr. Adams.

It would seem that Mr. Poor did not favor the Ogdensburg project, although it was apparently in conformance with his railroad theories. He was at this time working for the creation of his railroad to Chicago, which followed a more southern route, and in the absence of a clear statement his objections are liable to the suspicion of a personal interest. Perhaps he believed that the Grand Trunk Line from Montreal answered the purpose well enough.

The Portland & Ogdensburg Railroad was incorporated in 1867. The leaders of the enterprise were Samuel J. Anderson, who became president, and John E. Anderson, who became chief engineer. To aid in construction the City of Portland offered to loan the company $700,000 on the same terms as the original loan to the Portland & Rochester Railroad. But the promoters refused the assistance in the form of a loan, and by special act of the legislature in 1868, followed by a city election, the city actually purchased $714,300 par value of the capital stock. The amount received from all other sales of stock was about $335,000. With these funds available, the road was put under construction in 1869 and was completed to West Baldwin during 1870. In November, 1870, in order to secure additional funds, the company issued $800,000 first mortgage six per cent bonds, due in thirty years, which bonds were sold at about 82 per cent. When the road was opened to North Conway in 1871, all the proceeds of stock and bonds had been expended, and the company was heavily in debt.

It was the desire of the promoters to extend the road to the Connecticut River in order to connect with the Vermont division. In order to finance further construction another mortgage was created in the amount of $3,300,000, of which amount $800,000 was reserved to provide for bonds then outstanding. The available balance of $2,500,000 was secured by first mortgage on the proposed section from North Conway across New Hampshire and by second mortgage on the completed road between Portland and North Conway. In 1872 the legislature by special act authorized Portland to grant further aid up to $2,500,000, subject to a two-thirds vote. There was strong opposition to this proposition in Portland, led by Thomas B. Reed who was then beginning his political career, and it failed in the first election, but in a second election it was carried, the directors having agreed to call upon the city for only $1,350,000. The remainder of the issue was taken by the contractors.

A contract for remaining construction was made with Fuller & Harding, who agreed to build the mountain section for $2,000,000 in cash, or for $2,300,000 if half in cash and half in bonds. The company elected to pay the larger amount in the manner specified. The contractors could not sell the bonds during 1872, and the work was delayed for lack of funds. The financial panic in 1873 caused serious losses to Fuller & Harding in other ventures, and made the sale of the Ogdensburg bonds impossible. In 1874 the contractors failed, having built the road as far as Crawford Notch. The company assumed charge of construction, and the road reached Fabyans in August, 1875. In December of that year connection with the Vermont division was established by an arrangement with the Boston, Concord & Montreal Railroad.

The building of the mountain section was considered an engineering accomplishment of great merit which established the fame of John F. Anderson, the engineer who planned the road. From tide-

water at Portland the road ascends to an elevation of 680 feet at Upper Bartlett with a maximum grade of 80 feet to the mile. Above Bartlett the height increases within a distance of fourteen and one half miles to a maximum elevation of 1900 feet with the steepest grade about 115 feet to the mile. The cost of operation on such a grade, today practically prohibitive, was then considered of minor importance, and special emphasis was laid on the argument that the heavy traffic would move down the grade as the products of the west moved on their way to Portland, "the ocean gateway of North America".

The section of road between Portland and Bartlett had been built without difficulty and at reasonable cost, and was by itself a paying proposition. But the management, being eager to reach the final objective, by continuing construction through the mountains burdened the profitable section of road with the interest charges on an expensive section of unprofitable road, had expended the entire amount received from Portland, and had created a floating debt of about $400,000. In 1875 interest was defaulted on the consolidated mortgage, of which Portland held $1,350,000. The balance of $918,000 was pledged to secure loans. In July, 1876, interest was only partially paid on the first mortgage, and defaulted altogether in January, 1877. On that date the arrears in interest on the bonded debt was about $155,000. (The subsequent history of the Portland & Ogdensburg appears in the Maine Central history.)

Westbound RY-2 with two GP-38's, two GP7's and an RS11 cast their reflection in Pequaket Pond in Brownfield, October 1974. *Ron Johnson*

[RIGHT:] **Eight units head up eastbound YR-1 through Hiram December 4, 1976. The extra four locomotives was due to a wreck several days before.** [BELOW:] **Guilford's "Safety Express" passes by Sebago Lake September 1983.** *Both photos Ron Johnson*

Chapter Eight

Knox & Lincoln to Rockland
Somerset up the Kennebec Valley

This scene shows a gravel train on the Knox & Lincoln during the building of the line. *Ron Johnson collection*

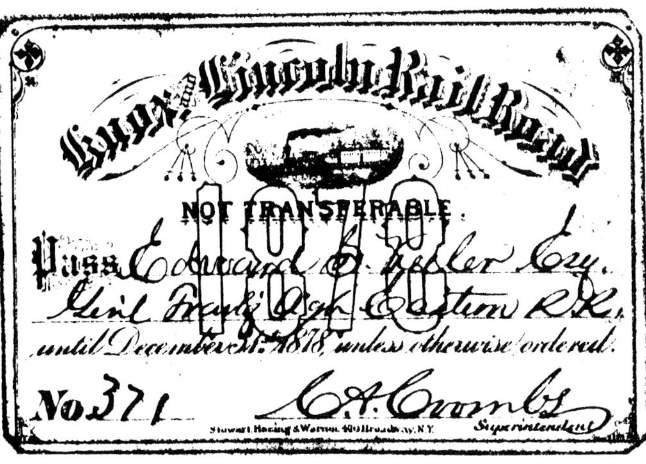

Richard Dole collection

Maine Central 4-4-0 152 is eastbound over the diamond with the narrow gauge Wiscasset, Waterville & Farmington at Wiscasset in the early 1900's. *470 Railroad Club collection*

The idea of a railroad from the Kennebec River to Rockland first appears in the charter of the Penobscot & Kennebec Railroad Company granted by the legislature in 1849. The confusion due to the identity in name with the railroad chartered to build between Waterville and Bangor was immediately recognized, and the same legislature changed the name to the Penobscot, Lincoln & Kennebec Railroad. The long list of incorporators includes the names of many prominent coast families. The charter was kept alive by legislative enactment, and in 1864 the charter was amended by changing the name to the Knox & Lincoln Railroad Company. By the same act the location of the road was authorized from Rockland through the counties of Knox and Lincoln to a point on the west side of the Kennebec River between the south line of Bath and the north line of Richmond, to connect with the Portland & Kennebec Railroad.

The town of Wiscasset was sponsor for a project which then existed on paper in the name of the Wiscasset & Kennebec Railroad, which company made a survey in 1866 for a route from Wiscasset to Harwoods Crossing on the Portland & Kennebec, and for alternative routes to Bath and Richmond. Assurances of the early construction of the Knox & Lincoln line caused the abandonment of this project

The cities and towns along the route were authorized to issue bonds to the railroad company to aid in construction in the following amounts: Rockland $400,000; Thomaston $200,000; Warren $50,000; Waldoboro $150,000; Damariscotta $100,000; Newcastle $100,000; Nobleboro $25,000; Wiscasset $150,000. These loans were to be secured by mortgage on the railroad, and were conditional upon prior expenditure of at least $300,000 raised by the sale of stock.

The original subscription for stock totalled $370,000, of which amount the City of Bath bought $125,000; Wiscasset $15,000; Waldoboro $10,000; Thomaston $25,000; and Rockland $100,000. The survey was completed late in 1867, and a route was established with a maximum grade of 53 feet to the mile. The line finally adopted was so distant from the village of Warren that aid could not be granted by that town. The first estimate of cost was about $1,464,624. The original city and town loans issued in aid of construction totalled about $1,300,000.

In 1867 by legislative action the City of Bath was authorized to loan its credit up to $600,000, provid-

[ABOVE:] **Maine Central's car ferry and station are pictured at Woolwich. The ferry ran back and forth across the Kennebec River between Bath and Woolwich.** *Richard Sanborn via Russell Monroe collection* [BELOW:] **The Carlton highway and rail bridge was completed in 1927. Doubleheaded locomotives 370 4-6-0 and 527 2-8-0 are westbound off the bridge at Bath on July 10, 1940.** *Howard Kirkpatrick*

Brand new 660 HP S-1 953 was the first diesel to operate on the Rockland branch and is shown switching at Bath in February 1941. *Howard Kirkpatrick*

[RIGHT:] **Tiny gas switcher 1 was leased by the Kennebec Wharf & Coal Co. of Bath after the abandonment of the Androscoggin & Kennebec electric line in 1937. It was built by Whitcomb in 1932.** [BELOW:] **Freshly overhauled Big 0 4-6-0 407 really shines as it pauses at the Bath station in February 1941 with an eastbound passenger train.** *Both photos Howard Kirkpatrick*

[LEFT:] **Classic Downeast railroading at its best is presented at Warren around 1911, complete with horse and buggy and lunch basket.** *Richard Dole collection*

[RIGHT:] **One more scene at Bath shows MEC RS2's 554 and 555 with an east-bound freight meeting RS11 801 in July 1963.** *Robert Baker*

Georges Valley 4-4-0 4 simmers with an ancient coach at the end of the line at Georges Valley in the early 1900's. *Russell Monroe collection*

Pacific 458 is westbound across the Sheepscot Inlet trestle at South Newcastle with Train 52 in 1948. *William Gale from the 470 Railroad Club collection*

ed the western terminus should be at Bath, and the Town of Richmond $150,000 provided the western terminus should be at Richmond. Before that time there had been considerable argument regarding the best plan for crossing the Kennebec River, and there were many who favored a bridge at Richmond. However, the amount of assistance offered by Bath summarily disposed of the Richmond bridge plan, and the project went forward under the leadership of Oliver Moses of Bath. Moses was one of the most active businessmen of that day. He was President of the Androscoggin Railroad and had taken a leading part in building the Androscoggin extension from Leeds to Brunswick. After this railroad was built he was active in the development of water power on the lower Androscoggin River, and was one of the founders of the Worumbo Manufacturing Company in 1865. In 1870 the Knox & Lincoln was authorized to operate a ferry at Bath in connection with its railroad business, and to erect wharves and acquire other necessary property. In 1869 a charter was granted to the Penobscot Bay & River Railroad to build a road from Rockland to Bangor, and it was planned that this road should be leased to the Knox & Lincoln when completed.

The magnitude of this undertaking was not fully appreciated by its promoters; and as the work progressed the original estimates of cost were found to be far too low. There had never been a railroad built in Maine, and indeed few anywhere else, through country possessing the characteristics of the coast of Maine between Pemaquid and Penobscot Bay. Other Maine railroads had followed the easy slopes of the river valleys, but no river route was available for any considerable distance along this line. A large amount of costly rock work was encountered, and expensive fills and bridge work were necessary in crossing the heads of the bays and the tidal rivers.

In 1870 all available funds had been expended, and in the fall of that year the cities and towns by special elections voted to raise their respective quotas of a new loan of $475,000, and these votes were made valid by the legislature of 1871. A second mortgage was put on the property to secure these loans. But the estimate of cost of completion had again been too optimistic, and before the summer of 1871 it was apparent that more money would be necessary. Again each city and town voted its quota of a new loan of $650,000, and these votes were made valid by the legislature of 1872. The total amount of city and town bonds outstanding, representing loans to the Knox & Lincoln and secured by first, second and third mortgages, was $2,395,000.

Trains were running over the road in November, 1871, but it was not completed until the following year. The final cost was about $2,700,000, about $55,000 per mile. An attempt was made to lease the property to the Maine Central Railroad, but that company's best offer was to operate the road at cost for five years. Independent operation continued under a board of directors representing the cities and towns, which held among them a large majority

The Limerock Railroad interchanged with the Maine Central at Rockland. In July 1936 0-4-0T 4 hauls a cut of loaded limerock cars at the north end of the line. *Beverley Historical Society from the collection of Russell Monroe*

of the stock. (The subsequent history of the Knox & Lincoln appears later.)

Two other short lines connected with the Knox & Lincoln. One was an industrial road called the Limerock Railroad, chartered in 1864 in Rockland. The 5 miles of track reached the quarries in the area. The line operated until the mid 1930's. Another shortline called the Georges Valley Railroad began operations from Warren in 1893. Later in 1899 it was renamed the Knox Railroad. Owned by the Great Northern Paper Company, the Knox Railroad lasted until the late 1930's.

It was natural that the citizens of Belfast, having been the leaders in the first important railroad project, should have continued their efforts to secure railroad facilities. In 1848 a charter was granted for a railroad from Belfast to Waterville, to connect there with the Androscoggin & Kennebec road, which was then under construction; but this plan was abandoned. In 1853 Albert J. Jewell conceived the idea of a railroad to Moosehead Lake, and a charter was granted to the Belfast & Moosehead Lake Railroad. The plan was to build a road from Belfast to Newport and from Newport through Dexter and Dover to Greenville. The charter of the Dexter & Newport Railroad, which was granted in 1853, authorized the Belfast & Moosehead Lake Railroad to buy from or build in the name of the Dexter & Newport Railroad the railroad between Newport and Dexter. The charter of the Belfast & Moosehead Lake Railroad expired on account of the inaction of the promoters.

This charter was revived in 1867 when the popular craze for railroad building made possible the financing of railroad construction on the credit of cities and towns. The City of Belfast voted to subscribe for $360,400 in common stock of the company, and individual subscriptions were received totalling about $156,000. The construction contract was for a broad gauge road to Newport at $25,900 a mile, payable $21,428 in cash and $4,472 in preferred stock.

The towns along the line, which had been authorized to buy stock in amounts up to twenty-five per cent of their respective valuations, were not enthusiastic to the extent of voting any material assistance, and Belfast was obliged to finance the company. In 1868 the city purchased $140,000 par value of preferred stock and later advanced a substantial amount for bonds and notes of the railroad com-

GP38 262 fields a short train across the unusual lift bridge spanning the St. Georges River at South Warren on April 11, 1978. *Ron Johnson*

pany. It soon became apparent that no money was available for building to Moosehead Lake, although the Dexter & Newport Railroad had built its part of the line in 1868. It was, therefore, proposed to change the terminus to Fairfield. This proposal was based upon an offer made by the then independent Portland & Kennebec Railroad to lease the Belfast road, and it was believed that the Portland & Kennebec management had in mind the construction of a line from Brooks to Bangor. This lease was approved by the citizens of Belfast, but the Board of Aldermen acting for the city refused to ratify it. This action caused great indignation, and added to the financial distress of the railroad company. It was claimed that the action of the Belfast aldermen in refusing to ratify the lease of the road to the Portland & Kennebec Railroad was the result of influence brought to bear by the Maine Central officials to prevent the consummation of the lease. It appears, however, that the Maine Central had promptly presented a counter proposition offering to lease the road upon terms which were regarded by the directors as more favorable to the company. In 1869 an agreement was made to lease the road, when completed, to the Maine Central, and to change the location of the terminus to Burnham. The annual rental agreed upon was $48,000, but the Maine Central refused to accept the road as first constructed. After defects in construction had been partially remedied the property was leased in 1871 to the Maine Central for fifty years at an annual rental of $36,000. The cost of the road was about $850,000.

For many years there was a dispute among the stockholders which finally ended in litigation regarding the disposition of the annual rental. Some of the stockholders favored the payment of dividends in the largest possible amount without making any attmept to reduce the debt, whereas the City of Belfast was committed to the policy of reducing the debt as rapidly as possible. The actions taken by Belfast in pursuance of this policy were later sustained by the Court. The debt was finally paid in full, and the present capitalization consists of $267,700 par value stock and $380,400 par value common stock. The City of Belfast owns 1396 shares of the preferred stock and all the common stock, except 200 shares which is owned by the town of Brooks.

From 1871 through 1925 this road was operated as part of the Maine Central system. The original lease expired in 1921, and was then renewed, subject to termination by either party on six months' notice. In July, 1925, the Maine Central management gave notice of its intention to terminate the lease on January 1, 1926.

The Dexter & Newport Railroad was chartered in 1853 to build a railroad from Dexter to Newport to connect with the Penobscot & Kennebec road which was then under construction. This project was part of the plan for the railroad from Belfast to Moosehead Lake. The charter was kept alive, but the company was not organized until 1867, when the Belfast & Moosehead Lake Railroad Company was revived. Construction of the road was made possible

Belfast & Moosehead Lake Ten-Wheeler 19 throws out a nice smoke plume with a two car train at City Point near Belfast. *Richard Sanborn via Russell Monroe collection*

by the loan of credit of the towns of Dexter and Corinna in the amounts of $125,000 and $50,000 respectively. The railroad was opened in 1868; and in February, 1869, apparently after the Belfast company had abandoned its plan to build to Newport, the road was leased to the Maine Central. Since that date this road has been part of the Maine Central system. The lease was later renewed for 999 years. This road was originally broad gauge.

The Somerset Railroad was chartered in 1860 to build a railroad in the Kennebec Valley between Waterville and Carratunk Falls through Fairfield, Norridgewock, Anson and other towns. Its proposed route followed the original line of the Somerset & Kennebec Railroad charter, the latter company never having built above Skowhegan. The location finally selected was to a connection with the broad gauge Maine Central road at Oakland (then West Waterville). Most of the stock of the company was owned by the towns of Norridgewock, Anson and Embden. In 1868 the Maine Central purchased $50,000 par value Somerset Railroad stock; and it was the original plan of the builders, apparently agreeable to both companies, that the road would be leased to the Maine Central. The Somerset road was opened to Norridgewock in 1873 and to Madison in 1875, and was gradually extended up the river. It was originally built broad gauge.

The proposed lease of the Somerset to the Maine Central was not executed. Contemporary railroad history indicates that the builders of the Somerset road soon became infected by the Quebec railroad virus and succumbed to that insidious and often fatal idea which has run through the record of Maine railroads from the beginning. In the early seventies several railroad projects were presented which were clearly parts of one plan, and it would appear that the parties had definitely established a community of interest on a working basis. This grand plan was for a railroad from Wiscasset to Quebec.

Of the histories of the coast towns which have aspired to greatness by reason of natural harbor facilities that of Wiscasset is perhaps the most disappointing. After the capture of Quebec and before the Revolution, when the British had established their supremacy on the North American continent, the British Admiralty, having made a survey of the harbor of Wiscasset, contemplated making this port the principal naval base in North America. In the early days of railroads Wiscasset, with Portland and Belfast, was considered one of the possible termini for a railroad to Quebec. The town finally secured railroad facilities by joining in the Knox & Lincoln enterprise, from which it emerged like the rest with a large financial loss. But it never abandoned its larger ambition, and in the seventies some of its citizens made heroic efforts to establish the town as the coast terminus of a railroad from the interior.

The Kennebec & Wiscasset Railroad was originally chartered to build from Wiscasset through Alna and Whitefield to the Kennebec River between Gardiner and Augusta. Wiscasset voted aid to the amount of $150,000; Alna voted $40,000, and Whitefield $150,000; and individual subscriptions were secured totalling $400,000. The success of the promoters depended upon their securing financial assistance from Augusta, which was denied. But it seems probable that Augusta would have joined if the Quebec road had been assured. Later the charter of the Kennebec & Wiscasset Railroad was amended to authorize the construction of a railroad north to a connection with the Bangor & Piscataquis Railroad, and the name was changed to the Wiscasset & Moosehead Lake Railroad. Towns along the line of the route were authorized to loan their credit to the extent of twenty per cent of their valuations, and St. Albans, Hartland, Canaan and Cambridge voted aid. Foreign capitalists were ready to invest in the company, but the necessary amount of municipal aid could not be secured.

Another link in the railroad to Quebec was to

MEC GP7's 573 and 571 cast their reflection in Sebasticook Lake while heading north for Dover-Foxcroft on April 19, 1976. *Ron Johnson*

Somerset 1 "Carratunk", built by the Portland Co. in 1873, looks sharp with its sunflower stack. It was sold by the Maine Central to the Somerset in 1900. *Richard Dole collection*

[RIGHT:] **A Somerset train casts a perfect reflection in the still waters of the Kennebec River at Norridgewock.** [BELOW:] **Trestlework is being built somewhere on the Somerset Railroad. Note 4-4-0 4 "Carrabassett" plus several wood sheathed freight cars.** *Both photos Richard Dole collection*

have been built in the name of the Messalonskee & Kennebec Railroad, chartered in 1874 to build from Augusta to West Waterville, there to connect with the Somerset road; and the Somerset was authorized to extend to the Canadian line. The Canadian portion of the line was in the process of construction by the Levis & Kennebec Railroad, which company built in 1874 about forty-three miles of road between Harlaka Junction and St. Joseph. It was the definite plan of this company to connect with the Somerset road, and it was stated that Wiscasset was the ultimate objective. The panic of 1873 practically stopped the flow of capital into railroad construction, and the program became impossible to carry out. The Levis & Kennebec road was sold to the Quebec Central in 1881, and is now part of the Canadian Pacific system. (The later history of the Somerset road appears hereafter.)

The Bangor & Piscataquis Railroad was chartered in 1864 to build a railroad from Old Town to Moosehead Lake. The company was organized in 1867. The principal promoters were Hannibal Hamlin, Isaiah Stetson, George Stetson, Charles Stetson, A.G. Wakefield, Franklin A. Wilson and N.C. Ayer, all of Bangor, and A.M. Robinson of Dover. Hannibal Hamlin was the first president, but he soon resigned and Isaiah Stetson took his place. In 1868 the legislature authorized the City of Bangor to loan its credit to aid construction and the town of Dover was also authorized to assist. The company received about 75,000 acres of the lands which had been originally granted to the European & North American, 5 feet 6 inch gauge, and assumed the attendant obligation, real or implied, to build a railroad into Piscataquis County. The road was opened to Dover in December, 1869. It was built broad gauge, connecting at Old Town with the European & North American. The City of Bangor furnished most of the money that built the road. The promoters were confident of being able to secure a large amount of business through the development of the iron and slate resources in the territory. The company was soon in financial distress, and in 1872 was unable to pay in full the interest on the first mortgage. Probably the officers were glad to escape from the responsibilities when the opportunity to lease the road to the European & North American appeared. (The history of the Bangor & Piscataquis Railroad appears later.)

[ABOVE:] **Greenville Jct. hosts Bangor & Piscataquis 4-4-0 3 "Moosehead" and train on September 8, 1888. The B&P connected with the Canadian Pacific here.** *470 Railroad Club collection* [RIGHT:] **Bangor & Piscataquis 4 "Hamlin" and work train pose on the Bunker Brook trestle between Blanchard and Shirley about 1883.** *Richard Dole collection*

Chapter Nine

Final Change to Standard Gauge
Maine Central Dominated by the Eastern

All of these new railroads completed or in the process of construction from 1865 to 1870 brought again to the front the question of gauges. Thirty-five years of American railroading had never demonstrated the superiority of one gauge over another, although the gauge of four feet eight and one-half inches had been generally adopted as standard. It was vital to Maine that the question should be settled before more new construction should add to the already complex problem. And aside from the matter of gauge the advantages of unity of operation were becoming apparent. The financial losses already incurred, the economic wastes of the different gauges, the power of the Boston road over its small feeders, and the constant quarreling among Maine railroads gradually led a large majority to believe that consolidation of the Maine railroad system was absolutely essential.

The only railroad company in Maine which had displayed any outstanding ability in railroad management was the Portland & Kennebec Railroad of which Richard D. Rice was president. This company had acquired title to the Kennebec & Portland Railroad through foreclosure proceedings, and had been successfully operating the road and the leased Somerset & Kennebec since 1864. The title of this company to the property was still in question, having been in litigation for several years, and there were many who questioned the good faith in the original Williams transaction by which the Rice group had come into possession of the road.

Apparently those favoring consolidation believed that the situation warranted desperate measures. In May, 1870, the directors of the Portland & Kennebec and of the Maine Central Railroad executed a lease of the property of the former company and an assignment of its 999 year lease of the Somerset & Kennebec property to the Maine Central Railroad for 999 years. A contract of the same date provided for the resignation of at least four of the Maine Central directors and the election of four of the Portland & Kennebec directors in their places. The lease would become void in the event of a court decision against the Portland & Kennebec stockholders with respect to their title to the property. The gauge of the Maine Central would be changed to standard and a line of that gauge would be built from Danville to connect with the Portland & Kennebec main line near Yarmouth.

A special meeting of the stockholders to approve this lease was called on May 31, 1870. The advocates of the broad gauge, the old stockholders of the Ken-

Train 10 with engine 466 comes off the Lower Road with Back Road on the left at Royal Jct., originally Cumberland Jct., on April 11, 1946. The tower is pictured on the left from where the first picture was taken. *470 Railroad Club collection*

[ABOVE:] **Symbol freight BASE (Bangor-Selkirk) passes under an old wooden private automobile bridge at West Falmouth with a Boston & Maine GP40-2 in the lead in August 1984.** [BELOW:] **Maine Central BR-4 (Bangor-Rigby) with U18B, GP7R and GP7 pulls through the snow in January 1981 at Yarmouth.** *Both photos Ron Johnson*

nebec·& Portland, and even the Maine Central stockholders were taken by surprise. Mr. Poor, the leading advocate of the broad gauge, appeared at the meeting and in a long speech denounced the whole proceeding and the parties to it. A bare majority of the stock was represented at the meeting and the motion for ratification of the lease and contract was carried by vote of less than half of the stock.

Mr. Poor commenced a suit in equity, seeking to restrain the Maine Central directors from carrying out the provisions of the contract, and he attempted to get a receiver appointed, but the motion was dismissed, as was also a later petition, the Court holding that a change of gauge would be beneficial to all parties to the contract. Other efforts failed to prevent the consummation of the lease, and in 1872 the legislature passed an act expressly recognizing its validity.

In the meantime the provisions of the contract were carried out. The title of the Portland & Kennebec Railroad to its property had been confirmed by the courts, and the new Maine Central board of directors had been elected as follows: Amos D. Lockwood, Richard D. Rice, Abner Coburn, George M. Patten, Reuben B. Dunn, John B. Brown and James F. Rawson. Richard D. Rice became president. In November, 1870, the gauge of the road from Waterville to Bangor was changed to standard, and through trains began running between Bangor and Boston. Freight between Bangor and Boston which formerly required four days in transit now moved between cities in one day. The extension from Danville to Cumberland Junction was completed in November, 1871, and in the same month the gauge became standard on the entire Maine Central main line. In 1872 the only broad gauge roads in Maine were the Atlantic & St.

Lawrence, the European & North American, the Bangor & Piscataquis, the Portland & Oxford Central and the Somerset Railroad. Within a few years all of these roads changed to standard gauge.

The Maine Central Railroad, by reason of its lease of the Portland & Kennebec and the Somerset & Kennebec in 1870, the Androscoggin, the Leeds & Farmington, and the Belfast & Moosehead Lake Railroad in 1871, became a railroad of considerable importance, operating 357 miles of road with gross earnings over $1,500,000. In 1871 the total interest-bearing debt was $7,989,014 and the capital stock $3,434,520. The new dignity of the company and the aggressive policy of the Rice management first appeared in a change in the railroad's relations with the Boston road.

The owners of the Portland, Saco & Portsmouth Railroad had become dissatisfied with the terms of the lease of their road to the Eastern and the Boston & Maine Railroads because their six per cent dividends were being paid in depreciated currency instead of gold, and they decided to pay the stipulated penalty for breach of contract and to cancel the lease. The railroad system in Maine was beginning to produce a large amount of traffic and more lines were building with the promise of more business. The control of the Portland, Saco & Portsmouth road was essential to any railroad which wanted the Maine business, and this was fully recognized by its owners. It was said that the Maine Central promoted the cancellation of the Portland, Saco & Portsmouth lease by offering a rental of five per cent in gold instead of the six per cent rental then paid in currency. However, this rumor would seem to be at variance with the statement of President Rice in his report to the Maine Central stockholders.

In 1870 the lease was cancelled, and the owners of the road were free to trade with the three railroads, the Eastern, the Boston & Maine, and the Maine Central, and they traded so successfully that a lease to the Eastern at a ten per cent rental was executed in 1871. As soon as the Eastern acquired full control it refused permission to the Boston & Maine to run its trains over the road, and as a result the Boston & Maine was obliged to build its line from South Berwick to Portland. This extension was completed in 1873.

One branch line off the Boston & Maine was the Kennebunk & Kennebunkport Railroad. It was built in 1883 off the main line at Kennebunk and ran east 4½ miles. After being leased to the Boston & Maine, that road ran it until abandonment in 1925. Another branch was the 3.24 Orchard Beach Railroad. It began operations in 1880 and ran from Old Orchard to Camp Ellis. The line was leased by the Boston & Maine in 1893, who ran the trains until 1923. Still another short line was the York Harbor & Beach Railway. It opened in 1887 from Kittery and a connection with the Boston & Maine to Old Orchard Beach. It too was leased to the Boston &

[ABOVE and BELOW:] **Scarboro Beach is represented with two different views of westbound Boston & Maine trains in the late 1800's.** *Russell Monroe collection*

[BELOW:] **Boston & Maine 0-6-0 101 trundles down cobblestones and snow covered Commercial Street in Portland to a connection with the Grand Trunk. The Custom House with its tower is in the background in this early 1900's photo.** *Russell Monroe collection*

[ABOVE:] **The first train on the York Harbor & Beach Railroad pauses at Long Beach in 1887.** *Howard Moulton collection* [BELOW:] **The Old Orchard Beach Railroad boasted some unique equipment in the form of open side cars for tourists and 0-4-0 86 "Bay View".** *Beverley Historical Society from the collection of Russell Monroe*

Maine who ran it until abandonment in 1925.

The Orchard Junction Railroad operated a short time from Saco on the Portland, Saco & Portsmouth to Old Orchard Beach, a distance of 14 miles. It started running in 1881, however, rails were removed in 1885.

Having secured control of the only western outlet for Maine Central traffic, the Eastern made a contract with the Maine Central for its entire western business. Contrary to the intention and expectation of the Eastern management, the terms of this contract became so onerous upon the Eastern, especially in the item of car demurrage, that Mr. Lothrop, the new president of the Eastern, having exhausted all ordinary measures to get the contract amended, conceived the idea of buying the control of the Maine Central for the Eastern in order to get out of the contract. In pursuance of this plan 7619 shares of Maine Central stock were purchased at an average cost of around $70 a share. This stock was sufficient to enable the Eastern interests to control the election of the board of directors at the annual meeting of the Maine Central in March, 1873. The purchase of Maine Central stock was continued until 1875, making a final total of 15,274 shares which cost about $1,220,000.

In June, 1873, the new Maine Central board, now dominated by the Eastern interests, amended the contract of 1871, annulling the car demurrage clause. Other traffic contracts were made in 1873, 1874 and 1875. The Boston & Maine road having reached Portland, in 1874 the Maine Central executed a contract with that road, but the Eastern Railroad had all of the important advantages.

Chapter Ten

Panic of 1873 Limits Rail Building Maine Central Grows to Largest Mileage in New England

The late sixties was a period of national enthusiasm for railroad building, and attention had been especially directed to the building of railroads to the Pacific. Direct financial aid was given by the national government, but the more popular method of assistance was by grants of land. About 240,000 square miles of land, in area about eight times as large as the state of Maine, was given to the railroads. The evidence of this enthusiasm appears constantly in the records of the times until the early seventies. About 1870 was the beginning of a wave of discontent and an agitation against railroads which came largely from the inception of the "granger movement" in the west. The opponents of the railroads were not without ammunition for their attacks. There had been many scandals connected with the construction and capitalization of railroads, of which the more notable instances were the construction of the Central Pacific, the watering of the Erie stock, and the Credit Mobilier scandal which involved many nationally known men.

The amount of railroad construction in progress was beyond the resources of the nation to finance, and a large part of the investment in American railroads was European capital. The supply of funds from Europe ceased at the time of the Franco-Prussian War in 1871. The condition of national disorder, intensified by the popular agitation against capital, aggravated by the railroad wars, and increased by the conversion of liquid capital into fixed assets in the form of railroads, finally culminated in the panic of 1873.

From 1873 to 1879 there was no substantial improvement in business conditions. Railroad construction was at a standstill during these years; and many receiverships and reorganizations of railroads occurred on account of these events and conditions. In 1874 over $500,000,000 par value of American railroad bonds were in default.

If the people of Maine had considered the railroad problem in the light of Maine railroad experience, there would have been found few reasons that could justify the resentment against Maine railroads which presently appeared. The promoters of railroad enterprises in Maine had been full of trouble and acquainted with grief. The original stockholders of the Kennebec & Portland had been wiped out. The Androscoggin & Kennebec had never paid a dividend, and the Penobscot & Kennebec had defaulted on its bonds. The Androscoggin Railroad had swallowed the entire fortunes of some of its promoters. The Knox & Lincoln had cost nearly twice the original estimate. The Portland & Rochester and the Ogdensburg roads were already in serious difficulties. The Maine Central situation disclosed no more than a remote promise of dividends. The war of the gauges had been fought and won. Direct trains were running between Bangor and Boston. The railroad service in Maine was better than ever before, and there were more reasons for peace than had ever before existed. But in the revulsion of popular feeling these considerations seem to have been ignored.

The first tangible result of the agitation against railroads in Maine appears in the acts of the legislature of 1874, which imposed on railroads a tax of one and one half per cent on the value of the corporate franchise, and required Maine railroad companies to make a detailed return of the results of their operations to the Railroad Commissioners. By the law of 1874 the value of the franchise was determined by deducting from the market value of the stock the assessed value of real estate taxed by the cities and towns. The right of the state to levy such a tax was the subject of much heated debate; and Governor Nelson Dingley, whose newspaper was then engaged in criticism of the Maine Central management, considered the matter of sufficient importance to justify special mention in his annual message.

The Maine Central refused to pay the franchise tax in 1874, claiming that it was in violation of the original charters, and that these charters were contracts between the state and the railroad companies which could not be changed. The old railroad charters were practically all drawn in similar form, and in most cases the clauses relating to taxation provide that real estate shall be taxable locally, and that the shares of stock shall be taxable to the owner; that when the net income exceeds ten per cent of the cost the legislature can take for the state any portion of the excess; and that *no other tax shall ever be assessed on said corporation or on any of its privileges or franchises.* The Maine Central management claimed that this meant what it said. The question was in litigation for several years and was finally decided against the railroad in 1878. In that year, although its current earnings were not sufficient to cover its fixed charges, the Maine Central had to pay five years back taxes.

In 1875, on account of the business depression brought about by the panic of 1873, the earnings of the Maine Central declined, and continued to decline steadily for four years. Railroad gross earnings are considered a fair indication of the prosperity of the territory served; and a fair estimate of general business conditions in Maine during these years can be formed from the fact that the Maine Central gross earnings were over $2,000,000 in 1874 and less than $1,500,000 in 1878. In the late seventies, largely on account of curtailment in railroad operations and the consequent loss of steady work by railroad men, there occurred a series of railroad strikes. There were eight or ten of these outbreaks in different sections of the country. In February, 1877, the Brotherhood of Locomotive Engineers promoted a strike on the Boston and Maine. The Maine Central operating department was then controlled from Boston, and although the strike did not spread over the Maine railroads, the results were seriously felt in the movement of Maine traffic. In 1879 there was a substantial improvement in business, and the resumption of specie payments in that year helped to a restoration of confidence. Capital was again available for new enterprises, and railroad construction was soon resumed on the western roads. In Maine the ice business on the Kennebec was flourishing, and train loads of ice were being shipped to points as far west as St. Louis.

For the first few years of operation things had gone well with the European & North American. In 1872 the Maine and the New Brunswick divisions were consolidated under one management. A mortgage was created covering all of the property, subject to $2,000,000 in bonds on the New Brunswick division and $3,000,000 on the Maine division, and some bonds secured by this consolidation mortgage were sold.

The program of the European & North American management included the construction of a railroad from the Penobscot River toward Lake Megantic into Canada, thereby creating a direct route for commerce between the Province of Quebec and New Brunswick and Nova Scotia. In 1871, when the European & North American road was practically completed, a charter was secured for the Penobscot & Lake Megantic Railroad to build a railroad on a route which closely follows the present line of the Canadian Pacific from Mattawamkeag to Megantic. Before any work was done under this charter there appeared an opportunity to lease the Bangor & Piscataquis road upon favorable terms, and it was decided to adopt this route for the western extension. Accordingly, the European and North American leased the Bangor & Piscataquis road in 1873, and extended the road from Dover to Abbot.

About this time a railroad was in the process of construction between Bucksport and Bangor. The town of Bucksport, an important community at the head of winter navigation on the Penobscot River, had for many years been considered as a possible railroad terminus. As early as 1836 a railroad was proposed between Milford and Bucksport to provide a means for winter shipment of lumber. Many years later a charter was granted to the Penobscot & Union River Railroad to build from Bangor to Bucksport, and through Penobscot and Surry to Ellsworth, and the towns along the line were authorized to aid. The name of this company was later changed to the Bucksport & Bangor Railroad Company, which built a broad gauge road between Bucksport and Bangor. In 1874 the road was leased to the European & North American.

Ten-Wheeler 380 and Pacific 468 doublehead a freight train from Bucksport to Bangor in the summer of 1946. *Ray Tobey from the collection of C.B. Cobb*

The Calais bound passenger train with Pacific 454 pulls out of Bangor over the Penobscot River in 1946. It backed out of the station yard tracks on the left and then started up the grade out of town. *Howard Moulton from the collection of Russell Monroe*

The program of expansion was soon abandoned on account of financial difficulty. In 1875, default having occurred on the consolidated mortgage, the trustee of that mortgage, Benjamin E. Smith, took possession of the road and operated it for about a year. Interest was defaulted on the City of Bangor mortgage in July, 1875, and on the land grant bonds the following September. In 1876 the first mortgage on the New Brunswick property was defaulted, and the trustees of that mortgage took possession. The title to this property conveyed to the trustees was prior to the act of consolidation, and the result was a dissolution of the legal association between the Maine and New Brunswick companies. The New Brunswick Company was later reorganized as the St. John & Maine Railway, and is now a part of the Canadian Pacific system.

On account of this action on the New Brunswick division the holders of the $2,000,000 bond issue on the Maine property requested their trustees to take possession of the Maine division, and in 1876 the trustees, Hannibal Hamlin and William B. Hayford, took over the property and operated it for several years. Under the management of the trustees the earnings were devoted to improvement of the railroad property which was put in excellent condition. The leases of the Bangor & Piscataquis and the Bucksport & Bangor Railroads were promptly terminated. The trustees changed the gauge to standard on the European & North American in 1877, and the Bangor & Piscataquis followed suit the same year. The gauge on the Bucksport road was changed to 3 feet.

The trustees initiated proceedings for the foreclosure of the mortgage in September, 1877, and in September, 1880, the European & North American bondholders organized a new company of the same name, receiving stock in exchange for the $2,000,000 par value bonds and unpaid coupons. The $1,000,000 mortgage to the City of Bangor remained undisturbed. In 1881 the directors of the new company were Noah Woods, President; Sprague Adams; Nathan C. Ayer; Samuel H. Blake; C.P. Stetson; Franklin A. Wilson; John S. Ricker; T.J. Stewart; and H.N. Fairbanks. In 1882 the European and North American Railroad was leased to the Maine Central for 999 years.

After acquiring the European & North American, the Maine Central system included 470 miles of railroad. The earnings of the company were steadily improving, and in August, 1882, the first dividend of two per cent was paid on the stock. A proposal to lease the Knox & Lincoln Railroad was presented to the owners but was defeated by popular vote in the coast towns which controlled the road. The Bucksport & Bangor Railroad, having passed into the hands of the bondholders and been reorganized by them as the Eastern Maine Railway, was leased to the Maine Central in 1883, and the gauge was changed to standard.

The Maine Shore Line Railroad was incorporated in 1881. Its charter granted permission to build a railroad from the St. Croix River to Bangor. In 1883 the line between Brewer and Mt. Desert Ferry was put under construction and was opened in 1884. The road was built by the Maine Central under the terms of a perpetual lease, and the company was later merged in the Maine Central. A survey of a route through Washington County was made, and the County of Washington was authorized to guarantee

Maine Central facilities at Waukeag connected with the Mt. Desert ferry to Bar Harbor. The several mile branch came off the Calais line at Washington Jct. *Russell Monroe collection*

$650,000 in first mortgage bonds to aid in construction. It was expected that the road would be extended eastward; but this field was presently surrendered to the Washington County Railroad.

In 1884 the 524 miles operated by the Maine Central was the largest mileage under one management in New England. The improvement in earnings had continued, and six per cent dividends were paid on the stock in that year. The popular agitation against railroads had continued, and the tremendous losses involved in the reorganization of the unfortunate Maine companies seem to have aroused more derision than sympathy. The principle of taxation of the franchise had never been abandoned since the right was confirmed; but there had been several variations in the method of determination of the value of the corporate franchise.

During the period when the Eastern Railroad was acquiring control of the Maine Central, the Eastern management had incurred considerable criticism on account of expenditures made for improvement of its Boston terminal and for acquisition of many small properties, including the control of the Portland, Bangor & Machias Steamboat Company. These unfortunate expenditures are examples of many other injudicious actions which resulted in financial difficulties. There was a reorganization and many changes were made in the active management. A consolidation with Boston & Maine was arranged, and in 1884 the Eastern Railroad, carrying the control of the Portland, Saco & Portsmouth and the Maine Central, was leased to the Boston & Maine. At this time it was proposed to lease the Maine Central to the Boston & Maine. The proposal aroused great indignation among many Maine people, and this idea seems to have been abandoned promptly.

Maine Central Class E 4-4-0 58 poses on the trestlework approach to the Mt. Desert ferry. *Howard Kirkpatrick collection*

Chapter Eleven

Bangor & Aroostook Begins Building Portland & Ogdensburg Leased to Maine Central

The Boston and Maine Railroad was at this time committed to a policy of expansion which appears to have contemplated the control of all the railroad traffic in New England. As its railroad system grew in mileage and in earnings, its influence naturally increased, and the exercise of this influence in political matters was an important factor in much of the legislation of the states. To what extent the railroad political activities were inspired by ambition and selfishness, and to what extent they seemed necessary in self defense against popular agitation cannot now be determined. The railroad interests in Maine had an important influence on legislation; but there was no condition of corruption such as seems to have existed in Massachusetts and New Hampshire.

It had long been apparent that state regulation of railroads could not solve the question of the public duties of the roads or create any adequate or uniform regulation of rates. The problem of regulation was under consideration in Congress from the beginning of the popular agitation in the early seventies. During this period the theory of government ownership had many supporters. In 1887 federal regulation was adopted as a necessary compromise between government ownership and unrestrained private operation, and the Interstate Commerce Act was enacted by Congress. This law provided that all charges should be just and reasonable; forbade discriminations in the form of special rates and rebates, and between localities and classes of freight; forbade a higher charge for a short haul than for a long haul; prohibited pooling; and ordered publication of all rates and fares. The law was not a solution of the problem, and supplementary legislation gradually increased the powers of the Interstate Commerce Commission. In Maine the problem of readjustment to the new condition was the more difficult on account of the competition of water transportation which was not regulated by law. The Maine Railroad Commissioners were frank in the expression of their opinion that attempts to regulate business through commissioners were unwise and in most cases unwarranted.

The first important event in Maine Central history during the period of Boston & Maine control was the lease of the Portland & Ogdensburg Railway. The great expectations of the builders of this road had never been realized, for the operations of ten years had failed to produce any substantial amount of paying business. Efforts had been made

[ABOVE:] **A Boston & Maine westbound freight with three GP38-2's stretches out over the Scarborough salt marsh in the mid-70's.** *Ron Johnson* [BELOW:] **B&M Train 123 with Pacific 3700 is eastbound into Rigby Yard as seen from the window of PT Tower 1 on September 26, 1941.** *Francis Donahue*

to join in a system of roads to secure western traffic bound for the Atlantic coast. In 1881 an agreement was made with the Ogdensburg & Lake Champlain and the Rome, Watertown & Ogdensburg Railroads for establishing a through route from Chicago and St. Louis to Portland, but this plan failed to produce any favorable result. In 1883 the officials of the Canadian Pacific Railway, in their search for an Atlantic terminus for their transcontinental railroad, made an inspection of the Ogdensburg road and of the terminal facilities in Portland. Negotiations progressed to the point of securing options on waterfront property in South Portland. The public statements made by the president of the Canadian Pacific clearly indicate that the purchase of the Ogdensburg road was being seriously considered. The failure of the negotiations may have been caused, as many believe, by the activities of the Boston railroad interests, which were trying to block the sale of the Ogdensburg to the Canadian Pacific in the hope that Boston might be selected as the Atlantic terminus. But it seems more probable that political considerations were the more potent. The popular agitation in Canada in favor of Canadian ports for Canadian railroads must have been a strong factor, and was probably the deciding factor, in the eventual decision to establish the Atlantic terminus on Canadian soil.

The Portland & Ogdensburg Railroad Company had defaulted on its consolidated mortgage in 1876 and had remained in default. Interest was paid on the first mortgage until 1884, when a default on that mortgage occurred and the company went into receivership. It was promptly reorganized as the Portland & Ogdensburg Railway. The stock of the former company was wiped out. The holders of the consolidated mortgage received stock in the new company of a par value equal to the principal amount of the bonds plus accrued interest. The $800,000 first mortgage remained undisturbed.

The City of Portland had an investment of over $700,000 in the stock of the old company which became worthless. It owned $1,350,000 consolidated mortgage bonds which it had borrowed money to buy, and had loaned a substantial sum to the old company to prevent the foreclosure of the first mortgage. After the reorganization the city owned about 23,000 shares of stock in the new company, which was all it had to show for a cash investment of over $2,000,000, made largely with borrowed money on which it had paid and continued to pay interest. This stock was sold in 1908, most of it at $47.50 a share.

In 1888 the Portland & Ogdensburg Railway property was leased to the Maine Central for 999 years. The lease stresses the obligation of the lessee to work for western business, and especially mentions the possibility of securing traffic from the Canadian Pacific. By the terms of the lease the Maine Central guaranteed the bonds and agreed to pay dividends on the stock at one per cent annually for three years and at two per cent annually thereafter. After acquiring the road, the Maine Central extended the line from Fabyans to Scotts Junction, which completed the road to the western line of New Hampshire, and established a connection with the St. Johnsbury & Lake Champlain Railway. $1,008,000 bonds were issued in the name of the Portland & Ogdensburg and guaranteed by the Maine Central to finance this construction. In 1890 this division was extended by the lease of the Upper Coos Railroad from North Stratford to the Canadian border, and the Hereford Railway from the border to Lime Ridge, Quebec. The twenty miles of road between Quebec Junction and North Stratford was built after the Maine Central leased the property and was opened in 1891.

As time proved, the lease of these roads was one of the most serious mistakes in the history of the Maine Central Railroad. The road had little in common with the rest of the Maine Central system, and only a small fraction of its traffic went east of Portland. It was practically a separate railroad, involving new problems and new responsibilities. Apparently the Boston & Maine arranged the lease because it did not want the Ogdensburg for itself, but could not afford to let anyone else have it.

The town of Dover had established railroad communication with Bangor in 1869. About the same time the Dexter & Newport Railroad was opened, and the opportunity was presented for improving transportation facilities in Dover by building a railroad to Dexter, only sixteen miles away. Other towns became interested in the project, and it was finally proposed to build a railroad from Dexter to Brownville and to lease the road to the Maine Central. This was in the days of hectic enthusiasm for railroad building; and this project became impossible under panic conditions which soon appeared.

In the late eighties, largely through the efforts of Colonel J.B. Peakes, the project was revived, and the construction of the Dexter & Piscataquis Railroad between Dover and Dexter was made possible by the offer from the Maine Central to lease the road if built. In 1888 the Dexter & Piscataquis Railroad was leased to the Maine Central for 999 years. The lease of the Dexter & Newport Railroad was renewed for 999 years at the same time. The railroad between Dexter and Dover was opened in 1889.

The bad business conditions of the early nineties, which culminated in the "gold panic" of 1893, were especially difficult for the western railroads, and many prominent railroads went into receivership; but in Maine there was no serious business depression until 1894. The lumber business was depressed on account of decreasing construction, and the ice business had begun to decline. With the exception of 1894 the gross and net earnings of the Maine Central tended to increase year by year. The

Dover-Foxcroft station served as the terminus for the Maine Central branch out of Newport and the Bangor & Aroostook's line to Greenville. *Richard Sanborn from the collection of Russell Monroe*

credit of the company was of the highest order. Its four per cent bonds were selling around par, and in 1891, and again in 1893, common stock was sold to its stockholders at par.

The operation of the Knox & Lincoln Railroad under the supervision of the towns which owned it had not been financally successful; and it had been necessary to raise by taxation the money required to pay interest on the railroad aid bonds issued by the cities and towns. This unfortunate experience in railroad building by towns was the principal cause for the amendment to the Constitution of Maine which was made in 1877, and which limited the debt of cities and towns to five per cent of the assessed valuation, except for war purposes or on loans in anticipation of taxes. Efforts were made to sell or lease the railroad; but the proposal made by the Maine Central in 1881 to lease the road at two and one-half per cent for 979 years was rejected. In 1883, by vote of most of the towns, it was decided to sell the road outright for $1,400,000 if a purchaser could be found. Several years later Mr. Levi C. Wade, representing a syndicate which included several men then prominent in Maine Central affairs, bought the road for $1,300,000 in bonds and $200,000 in cash. The town of Waldoboro refused to confirm the sale, but its interest was so small that the town was eventually compelled to dispose of its interest along with the other owners. This syndicate sold the railroad to the Penobscot Shore Line Railroad Company. In 1891, the name of the company having been again changed to the Knox & Lincoln Railway, the property was leased to the Maine Central, the lessee assuming its bonds amounting to $1,380,000 and agreeing to pay an annual rental of five per cent on two thousand shares of stock. In 1901 the Knox & Lincoln Railway was merged in the Maine Central.

When the Province of British Columbia entered the union of Canadian provinces, the Dominion of Canada had agreed to build a railroad into that territory. The Canadian Government preferred that this road should be built by private enterprise. It appeared impossible to secure private capital to undertake such an enterprise; and in 1881 Parliament granted to the newly organized Canadian Pacific Railway a subsidy of $25,000,000 and gave the company 25,000,000 acres of land to aid in construction, and also turned over to the Canadian Pacific about 700 miles of railroad previously built by the Dominion government. The activities of the Canadian Pacific builders were early directed to securing an Atlantic terminus.

With the Grand Trunk terminal in Portland it was natural that the possibilities of that port should be considered. The Ogdensburg road was for sale,

Bangor & Katahdin Iron Works 4-4-0 1 and train sits in front of the Katahdin Iron Works. The locomotive was former Maine Central 43. *Richard Dole collection*

and this route provided access to Portland. Although overtures were made by the representatives of Boston and of other Atlantic ports seeking the establishment of the Canadian Pacific port in their respective cities, it would appear that Portland was the port most seriously considered. From Minneapolis to Portland via the Canadian Pacific-Ogdensburg route was about seventy-five miles shorter in distance than the then existing railroad route from Minneapolis through Chicago to New York City; and a terminus in Portland, as compared with Halifax, would save about 400 miles in distance. The economic advantages afforded by the shortest route were sacrificed, however, by reason of political considerations, and the decision was finally made in favor of Canadian ports.

In 1885 the International Railway of Maine, a companion enterprise with a Canadian company of the same name, having acquired the old charter of the Penobscot & Lake Megantic Railway, undertook the construction of a railroad from Lake Megantic across Maine to Mattawamkeag. The company was generously assisted by a subsidy from the Dominion of Canada. In 1886 the company sold its property, rights, and franchises to the Atlantic & Northwest Railway, which company promptly leased the property to the Canadian Pacific. The Canadian Pacific completed the railroad, and it was opened to Mattawamkeag in 1889. The New Brunswick Railway, which controlled the St. John & Maine Railway, was leased in 1890. A contract was made between the Canadian Pacific Railway and the Maine Central for joint use of the European & North American line between Mattawamkeag and Vanceboro, giving the Canadian Pacific a connection between its own roads, and this section now forms part of the Canadian Pacific main line to Halifax and St. John.

In 1892 the Bangor & Aroostook Railroad began its activities by leasing the Bangor & Piscataquis Railroad and the Bangor & Katahdin Iron Works Railroad. The road was built to Houlton the next year and was gradually extended. The connection with the Maine Central was at Old Town until 1905. From this source a large amount of business came to the Maine Central.

The declaration of war with Spain caused a sudden decrease of manufacturing in Maine, and as a result there was a sharp decline in the gross earnings of the Maine Central, but comparatively little change in the net earnings. The textile and lumber mills curtailed operations for a few months, but prosperity was soon restored. In 1899 the total funded debt of the Maine Central was $10,792,192 and of the leased lines $7,138,500. The par value of the outstanding Maine Central stock was $4,975,600 and of the leased lines $9,325,938. In that year Mr. Lucius Tuttle, for many years president of the Boston & Maine, became president of the Maine Central. In 1900 an issue of Portland & Ogdensburg 3½s were sold around par, and Maine Central 4s sold at a substantial premium.

[OPPOSITE PAGE:] **The westbound "Scoot" train glides across Onawa trestle as seen from Ship Pond Stream near the end of steam on August 22, 1959.** [RIGHT:] **Canadian Pacific RS3 8451 and two B units provide the muscle for a westbound freight across Onawa trestle on the same day.** *Both photos Russell Monroe*

An eastbound mixed train behind Ten-Wheeler 2597 approaches Jackman station on October 18, 1958. *Russell Monroe*

[ABOVE:] Three CP RS3's haul a westbound freight past the enclosed water tank at Onawa, halfway between Greenville and Brownville Jct. on August 22, 1959. *Russell Monroe* **[BELOW:] The once a week CP local with RS23 8022 waits with two cars beside the Houlton station while customs duties are performed before heading back into Canada via Debec Jct. on September 15, 1980.** *Ron Johnson*

On a frosty December 20, 1958 CP FP7A 4022 and B haul a westbound piggyback and general freight train through Greenville past the frozen waters of Moosehead Lake on the right. *Russell Monroe*

From the frozen Moosehead Lake a westbound CP freight train 949 with two big C630's and an M630 slice through fresh snow at Harford's Point near Greenville in February, 1985. *Ron Johnson*

CP C630 4500 passes the trim Greenville station on August 15, 1984. *Ron Johnson*

[RIGHT:] **Eastbound CP M636 4713 emerges from the unusual "covered wagon" style bridge over the Penobscot River at Mattawamkeag in June 1985.** [BELOW:] **CP S2 7097 shuffles cabooses around Brownville Jct. yard as an eastbound CP freight with GP35 5008 enters the scene on March 27, 1976.** *Both photos Ron Johnson collection*

[BELOW:] **Two CP RS10's and a B unit lift a westbound train out of Brownville Jct. on January 12, 1964.** *Russell Monroe collection*

Chapter Twelve

Laying Rails through Washington County
Narrow Gauge Fever

[ABOVE:] **Washington County 4-4-0 1 was built by Brooks in 1898.** *Russell Monroe collection* [BELOW:] **St. Croix & Penobscot 0-4-0 1 "G.M. Porter" was built by Norris in 1867. It was sold to the Washington County Railroad in 1898 and scrapped in 1899.** *Richard Dole collection*

In 1904 the Maine Central acquired control of the Washington County Railway. The history of that railroad had been one of grief. The citizens of Washington County had wanted a railroad for many years, and had joined in supporting the European & North American project when it was originally proposed to build that road from Bangor to Calais. One of the first Maine railroad charters was to the Calais Railway in 1832, and a horse railroad was soon after in operation between Calais and Milltown. In 1849 the company became the Calais & Baring Railway Company, and the road was extended to Baring and put in operation by steam in 1852. It was part of the original plan of the European & North American to include this road in its line to St. John. The Lewy's Island Railroad was incorporated in 1854 and opened in 1856 between Baring and Princeton. The City of Calais loaned this company $150,000, secured by mortgage on the road. This mortgage was defaulted, and the city took possession of the railroad in 1862 and operated it until 1870, when it was sold to the St. Croix & Penobscot Railroad Company.

In 1870 the name of the Calais & Baring Railroad was changed to the St. Croix & Penobscot Railroad Company, and the company was authorized to extend the road through Princeton to some point on the European & North American between Milford and Lincoln. The Lewy's Island Railroad was immediately acquired as the first step, and the plan was to build to Passadumkeag, but nothing further was done. The existing road was operated by the company with indifferent success.

The Washington County Railroad was incorporated in 1893 to build a railroad from Calais to a connection with the Maine Central Railroad in Hancock County, with a branch to Eastport. The list of incorporators includes the names of the most prominent men in Washington County. A native of Steuben, John Moore, then a member of the New York Stock Exchange firm of Moore & Schley, took a prominent part in financing the construction. The County of Washington purchased $500,000 par value of preferred stock, issuing its bonds to secure the money required.

The contractors acquired the St. Croix & Penobscot Railroad by purchase of the bonds of the Calais & Baring Railroad and by foreclosure of the mortgage securing those bonds which was then in default, and by purchase of the City of Calais interest

[RIGHT:] **A Washington County passenger train waits at the Princeton station in the late 1800's.** *Richard Sanborn collection via Russell Monroe* [BELOW LEFT:] **The Quoddy Railroad consisted of a spur off the Eastport branch into the Passamaquoddy Indian Reservation and used MEC power.** *Both passes Jim McFarlane collection*

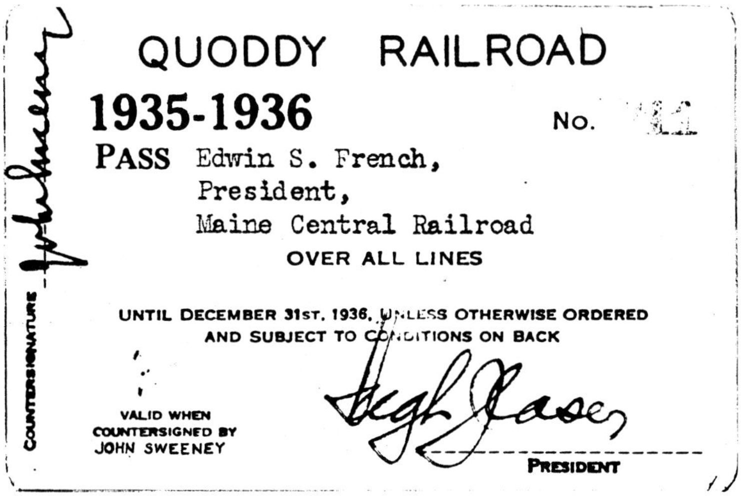

QUODDY RAILROAD

1935-1936 No.

PASS Edwin S. French,
President,
Maine Central Railroad
OVER ALL LINES

UNTIL DECEMBER 31st, 1936, UNLESS OTHERWISE ORDERED AND SUBJECT TO CONDITIONS ON BACK

VALID WHEN COUNTERSIGNED BY JOHN SWEENEY

PRESIDENT

COUNTERSIGNATURE

St. Croix & Penobscot R.R.

PASS

Until December 31st, 1876 unless otherwise ordered.

NOT TRANSFERABLE. W. W. Sawyer SUPT.

[BELOW:] **Maine Central GP7 581 hauls piggyback cars out of New Brunswick, Canada across the St. Croix River back into Maine at Woodland in April 1984. The train is traversing former Lewy's Island and St. Croix & Penobscot trackage.** *Ron Johnson collection*

[RIGHT:] **An eastbound Washington County freight train with 4-6-0 7 crosses a bridge at Dennysville in the late 1800's. Note the eagle on the second dome of the locomotive.** *Richard Dole collection* [BELOW:] **WC 4-6-0 34 built by Brooks in 1898 is reflected in the still back water of the St. Croix River at Woodland in the early 1900's.** *Richard Sanborn collection via Russell Monroe*

[LEFT:] **Washington County 4-4-0 22 poses with a passenger train below Schoodic Mountain in the late 1800's.** *Richard Sanborn collection via Russell Monroe* [BELOW:] **MEC RS2 554, RS3 557 and 44 tonner 14 layover at the Calais enginehouse in October 1974.** *Ron Johnson*

[LEFT:] **Eastbound Train 116 with E7 710 is ready to depart Calais in 1956, the last year of passenger service on this line. It is 133 miles to Bangor.** *470 Railroad Club collection*

[ABOVE:] **Ayer's Jct. in 1937 hosts two trains. MEC 4-6-0 389 on the left is from Calais bound for Bangor and 4-4-0 246 has just arrived with a combine from Eastport.** *Howard Kirkpatrick collection* [BELOW:] **Light rail prompted the use of 44 tonners on the 16 mile Eastport branch. Westbound 44 tonner 16 with two hopper cars cross a meandering stream at Pembroke in October 1974. The unusual bridge is actually a former turntable.** *Ron Johnson*

Station, freight house and water tank still exist at Cherryfield in a scene that shouts Downeast railroading. BC-1 (Bangor-Calais) is running very late with 30 or so 10 mph speed restrictions in this boggy county in the Spring of 1984. *Ron Johnson*

Eastbound BC-1 with GP7 569, masquerading as a Delaware & Hudson locomotive of Guilford Industries and GP7 565 pull a short train alongside the lowering tidal waters of the East Machias River at its namesake in April 1985. [OPPOSITE PAGE BOTTOM:] **A going away afternoon shot of the same train is lensed from the cliff above the Downeast village of East Machias.** *Both photos Ron Johnson*

[TOP:] **In more prosperous days on the Calais line BC-1 threads through Machias in the Spring of 1984 before traffic was rerouted via Mattawamkeag and the Canadian Pacific.** *Ron Johnson*

in the St. Croix & Penobscot Railroad. The road was completed in sections in 1898, and parts of the railroad were operated during that year by the contractors. The mileage built was about 119 miles, which with the St. Croix & Penobscot Railroad made the total mileage about 136 miles. It was finally completed and opened throughout in 1899. The cost of the road was nearly $5,000,000, which had been financed by the issue of $2,320,000 five per cent bonds, due in 1948; by the $500,000 subscribed by the county for preferred stock; and by the sale of $1,500,000 par value common stock.

The earnings of the railroad failed to confirm the estimates of its promoters, and were hardly sufficient to cover the expenses of operation. The mortgage was subsequently foreclosed, the original stockholders, including the County of Washington, losing their entire investment; and the property was sold to a group of New York capitalists, by whom the company was reorganized as the Washington County Railway Company. This company created a mortgage securing $2,500,000 three and a half per cent bonds and issued $2,500,000 par value of common stock. In 1904 the Maine Central secured control of the company by assuming the bonds, of which the Maine Central received $250,000 par value as a condition of the sale, and by taking over the stock. It was believed at that time that the traffic would increase and that the road could be made to pay if operated under the supervision of the Maine Central management, and during the next six years the earnings did increase substantially. The railroad was operated as a separate company until 1911 when it was merged in the Maine Central Railroad Company.

The traffic on the Bangor & Aroostook Railroad had increased rapidly, especially on account of the development of the Great Northern Paper Company; and by 1904 it had grown to the point where the terminal facilities at Old Town and Bangor were inadequate. The only practical outlet for the freight business originating on the Bangor & Aroostook had been over the Maine Central line, and the management believed that a seaport terminal would be advantageous in handling coal and other heavy freight and in securing favorable divisions of rates on freight business with other railroads. In 1905 the Northern Maine Seaport Railroad was built from South Lagrange south to a connection with the Maine Central at Northern Maine Junction, and to Searsport on Penobscot Bay. From an operating standpoint the new road was an advantage to both railroads by eliminating a large amount of southbound traffic on the steep grade out of Bangor.

A short lumber line called the Cobbosseecontee Railroad began service out of Gardiner on the Maine Central up the same named stream 1.1 miles to Dam No. 8. It was later controlled by the Maine Central.

In 1907 the Maine Central purchased control of the Somerset Railway. This company was successor to the Somerset Railroad which had built the railroad between Oakland and Madison in the early seventies. The former company had extended the road to North Anson in 1877. In 1879 it defaulted on its mortgage, and in 1883 the bondholders took the road and reorganized as the Somerset Railway in 1884. The old plan of including the Somerset road in a railroad line from Quebec to tidewater was revived in modified form when the Canadian Pacific system was being formed, and the hopes of Wiscasset were renewed by the activities of prominent citizens who tried to persuade the Canadian Pacific management to make Wiscasset the Atlantic terminus of that road. When it became apparent that this project could not succeed, an effort was made to connect

Somerset (1st) 1 "Somerset" poses with a train at Madison on a snowy day in the late 1800's. This engine was originally PS&P 6 built by Hinkley in 1869 and later became Eastern 90.

This unique cedar shingled station at Lake Moxie was on the upper portion of the Somerset line to Kineo. *Both photos Richard Sanborn collection via Russell Monroe*

the Somerset with the Canadian Pacific by the construction of a railroad from North Anson to Lake Megantic. This railroad was to be built by the Carrabassett & Canadian Railroad up the valley of the Carrabassett, crossing between Mt. Abram and Mt. Bigelow into the valley of the Dead River, and following that river to the boundary. The survey disclosed a line more favorable in grade than any previously discovered. The promoters of this railroad company contemplated the construction of a railroad line to an Atlantic terminus at Wiscasset; but no construction work was ever done on either line.

In the middle eighties, while the terminus of the Somerset was at North Anson, a project appeared on paper known as the Boston & Quebec Air Line Railroad. The promoters of this project applied for a charter to build a railroad from Skowhegan up the Kennebec River to The Forks, north to Moose River, and from the Moose River valley northeast to the boundary near Bald Mountain. The Quebec Central made a survey for a railroad to connect at the Canadian line. The management of the Somerset road opposed the granting of this charter and the Railroad Commissioners refused to grant it; but in resisting this invasion of its territory the Somerset management was practically obliged to agree to extend its own line; and the road was extended to Solon in 1889 and to Bingham in 1890.

In 1903 John F. Hill of Augusta became interested in the Somerset road, and with William T. Haines, Weston Lewis, William M. Ayer and others he accomplished the extension from Bingham to Moosehead Lake and opened the road to the Lake in 1906. Under Maine Central control the railroad was operated as a separate road until 1911 when it was merged in the Maine Central Railroad.

Two different views of the Kineo Station of the Maine Central on the shores of Moosehead Lake in the early 1920's show the interesting operations at the end of the Somerset line. In the top view one can see the plush summer resort, Mount Kineo House, in the distance, owned by the Maine Central. In the picture below the entire rail facilities are in view taken from a boat, the only way to get across to the resort. *Both photos Richard Sanborn via Russell Monroe*

A short train out of Bingham is returning to Waterville and is shown crossing the raging waters of the Kennebec River at Solon on May 13, 1978. This was the last year of train operations to Bingham before the tracks were pulled back to North Anson. *Ron Johnson*

In the same year when control of the Somerset Railway was purchased the Maine Central leased the Portland & Rumford Falls Railroad which controlled the line between Rumford Junction and the Rangeley Lakes. The development of this railroad involves the history of smaller roads which extends back to the beginning of railroads in Maine.

The Buckfield Branch Railroad was chartered in 1847 to build a railroad from Mechanic Falls on the Atlantic & St. Lawrence route to Buckfield, and to extend from Buckfield to Canton. The road to Buckfield was built in 1849. The original stockholders sustained severe losses, having to pay double assessments, and in 1857 the property was sold to Francis O.J. Smith of Portland. The Portland & Oxford Central Railroad was then organized and took over the property with a charter authorizing the construction of a railroad from Mechanic Falls to Portland. The road was idle for several years prior to 1863 when operations were resumed; and in 1870 the road was extended to Canton. Its operations were not profitable, and through neglect of the owners the road became so unsafe that the charter was revoked in 1874. In that year the Rumford Falls & Buckfield Railroad Company was organized with authority to take over the location of the Portland & Oxford Central and to extend to Rumford Falls. In 1878 the new company came into possession as receiver, and the railroad was repaired, the gauge was changed to standard, and operations were again resumed.

In 1890 the Portland & Rumford Falls Railway was incorporated, and in the same year leased the Rumford Falls & Buckfield Railroad Company. Two years later the road was extended to Rumford Falls, and in 1893 was extended from Mechanic Falls to a connection with the Maine Central at Rumford Junction in Auburn. In 1897 a branch line was built from Canton to Chisholm, and in 1899 to Livermore Falls. The Rumford Falls & Rangeley Lakes Railroad Company was incorporated in 1894 to build from Rumford Falls to the Rangeley Lakes. The road was gradually extended and reached Oquossoc in 1902. Both companies were controlled by the same interests.

The operations of Hugh J. Chisholm and his associates in the development of railroads, water power and manufacturing in the Androscoggin Valley, especially in Rumford Falls, fall more naturally in the field of industrial history; but it was the railroad which made possible the industrial development. Few men have risked more for the accomplishment of a purpose, and few have lived to see their efforts so nobly rewarded, as did the group which followed Mr. Chisholm in these enterprises. The whole project was well conceived and ably managed, and, although the undertaking involved considerable risks during the construction period, the profits began to be realized almost as soon as the completion of the work.

In 1907 the Chisholm group, now fortified by the success of all their enterprises, formed a company called the Portland & Rumford Falls Railroad which contemplated the construction of a railroad from Portland to the Province of Quebec, utilizing their existing lines between Auburn and the Rangeley Lakes. For terminal purposes valuable real estate was purchased in Portland. The creation of such a railroad was apparently more than President Tuttle was prepared to endure. Within a few months after its incorporation the Portland & Rumford Falls Railroad, which carried control of the Portland & Rumford Falls Railway and the Rumford Falls & Rangeley Lakes Railroad by lease, was leased to the Maine Central at an annual rental of $328,000. The earnings of these railroads at that time fully justified the amount of rental guaranteed by the lease.

The extension of this line into Quebec was later planned by the Maine Central management, and the Rangeley Lakes & Megantic Railroad was formed to build from Oquossoc to Lake Megantic, primarily for the purpose of opening a new supply of pulpwood for the paper mills on the Androscoggin River. The Maine Central bought the stock of the new company and with the proceeds the road from Oquossoc to Kennebago was built. The plan of the extension to Quebec was abandoned, and the railroad as built became the property of the Maine Central through consolidation in 1914.

Rumford Falls & Buckfield 3 poses with a crew amid some typically deep snow in up country Maine during the 1880's. *470 Railroad Club collection*

A broad side view is presented of handsome 4-4-0 3 of the Rumford Falls & Buckfield built by Rhode Island in 1883. *Russell Monroe collection*

The Rumford Falls & Rangeley Lakes Railroad ran 36 miles from Rumford Falls to Oquossoc. 2-6-0 2 was built by Baldwin in 1895 and eventually became MEC 162. *Russell Monroe collection*

The original Poland Spring station features some classic 1890's appointments. Note the P&RF train, horses and buggies and baggage cart loaded with various goodies. *470 Railroad Club collection*

A MEC Ten-Wheeler pauses on the deck bridge over the Nezinscot River at East Sumner before heading south for Buckfield in 1915. *Richard White collection*

DR-2 (Rumford-Rigby) glides through West Peru with ex-RI U25B 231 and U18B 408 in the lead. One may look across the Androscoggin River to Dixfield and the twin peaks of Sugarloaf and Pauls Bluff. *Ron Johnson*

Portland & Rumford Falls 4-4-0 3 "Buckfield" sits in front of the original Rumford Falls depot in the 1890's. *470 Railroad Club collection*

[ABOVE:] **The second station in downtown Rumford boasted an impressive clock tower as seen in the 1890's.** *470 Railroad Club collection* [BELOW:] **A Maine Central mixed train is stopped at the Oquossoc station, 36 miles above Rumford.** *Richard Sanborn collection via Russell Monroe*

Perhaps some people have seen this outside view of the unique log cabin station at Bemis on the north end of the Kennebago line but how many persons have looked at a picture of the interior of the station? Look closely for details including the Moosehead and ticket office. *470 Railroad Club collection*

[TOP:] **In 1933 the Maine Central abandoned 11 miles of track between Oquossoc and Kennebago. The Kennebago Bus Co. was formed to operate over this section of line. They used a 20-passenger bus converted to run on rails along with a trailer shown on the Oquossoc table in 1936. In March of that year floods wiped out the line to Rumford for good. Today the rail car resides at Clark's Trading post in Lincoln, N.H.** *Howard Kirkpatrick collection* [ABOVE:] **Sebasticook & Moosehead 4-4-0 1 "Hartland", built by Taunton in 1866, pauses at Pittsfield with car 3 in the early 1900's.** *Richard Dole collection*

The first train in Harmony arrives on August 19, 1912 with 4-4-0 60. *Richard Dole collection*

In June, 1907, the New York, New Haven & Hartford Railroad secured control of the Boston & Maine. The New Haven management was committed to a policy of expansion which involved the purchase of properties directly or indirectly connected with railroad operation in New England, including electric railways, steamship lines and tourist hotels. Under Boston & Maine influence the Maine Central had secured control of most of the railroad system in Maine, and in the process had acquired some roads which later became a heavy burden upon the company. Mr. Charles S. Mellen, president of the New Haven, succeeded Mr. Tuttle as president of the Maine Central in 1910, and under his leadership the company adopted a program of expansion into new fields.

Early in 1911 the Maine Central acquired the Sebasticook & Moosehead Railroad. The original company of this name was incorporated in 1886, and it was the plan of the promoters to build a railroad from Pittsfield through Hartland, Harmony, Wellington and other towns, connecting with the Bangor & Piscataquis Railroad near Monson. The company built eight miles between Pittsfield and Hartland, and opened this line in 1886. The company was soon in receivership, and the road was sold on execution to pay debts. Operations were continued by a receiver. The road was extended to Harmony in 1901. In 1903 the bondholders of the old company, having foreclosed the mortgage, organized a new company of the same name; but the new company never operated the road, which remained in the possession of the receiver until it was sold to the Maine Central.

On June 30, 1910, the par value of Maine Central stock outstanding was $4,976,300. A year later it stood at $9,950,000. And on June 30, 1913, the amount had reached $24,516,300, plus subscriptions unpaid which presently brought the total to $24,888,100. During the same period the funded debt decreased about $17,000,000. In 1912 a large amount of bonds matured and these were paid from the proceeds of the sale of common stock. In 1911, by legislative act, the controlled Washington County Railway, Somerset Railway, and the Sebasticook & Moosehead Railroad were merged with the Maine Central Railroad.

Between 1880 and 1900 there had been built in Maine several narrow gauge railroads. The financial experiences in the railroad field in the early seventies had demonstrated the folly in the theory that a railroad would in itself bring prosperity to the communities which it served, and the smaller towns were seeking for a method of transportation which was within their means.

The first narrow gauge railroad in Maine was built between Farmington and Phillips in 1880. The first 24 inch gauge engine in the United States ran on this road. This was the Sandy River Railroad, and it was built from the material formerly used on the Bedford and Billerica road. The owners of the Billerica road, having failed to make it pay where first located, loaded all the material on a train and shipped it to Farmington. During the next twenty years there was built a system of narrow gauge roads above Phillips into the Rangeley and Dead River regions. These other two foot gauge railroads included the Franklin & Megantic, Madrid, Eustis and the Kingfield & Dead River Railroads. Excepting the Sandy River Railroad none of these small roads had paid. In 1908 Josiah S. Maxcy and Weston Lewis, who had for several years owned and operated profitably the Sandy River Railroad, acquired and merged most of the small roads above Farmington, forming the Sandy River & Rangeley Lakes Railroad. Messrs. Maxcy and Lewis successfully operated the consolidated properties until 1911, when they sold the stock to the Maine Central.

While on the subject of narrow gauge railroads, the Kennebec Central Railroad should be mentioned. It ran from Randolph on the Kennebec River opposite the city of Gardiner to the National Soldiers'

Home at Togus, five miles. It opened for traffic in 1890 and hauled mainly coal and passengers for the Home until 1929 when operations ceased.

The Bridgton & Saco River Railroad was built in 1881 from a junction with the Ogdensburg road to Bridgton and was later extended to Harrison. The most interesting material in the history of this road is in the arguments relative to its probable value to Bridgton. One advocate claimed that the small stream which flows through the town of Bridgton was capable of turning the wheels of all the mills of Lewiston. On the whole, this narrow gauge road was a paying proposition. In 1912 the Maine Central purchased the stock of this company, and operated the line until 1927. The railroad was abandoned in 1941.

The ambition of Wiscasset for a railroad connection with the interior was not to be entirely denied. In 1894 construction was actually started on the Wiscasset & Quebec Railroad. But the name of the company was grander than its property, and its resources were slender for its ultimate design. A roadbed was graded through Alna, Whitefield, Windsor, China, Albion and Unity to Burnham, and in 1895 rails were laid to Albion. The road was built with a 24 inch gauge, but the plan was to change to standard gauge when justified by traffic. The road was unprofitable and the company was soon reorganized. In 1901 Mr. Leonard Atwood of Farmington conceived a plan for the creation of a narrow gauge railroad system which would connect the narrow gauge lines in the Rangeley region with the Wiscasset road. The Wiscasset, Waterville & Farmington Railway was organized, and that company took over the Wiscasset & Quebec road, the charter of the Waterville & Wiscasset Railroad, and the Franklin, Somerset & Kennebec Railway, the latter company having a charter authorizing the construction of a road from Waterville to Farmington. The Wiscasset line was extended to Winslow and piers for a bridge across the Kennebec were erected, while some work was done west of the river. The new company soon failed, and the railroad from Wiscasset to Winslow, having been mortgaged to secure bonds, was sold under foreclosure proceedings. Mr. Carson Peck of New York owned a substantial amount of the bonds and he purchased the property to protect his investment in it. The road from Albion to Winslow was later abandoned. The line from Wiscasset to Albion was operated by Mr. Peck, or by his heirs, until 1925, when the road was purchased by a group of individuals in order to prevent its abandonment.

The charter of the Portland Union Railway Station Company was amended in 1911, and its powers were enlarged and its name changed to the Portland Terminal Company. This company acquired by purchase and lease from the Boston and Maine and Maine Central Railroads all of their railroad property owned or leased in Portland, South Portland and Westbrook and has since operated this property for the joint benefit of the Maine Central and Boston & Maine.

The Maine Central had acquired as part of the Somerset Railway purchase the Kineo House and other property at Moosehead Lake. In 1912 the company acquired the stock of the Ricker Hotel Company (now the Sam-O-set Company) which owned "The Sam-O-set" hotel at Rockland, and the Kineo property was sold to this company which operates the hotel properties. The Mellen management contemplated the purchase and construction of other hotels, and for that purpose acquired land at Bar Harbor. The Interstate Commerce Commission did not view with favor this growth in the hotel business, and the activities of the Maine Central in that field became restricted to the supervision of operation of the existing hotel properties.

Wiscasset, Waterville & Farmington locomotive 7 pauses at China Lake to load passengers and milk. *Russell Monroe collection*

Wiscasset was the terminus of the WW&F where it crossed the Maine Central and struck out over the water on a series of wood pile trestles because of space limitations. Note the ball signals at the diamond where the two foot gauge line crossed the standard gauge track. *All photos Russell Monroe collection*

[LEFT:] **Kennebec Central engine 3 and combine pose at Randolph on the occasion of the last train.** *Russell Monroe collection* [BELOW:] **Two scenes at Bridgton Jct. show B&SR 2-4-4 5 arriving at the station in August 1908 and another locomotive on the turntable.** *470 Railroad Club collection*

B&H locomotive 8 rounds a curve in a scenic setting on a special excursion July 14, 1940 near the end of total services. *470 Railroad Club collection*

[RIGHT:] **B&H 8 stops for a few minutes beside Hancock Lake on an excursion on July 14, 1940.** *470 Railroad Club collection*
[BELOW:] **Sandy River 4, built by the Portland Co. in 1890 is on lease to the Franklin & Megantic. It is ready to haul a pulpwood train in 1898.** *Russell Monroe collection*

[BELOW:] **This picture shows a nice overview of Phillips with station, enginehouse, ball signal and locomotive 24.** *Russell Monroe collection*

Train time at Strong in 1934 sees SR&L rail bus and mixed train with locomotive 24 side by side. *470 Railroad Club collection*

Eustis Railroad 9 has a pulpwood train in tow at Bigelow in 1906. It is operating on the Kingfield & Dead River while under lease to the Franklin & Megantic. *Russell Monroe collection*

Phillips & Rangeley 2 is pictured at Marbles in 1904. *Russell Monroe collection*

Chapter Thirteen

Restoring the Maine Central to Maine People

In 1914 the Boston & Maine and the New Haven Railroads were in financial straits. The expansion program of the Mellen management had been viewed with misgivings by many in Maine, and when the result appeared in the insolvent condition of the Boston & Maine, an opportunity appeared for restoring the control of the Maine Central to Maine people. The railroad had been controlled by capital foreign to Maine for more than forty years. The reacquisition of the Maine Central is one of the few instances, and by far the most notable instance, where Maine people have cooperated in an effort to regain control of their own economic destiny.

The Boston & Maine owned 25,160 shares of the total amount of 49,763 shares of Maine Central stock. The purchase of this stock was financed in the first instance through Maine Railways Companies, which was a trust with Charles O. Bancroft, Morris McDonald, who had succeeded Mr. Mellen as President in 1913, and Harry M. Verrill, all of Portland, Trustees. The Maine Central Railroad bought and paid $3,000,000 for 30,000 shares, which was the entire capital of the trust. The Maine Railways Companies issued $12,202,000 in five per cent notes due April 1, 1919, and with the proceeds of sale of the notes and shares this trust purchased at $95.25 a share the 159,601 shares of Maine Central stock. The stock purchased was pledged as collateral security for the Maine Railways Companies notes.

It was beyond the capacity of Maine investors to absorb the total amount of Maine Central stock available, and the problem of distribution was the more difficult on account of the European war. The income of the Maine Railways Companies from dividends was more than sufficient to pay its interest charges and five per cent dividends, and the trust made some progress in retiring its notes from its surplus income. In 1915, in order to facilitate the financial operations of the Maine Railways Companies, the legislature authorized the Maine Central to retire $10,000,000 par value of its common stock and to issue in place thereof an equal par value of bonds, notes, or preferred stock. The Maine Central thereupon issued and sold $7,000,000 par value first and refunding mortgage four and one-half per cent bonds, due in December, 1935, and $3,000,000 par value five per cent cumulative preferred stock, and retired 100,000 shares of common stock. The balance of the common stock held by the Maine Railways Companies was distributed in 1916 by a Maine syndicate of investment dealers. As a result of these operations the number of stockholders almost doubled in two years while the amount of common stock outstanding became about half the previous amount. The Maine Central in the process acquired 28,815 shares which are held as an asset in the treasury of the company.

Conditions which could not have been foreseen by the men who sponsored this change in capitalization and stock control caused substantial losses to the purchasers of the stock and weakened the financial structure of the Maine Central Railroad Company. The United States became engaged in the World War in 1917, and the emergency made necessary the operation of the railroads by the Federal Government. The changes inaugurated during the period of Federal control, for which the corporate management was in no way responsible, resulted in the railroad being returned to private operation in 1920 in a desperate financial condition, and it has required years to regain for the company a condition of prosperity and sound credit.

The government Railroad Administration took over the railroads on January 1, 1918, and returned them to the owners on March 1, 1920. The government guaranteed a "Standard Return" equal to the average annual railway operating income for the three years ending June 30, 1917, and in the case of the Maine Central this amount was $2,955,696.88. Before and during this period of Federal control there had been tremendous increases in wages of railroad employees by authority of the National Government. The agreement to return the railroads to their owners in as good condition as when taken was not carried in most cases, and certainly was not with the Maine Central.

The Transportation Act, enacted by Congress before the railroads were returned by the government, established a new basis of rates which caused great hardship for the Maine Central and other New England roads. Rates were established for groups of railroads regardless of the effect on any one company. The Eastern group included roughly all railroads east of Chicago and north of the Potomac and Ohio Rivers. Increases in rates being absolutely necessary, the Interstate Commerce Commission authorized an increase of forty per cent in freight rates in the Eastern group and a small increase in passenger rates. The burden of the increase being on freight, the result was to the disadvantage of any railroad whose freight traffic composed a lower percentage of its total business than the average percentage of freight in the total business in the whole Eastern group. The percentage of freight traffic was far below this average on the New Haven, Boston & Maine, and Maine Central. These railroads petitioned for relief by readjustment in the division of rates with the trunk lines on through freight traffic. It was nearly two years before this request was granted, and then the increase allowed was materially less than appeared reasonable and necessary.

During the period of Federal control and the Guarantee period the actual earnings of the Maine Central resulted in a deficit of $2,399,181 after paying fixed charges in 1918, and in similar large deficits in 1919 and 1920. But the payment of the "Standard Return" by the government made possible the payment of interest and dividends. Upon the termination of the "Standard Return" in the fall of 1920 it became necessary to cease paying dividends on the preferred and common stocks. This was the inevitable result of conditions caused by government control.

In 1921 there was a deficit of $2,165,361 after the payment of fixed charges. Practically helpless to alter the situation with rates and wages fixed by government authority, the management devoted its efforts to restoring the railroad and equipment to its former excellent condition, and directed its attention to the possibility of securing some measure of relief. The only item in the company's budget in which a prompt reduction could reasonably be expected was the tax paid to the State of Maine.

Taxation of railroad franchises had been continued by the state since its original adoption in the early seventies, and the method of automatic assessments based on a definite percentage of gross earnings had been in effect since 1881. Prior to 1901 the maximum rate had been three and one-quarter per cent. The rate was increased steadily until 1911 when it became five and one-half per cent. In that year the Maine Central and controlled companies paid about $422,000 as an excise tax to the state. The tremendous increase in gross earnings caused by rate increases during and after the war were not an indication of greater value in the railroad or in the franchise. The value of the franchise depended upon the profits from operation of the railroad, and without profits the franchise was a liability instead of an asset. In 1921, when operations resulted in a deficit of over $2,000,000, the excise tax paid to the State of Maine was $972,863, and total taxes paid amounted to $1,263,982.

In 1921 a request was made to the legislature to reduce the rate of taxation on gross earnings from five and one-half to four and one-half per cent. This measure of relief was refused by the legislature. In 1925 a new proposition was presented in the form of a proposed tax law known as the "gross-net plan" by which the rate of tax on gross earnings would vary in accordance with the ability of a railroad company to pay, the proposed rates ranging from a minimum of three per cent to a maximum of five and one-half per cent of gross earnings. This measure was scientifically devised and had been recommended by authorities on taxation. It commanded the almost unanimous support of the leading businessmen in Maine and of many members of the legislature, and its enactment was expected. The bill passed in both branches of the legislature, but was vetoed by Governor Brewster.

The suspension of dividends on the stocks in 1920, although inevitable under the conditions following the termination of the "Standard Return", was not likely to increase the goodwill of the stockholders toward the management, and there presently appeared opposition to the policies of the management and criticism of officials and directors. The first evidence of organized opposition appeared in 1922 upon the announcement of the management of its intention to cease paying interest on the bonds of the Sandy River & Rangeley Lakes Railroad and to abandon the road. The bonds of this company were owned in large amounts by savings banks, and many of these banks had substantial holdings of Maine Central stock. Negotiations having failed to secure any compromise on this matter, the Sandy River and Rangeley Lakes Railroad defaulted on its bonds and went into the hands of receivers, who have since operated a portion of the road.

After a tremendous loss in 1921 there was a substantial improvement which resulted in a surplus after fixed charges in 1922 of $551,157; but the paralysis in traffic on account of the severe winter in 1923 and of the flood on Maine rivers which occurred the following spring caused substantial losses, and the result for the entire year showed fixed charges barely earned.

Many stockholders were discouraged by this showing. Opposition to the management and to certain directors had continued, and early in 1924 a campaign was started among the stockholders to secure the election of some new directors. On March 28 the management issued an announcement of the financial program of the directors which proposed the settlement of accumulated preferred dividends by the issue of additional preferred stock and the resumption of regular preferred dividends in December. It was intimated that this action would make possible the payments of dividends on the common stock early in 1925. The effect of such action would have been to compromise the claim of the preferred stockholders to cash dividends in order that the common stock might sooner receive dividends.

The management, by virtue of its superior position and greater diligence in securing proxies, controlled a large majority of the stock represented at the annual meeting, and the old board of directors was re-elected. The proposal for settlement of preferred dividends in stock instead of cash was also carried, but this plan was never put into execution. Regular cash dividends on the preferred stock were resumed in December, 1924, and the accumulated

MAINE CENTRAL RAILROAD

MAINE CENTRAL RAILROAD

PORTLAND DIVISION

SCHEDULE OF PASSENGER TRAINS IN EFFECT JUNE 25, 1917

PORTLAND to ROCKLAND and to BANGOR via AUGUSTA.

BANGOR via Augusta and Rockland to PORTLAND and BOSTON

Portland to Rumford, Farmington, Rangeley, Moosehead Lake and Skowhegan via Lewiston.

Skowhegan, Moosehead Lake, Rangeley, Farmington and Rumford to Portland via Lewiston.

Bath to Brunswick, Lewiston and Leeds Junction.

Leeds Junction, Lewiston and Brunswick to Bath.

Harmony Branch

Nos. of Trains.	803	805
STATIONS.	A M	P M
Pittsfield lv	11†00	5†05
West Palmyra	11f10	5f13
Thompson's	11f15	5f18
Hartland	11 45	5 23
Wild Goose Club	11f55	5f33
Mainstream	12f05	5f40
Harmony .... ar	12 15	5 45

Nos. of Trains.	802	804
STATIONS.	A M	P M
Harmony lv	7†00	1†30
Mainstream	7f05	1f45
Wild Goose Club	7f12	1f55
Hartland	7 20	2 35
Thompson's	7f27	2f45
West Palmyra	7f33	2f55
Pittsfield .... ar	7 40	3 10

Waterville and Burnham Junction to Belfast.

Nos. of Trains.	131	333	135
STATIONS.	A.M.	A.M.	P.M.
Bangor lv	6†45	......	12†40
Waterville	7 18	10†15	3 26
Benton	7 25	10 22	3f32
Clinton	7 34	10 31	3 42
Burnham Junction	8 25	10 50	4 05
Winnecook	8f35	11f00	4f15
Unity	8 44	11 30	4 23
Thorndike	8 52	11 45	4 32
Knox	9f00	11f55	4f40
Brooks	9 15	12 57	4 55
Waldo	9f25	1f15	5f05
City Point	9f35	1f40	5f15
Belfast .... ar	9 40	1 50	5 20
	A.M.	P.M.	P.M.

Belfast to Burnham Junction and Waterville.

Nos. of Trains.	132	134
STATIONS.	A.M.	Noon
Belfast lv	6†55	12†30
City Point	7f00	12f35
Waldo	7f10	12f45
Brooks	7 22	12 57
Knox	7f34	1f09
Thorndike	7 40	1 15
Unity	7 48	1 23
Winnecook	7f58	1f30
Burnham Jct. ...... ar	8 10	1 40
Clinton .... ar	8 28	......
Benton .... "	8 38	......
Waterville .... "	8 44	2 25
Bangor .... ar	11 52	3 05
	A.M.	P.M.

Newport Junction to Dover and Foxcroft

Nos. of Trains.	83	87
STATIONS.	A.M.	P.M.
Portland lv	......	12†50
Waterville	7†18	3 26
Bangor	6 45	3 45
Newport Jct. lv	8†15	4†50
Camp Benson	8f19	4f54
Corinna	8 30	5 05
Lincoln Mills	8f36	5f11
Moodys	8f38	5f13
Dexter	8 48	5 23
Silvers Mills	8f58	5f33
West Dover	9f01	5f36
Starbirds	9f05	5f40
Dover & Foxcroft ar	9 15	5 50
	A.M.	P.M.

Dover and Foxcroft to Newport Junction

Nos. of Trains.	84	88
STATIONS.	A.M.	P.M.
Dover & Foxcroft lv	6†35	3†20
Starbirds	6f46	3f31
West Dover	6f48	3f33
Silvers Mills	6f52	3f37
Dexter	7 02	3 47
Moodys	7f10	3f55
Lincoln Mills	7f12	3f57
Corinna	7 20	4 05
Camp Benson	7f30	4f15
Newport Jct ...... ar	7 35	4 20
Bangor .... ar	9 05	5 20
Waterville	8 44	5 45
Portland .... ar	11 50	8 30
	A.M.	P.M.

Livermore Falls Branch.

Nos. of Trains.	221	223
STATIONS.	A.M.	P.M.
Canton lv	10†21	3†40
Meadowview	10f36	3f55
Riley's	10 42	4 01
Jay Bridge	10 47	4 06
Livermore Falls .ar	10 53	4 12

Nos. of Trains.	220	222
STATIONS.	A.M.	P.M.
Livermore Falls .. lv	9†45	3†00
Jay Bridge	9 51	3 06
Riley's	9 56	3 11
Meadowview	10f02	3f17
Canton .... ar	10 10	3 25

REFERENCES:

* Daily, Sundays included. † Daily, except Sundays. ✱ Daily commencing June 26th. f Stops on signal or on notice to conductor. * Carries no coaches. Pullman passengers only. ✚ Passengers for Farmington Branch leave Lewiston 8.50 a.m., Greene 9.02 a.m. E Stops to leave passengers for Poland Spring and points east of Rumford Jct.

‡ Except Saturdays. ¶ Daily, except Mondays. s Saturdays only. B Stops to take passengers. c Stops to leave passengers.

§ Sundays only. () Restaurant.

x Passengers from Farmington Branch arrive Greene 6.04 p.m., Lewiston 6.15 p.m. w Stops to leave passengers holding tickets, not mileage, from Portland and points West. Ⓐ Stops to leave passengers from Lake Moxie and points east and to take passengers for points west of Deadwater. K Stops to take passengers holding tickets, not mileage, for Portland and points west. J Stops to leave passengers from points east of Leeds Junction.

p Stops to leave passengers holding tickets, not mileage, from B. & A. R. R. or points east of Bangor. R Stops to take Pullman passengers holding tickets, not mileage, for Portland and points west, and to leave Pullman passengers holding tickets, not mileage, from points east of Waterville and from the Kineo Branch. Y Stops to leave passengers from west of Deadwater and to take passengers for Lake Moxie and points east.

T Stops to take passengers holding tickets, not mileage, for points east of Freeport.

NOTE—Trains Nos. 89-90-91-94 will stop on signal between South Gardiner and Augusta at Church Crossing, Bradstreet's, Cove, Oaklands, North St., Farmingdale, Millikens, Lowells, Wilders and Shoe Shop.

At stations where no time is given, trains do not stop.

TICKETS SOLD AND BAGGAGE CHECKED THROUGH TO ALL PRINCIPAL POINTS. UNAVOIDABLE DELAYS EXCEPTED AND SUBJECT TO CHANGE WITHOUT NOTICE. AMERICAN EXPRESS COMPANY TRANSACTS BUSINESS ON THIS LINE.

RAILROAD CONNECTIONS. At Portland, Deering Junction, with Boston & Maine Railroad. At Yarmouth Junction, Danville Junction, and Mechanic Falls with Grand Trunk Railway. At Wiscasset with Wiscasset, Waterville & Farmington Railroad. At Warren with Georges Valley Railroad. At Farmington with Sandy River & Rangeley Lakes Railroad. At Northern Maine Junction, and Dover and Foxcroft with Bangor & Aroostook Railroad.

D. C. DOUGLASS, GENERAL MANAGER.

GENERAL OFFICES: PORTLAND, ME.

M. L. HARRIS, GENERAL PASSENGER AGENT.

ADV. FORM 301. 6-22-17—4000.

Ron Johnson collection

MAINE CENTRAL RAILROAD

New York, Boston and Portland to Bangor and Bar Harbor

Miles from Portland	Nos. of Trains / STATIONS	WEEK DAYS						SUNDAYS				
		*127	*127 *121	*153	*153 †115	†29 †129	†11	*127	*127 *121	*127 §741	*153	§711
		P. M.	P. M.	P. M.	P. M.	A. M.	A. M.	P. M.	P. M.	P. M.	P. M.	A. M.
	New York } Via Worcester ... lv	......	......	*7 30	*7 30	......	......	......	......	......	*7 30	......
	Portland } ar	......	......	*6 00	*6 00	......	......	......	......	......	*6 00	......
	Boston } via Portsmouth ... lv	*10 00	*10 00	......	......	......	†10 00	*10 00	*10 00	*10 00	......	*9 00
	Portland } ar	*1 10	*1 10	......	......	......	†12 35	*1 10	*1 10	*1 10	......	*12 15
	Boston } via Dover ... lv	......	......	......	......	†8 00	†8 55	......	......	......	......	§9 10
	Portland } ar	......	......	......	......	†10 50	†12 25	......	......	......	......	§12 30
		A. M.	A. M.	A. M.	A. M.	A. M.	Noon	A. M.	A. M.	A. M.	A. M.	Noon
0	**Portland** ... () lv	*1 20	*1 20	*6 20	*6 20	†11 00	†12 45	*1 20	*1 20	*1 20	*6 20	§12 45
136	**Bangor** ... () ar	*5 35	*5 35	*10 05	*10 05	†3 05	†4 50	*5 35	*5 35	*5 35	*10 05	§5 20
		A. M.	A. M.	A. M.	A. M.	P. M.	P. M.	A. M.	A. M.	A. M.	A. M.	P. M.
136	**Bangor** ... () lv	*5 50	*6 10	*10 15	†10 45	†3 20	†5 10	*5 50	*6 10	§8 00	*10 15	§5 35
137	Brewer Junction	......	6 16	......	10 51	......	5 16	......	6 16	8 07	......	5 40
146	Holden	......	6 36	......	11 12	......	5 35	......	6 36	8 27	......	f5 58
148	Egery's Mill	......	......	......	f11 15	......	......	......	......	f8 30	......	......
150	Phillips Lake	......	f6 42	......	f11 19	......	f5 42	......	f6 42	f8 34	......	f6 04
153	Green Lake	......	6 50	......	11 29	......	f5 50	......	6 50	8 42	......	f6 12
157	Nicolin	......	7 00	......	f11 39	......	f6 00	......	7 00	8 51	......	f6 21
163	Ellsworth Falls	......	7 12	......	11 52	......	6 12	......	7 12	9 05	......	6 34
165	Ellsworth	6 55	7 18	11 16	11 58	4 21	6 18	6 55	7 18	9 11	11 16	6 40
167	**Washington Junction**	......	*7 25	......	12 08	4 33	f6 24	......	*7 25	f9 18	......	f6 47
171	Franklin Road	......	......	......	12 17	......	f6 32	......	......	9 26	......	6 56
175	Hancock	......	......	......	12 26	......	6 40	......	......	9 35	......	7 05
176	Waukeag, Sullivan Ferry	7 18	......	11 38	12 29	4 50	6 43	7 18	......	9 38	11 38	7 08
178	**Mt. Desert Ferry** ... ar	*7 25	......	*11 45	†12 35	†5 00	†6 50	*7 25	......	§9 45	*11 45	§7 15
	Bar Harbor } Steamer	*8 20	......	*12 35	......	†5 45	†7 30	*8 20	......	......	*12 35	§7 55
	Seal Harbor	*9 05	......	*1 15	......	†6 25	†8 20	*9 05	......	......	*1 15	§8 45
	Northeast Harbor	*9 25	......	*1 35	......	†6 40	†8 40	*9 25	......	......	*1 35	§9 05
	Southwest Harbor	*9 40	......	*1 55	......	†7 00	†8 55	*9 40	......	......	*1 55	§9 25
	Manset	*9 45	......	*1 50	......	†6 55	†8 50	*9 45	......	......	*1 50	§9 20
	Sullivan } Steamer	†7 50	......	......	†12 55	......	......	......	......	......	§1 05	......
	Hancock Point	†8 10	......	......	†1 20	......	......	......	......	§10 00	§1 25	......
	Sorrento	†8 25	......	......	†1 30	†5 20	†7 10	......	......	§10 10	§1 40	§7 35
	Bar Harbor	†9 00	......	......	†2 10	......	†7 40	......	......	§10 45	§2 10	§8 05
		A. M.	A. M.	P. M.	P. M.	P. M.	P. M.	A. M.	A. M.	A. M.	P. M.	P. M.

* Daily, Sundays included. † Daily, except Sundays.
§ Sundays only. () Restaurant.
f Stops on signal or on notice to Conductor. s Saturdays only.

Train No. 11. Parlor Cars and Coaches Boston, via Portsmouth, to Bangor and Mt. Desert Ferry, Dining Car Boston, via Portsmouth, to Augusta, Buffet Service Augusta to Bangor and Mt. Desert Ferry, daily, except Sunday.

Train Nos. 29-129. Parlor Car Boston, via Dover, to Mt. Desert Ferry, Coaches Boston, via Dover, to Bangor and Bangor to Mt. Desert Ferry, Dining Car Boston to Bangor, daily, except Sundays.

Train No. 127. Sleeping Cars and Coaches Boston, via Portsmouth, to Mt. Desert Ferry daily.

Train Nos. 127-121. Broiler Buffet Sleeping Car Boston, via Portsmouth, to Calais, Coaches Boston, via Portsmouth, to Bangor and Bangor to Calais daily.

Train No. 153. Sleeping Cars New York to Bangor and Mt. Desert Ferry, daily. Buffet Smoker New York to Bangor for Pullman passengers only. Dining Car Portland to Bangor.

Train No. 711. Buffet Parlor Cars and Coaches Boston, via Portsmouth, to Bangor and Mt. Desert Ferry. Sundays only.

Bangor to Bucksport.

Mls	Nos. of Trains / STATIONS	†431	†433	†435	s437
		A. M.	A. M.	P. M.	P. M.
0	**Bangor** ... ()lv	†7 10	†11 50	†4 55	s6 55
2	Brewer Junction	7 16	11 57	5 00	s7 01
4	South Brewer	7 21	12 05	5 06	s7 06
6	North Orrington	f7 25	f12 10	f5 10	s7 f10
6	Pierce's	f7 27	f12 12	f5 12	s7 f12
7	Orrington	7 30	12 16	5 15	s7 15
10	South Orrington	7 36	12 25	5 21	s7 21
12	Hink's Landing	f7 40	f12 30	f5 25	s7 f25
13	North Bucksport	f7 43	f12 33	f5 28	s7 f28
15	Bucksport Center	7 48	12 42	5 33	s7 33
17	Chipman's	f7 53	f12 48	f5 38	s7 f38
20	**Bucksport** ... ar	†8 00	†1 00	†5 45	s7 45

MAINE CENTRAL RAILROAD

Bar Harbor and Bangor to Portland, Boston and New York

Mls.	Nos. of Trains / STATIONS	WEEK DAYS						SUNDAYS				
		†110	†122 †102	*156	*114 *2	*118	*120 *118	§764	*156	*114 *2	*118 *8	*120 *8
		A. M.	A. M.	P. M.	P. M.	P. M.	P. M.	A. M.	Noon	P. M.	P. M.	P. M.
	Bar Harbor	†6 10	†10 00	......	*3 30	......	......	......	......	*3 30	......	......
	Sorrento } Steamer	......	†10 30	......	*4 00	†5 20	......	......	§12 30	*4 00	......	......
	Hancock Point	†6 35	†10 40	......	*4 10	......	......	......	§12 40	*4 10	......	......
	Sullivan	......	†11 05	......	*4 35	......	......	......	§9 30	*4 35	......	......
	Manset } Steamer	......	†9 00	*1 05	†1 50	*6 55	......	......	*1 05	......	*6 55	......
	Southwest Harbor	......	†9 10	*1 15	†2 35	*7 25	......	......	*1 15	......	*7 25	......
	Northeast Harbor	......	†9 25	*1 30	†2 50	*7 40	......	......	*1 30	......	*7 40	......
	Seal Harbor	......	†9 45	*1 50	†3 10	*8 00	......	......	*1 50	......	*8 00	......
	Bar Harbor ... lv	......	†10 50	*3 00	▲†4 10	*9 00	......	§5 20	*3 00	§4 15	*9 00	......
0	**Mt. Desert Ferry** ... lv	†7 00	†11 45	*3 40	*5 00	*9 50	......	§6 05	*3 40	*5 00	*9 50	......
3	Waukeag, Sullivan Ferry	7 07	11 51	3 47	5 07	9 57	......	6 12	3 47	5 07	9 57	......
4	Hancock	7 15	11 54	......	5 10	......	......	6 15	......	5 10	......	......
8	Franklin Road	f7 22	......	......	5 19	......	......	6 23	......	5 19	......	......
11	**Washington Junction**	7 30	12 16	......	f5 28	......	*10 30	f6 32	......	f5 28	......	*10 30
14	Ellsworth	7 37	12 23	4 11	5 35	10 21	10 37	6 39	4 11	5 35	10 21	10 37
15	Ellsworth Falls	7 42	f12 28	......	5 40	......	10 42	6 47	......	5 40	......	10 42
21	Nicolin	f7 55	f12 41	......	6 00	......	f10 55	f7 00	......	6 00	......	f10 55
25	Green Lake	8 04	f12 51	......	6 12	......	11 04	f7 08	......	6 12	......	11 04
29	Phillips Lake	f8 11	f12 58	......	f6 20	......	f11 11	f7 14	......	f6 20	......	f11 11
31	Egery's Mill	f8 14	......	......	f6 23	......	......	......	......	f6 23	......	......
32	Holden	8 18	f1 06	......	6 27	......	11 18	f7 20	......	6 27	......	11 18
42	Brewer Junction	8 38	1 24	......	6 44	11 24	11 38	7 37	......	6 44	11 24	11 38
43	**Bangor** ... () ar	†8 45	†1 30	*5 10	*6 50	*11 30	*11 45	§7 42	*5 10	*6 50	*11 30	*11 45
	Bangor ... () lv	......	†1 50	*5 20	*8 00	✠12 05	✠12 05	§7 50	*5 20	*8 00	¶12 40	¶12 40
178	**Portland** ... () ar	......	†5 55	*9 25	*12 50	✠4 05	✠4 05	§12 20	*9 25	*12 50	¶5 00	¶5 00
			P. M.	P. M.	Night	A. M.	A. M.	Noon	P. M.	Night	A. M.	A. M.
	Portland } via Portsmouth ... lv	......	†6 05	......	*1 05	✠4 15	✠4 15	§12 35	......	*1 05	......	......
	Boston } ar	......	†9 10	......	*5 10	✠7 15	✠7 15	§3 50	......	*5 10	......	......
	Portland } via Dover ... lv	......	†6 00	......	......	......	......	§12 25	......	......	¶5 10	¶5 10
	Boston } ar	......	†9 10	......	......	......	......	§3 45	......	......	¶8 30	¶8 30
	Portland ... lv	......	♦8‡35	*9 40	......	......	......	......	*9 40	......	......	......
	New York, via Worcester	......	♦7†48	*7 52	......	......	......	......	*7 52	......	......	......
		A. M.	A. M.	A. M.	A. M.	A. M.	A. M.	P. M.	A. M.	A. M.	A. M.	A. M.

* Daily, Sundays included. § Sundays only. ¶ Mondays only. () Restaurant.
† Daily, except Sundays. ▲ Sundays leave Bar Harbor 4.15 p. m.
‡ Daily, except Saturdays. *f* Stops on signal or on notice to Conductor.
♦ Saturday Night leave Portland 9.40 p. m., arrive New York Sundays 7.52 a. m.

Train Nos. 114-2. Sleeping Car Mt. Desert Ferry, via Portsmouth, to Boston daily, except Sundays, to August 8th inclusive. Commencing August 10th Sleeping Car will start from Bangor. Coaches Mt. Desert Ferry to Bangor and Bangor, via Portsmouth, to Boston daily.

Train No. 118. Sleeping Car and Coaches Mt. Desert Ferry, via Portsmouth, to Boston, except Sundays. Broiler Buffet Sleeping Car Calais, via Portsmouth, to Boston, except Sundays. ✠ Daily, except Mondays.

Train Nos. 118-8. Sleeping Cars Mt. Desert Ferry, via Dover, to Boston, Sundays only.

Train Nos. 120-8. Broiler Buffet Sleeping Car Calais, via Dover, to Boston, Sundays only. Coaches Calais to Bangor and Bangor, via Dover, to Boston.

Train Nos. 120-118. Broiler Buffet Sleeping Car Calais, via Portsmouth, to Boston, daily, except Sundays. Coaches Calais to Bangor and Bangor, via Portsmouth, to Boston.

Train Nos. 122-102. Parlor Cars, Mt. Desert Ferry, via Portsmouth, to Boston. Buffet Service to Augusta, Dining Car Augusta, via Portsmouth to Boston. Coaches Mt. Desert Ferry to Bangor and Bangor, via Portsmouth, to Boston.

Train No. 156. Sleeping Cars, daily, Mt. Desert Ferry and Bangor to New York. Dining Car Bangor to Portland and Buffet Smoker Bangor to New York for Pullman passengers only. Coach Mt. Desert Ferry to Portland. No coach passengers carried west of Portland.

Train No. 764. Parlor Car, Buffet Service, Mt. Desert Ferry, via Portsmouth, to Boston. Sundays only. ♦

Bucksport to Bangor.

Mls	Nos. of Trains / STATIONS	¶430	†432	†434	†436
		A. M.	A. M.	P. M.	P. M.
0	**Bucksport** ... lv	¶5 50	†8 30	†3 00	†6 05
4	Chipman's	¶5 f57	f8 37	f3 10	f6 12
6	Bucksport Center	¶6 02	8 42	3 18	6 17
7	North Bucksport	¶6 f06	f8 46	f3 23	f6 21
9	Hink's Landing	¶6 f09	f8 49	f3 26	f6 24
10	South Orrington	¶6 13	8 53	3 33	6 28
13	Orrington	¶6 19	8 59	3 43	6 34
14	Pierce's	¶6 f21	f9 01	f3 45	f6 36
14	North Orrington	¶6 f23	f9 03	f3 47	f6 38
17	South Brewer	¶6 28	9 08	3 53	6 43
19	Brewer Junction	¶6 35	9 14	4 00	6 49
20	**Bangor** ... ()ar	¶6 40	†9 20	†4 10	†6 55

Summer, 1914 Timetable

MAINE CENTRAL RAILROAD

New York, Boston, Portland and Bangor To Calais, Eastport and Princeton

Mls	Nos. of Trains	WEEK DAYS *127 †121	WEEK DAYS †29 †129 †429	SUNDAYS *127 §721
	STATIONS	P. M.	P. M.	P. M.
	New York, via Worcester lv	......	△†8 00	......
	Boston, via Portsmouth lv	*10 00	A. M.	*10 00
	Boston, via Dover lv	A. M.	†8 00	A. M.
	Portland lv	*1 20	†11 00	*1 20
	Augusta	*3 27	†12 08	*3 27
	Waterville	*4 03	†1 33	*4 03
	Bangor	*6 10	†3 20	*6 10
	Ellsworth	*7 18	†4 21	*7 18
		A. M.	P. M.	A. M.
0	**Washington Junction** lv	†7 35	†4 35	§7 30
10	Franklin	7 53	4 52	7 47
15	Schoodic	f8 04	......	......
17	Tunk Pond	f8 08	f5 07	f8 01
20	Goodwins	f8 14	f5 13	......
25	Unionville	8 23	5 21	8 15
29	Cherryfield	8 37	5 36	8 26
32	Dorman	f8 43	f5 42	f8 32
35	Harrington	8 51	5 51	8 39
39	Columbia	8 59	5 59	8 47
42	Columbia Falls	9 07	6 06	8 54
46	Jonesboro	f9 17	6 15	9 03
54	Whitneyville	9 31	6 29	9 16
58	Machias	9 43	6 39	9 26
60	Machiasport	f9 48	f6 43	f9 31
62	East Machias	9 55	6 49	9 37
63	Jacksonville	f9 58	f6 52	f9 40
75	Marion	f10 22	f7 17	f10 03
80	Dennysville	10 31	7 28	10 12
86	**Ayers Junction** ar	10 44	7 42	10 25
	Pembroke ar	11 03	7 57	10 42
	Eastport	11 40	8 28	11 13
86	**Ayers Junction** lv	10 50	7 47	10 27
89	Charlotte	f10 57	f7 55	f10 35
99	**St. Croix Junction**	11 18	f8 13	f10 53
100	Milltown	11 22	8 17	10 57
102	**Calais** ar	†11 30	†8 25	§11 05

EASTPORT BRANCH
Calais and Ayers Junction to Eastport

Mls	Nos. of Trains	WEEK DAYS †447	†449	†459	†451	SUNDAYS §705	§707
	STATIONS	A. M.	A. M.	P. M.	P. M.	A. M.	P. M.
	Calais lv	†7 50	......	......	†6 20	......	§6 20
0	**Ayers Junction** lv	†8 35	†11 00	†1 25	†7 48	§10 30	§7 05
4	Pembroke	8 46	11 09	1 43	7 57	10 42	7 14
9	Perry	9 02	11 22	2 05	8 10	10 55	7 27
11	Pleasant Point	f9 11	f11 29	f2 16	f8 17	f11 02	f7 34
16	**Eastport** ar	9 25	11 40	2 30	†8 28	§11 13	§7 45
	Campobello, Steamer	10 15	12 15	3 45	......	......	......
	Lubec, Steamer ar	†10 30	†12 30	†4 00	......	......	......

PRINCETON BRANCH
Calais to Woodland and Princeton

Mls	Nos. of Trains	WEEK DAYS †452	†454	†458	s456	SUNDAYS §706
	STATIONS	A. M.	A. M.	P. M.	P. M.	A. M.
0	**Calais** lv	†6 05	†10 45	†2 00	s10 30	§11 15
3	Milltown	6 13	11 08	2 15	s10 38	11 23
4	**St. Croix Junction**	6 17	11 18	2 26	s10 43	11 27
6	Baring	6 21	11 23	2 35	s10 47	11 31
11	Woodland Junction	6 36	11 52	2 55	s11 13	11 54
12	Woodland	†6 40	11 47	†3 00	s11 08	11 50
18	Baileyville	......	12 f10	......	f11 s32	f12 11
22	**Princeton** ar	......	†12 20	......	s11 43	§12 20

* Daily. Sundays included. † Daily, except Sundays. § Sundays only.
f Stops on signal or on notice to Conductor. s Saturdays only.
△ Sundays, leave New York at 7.30 P. M., arrive Portland 6.00 a. m. Mondays.

Train 29-129-429, Parlor Car Boston, via Dover, to Washington Junction and Dining Car and Coaches Boston, via Dover, to Bangor.

Trains 127-121 Broiler Buffet Sleeping Car Boston, via Portsmouth, to Calais and through coaches Boston, via Portsmouth, to Bangor and Bangor to Calais.

Trains 127-721, Broiler Buffet Sleeping Car Boston, via Portsmouth, to Calais and through Coaches Boston, via Portsmouth, to Bangor and Bangor to Calais.

MAINE CENTRAL RAILROAD

Calais, Eastport and Princeton to Bangor, Portland, Boston and New York

Mls	Nos. of Trains	WEEK DAYS †422- †122- †102	WEEK DAYS *120- †118	SUNDAYS *120- *8
	STATIONS	A. M.	P. M.	P. M.
0	**Calais** lv	†7 50	*6 20	*6 20
3	Milltown	7 58	6 28	6 28
4	**St. Croix Junction**	8 03	6 36	6 36
14	Charlotte	f8 22	f6 55	f6 55
17	**Ayers Junction** ar	8 30	7 02	7 02
	Eastport lv	7 30	6 20	§6 10
	Pembroke	8 02	6 51	6 41
17	**Ayers Junction** lv	8 35	7 14	*7 14
23	Dennysville	8 49	7 28	7 28
28	Marion	f8 59	f7 37	f7 37
39	Jacksonville	9 23	f8 01	f8 01
41	East Machias	9 28	8 06	8 06
43	Machiasport	f9 32	f8 10	f8 10
45	Machias	9 43	8 18	8 18
49	Whitneyville	9 54	8 29	8 29
57	Jonesboro	10 09	f8 43	f8 43
61	Columbia Falls	10 20	8 53	8 53
64	Columbia	10 29	9 01	9 01
68	Harrington	10 39	9 10	9 10
71	Dorman	f10 44	f9 15	f9 15
74	Cherryfield	10 55	9 26	9 26
78	Unionville	11 07	9 37	9 37
83	Goodwins	f11 18	f9 46	f9 46
86	Tunk Pond	f11 25	f9 52	f9 52
88	Schoodic	......	B9 55	B9 55
93	Franklin	11 43	10 06	10 06
102	**Washington Junction** ar	†12 03	*10 24	*10 24
		Noon	P. M.	P. M.
	Ellsworth	†12 23	*10 37	*10 37
	Bangor	† 1 30	*11 45	*11 45
	Waterville	† 3 25	☩1 44	¶2 28
	Augusta	† 4 05	☩2 19	¶3 00
	Portland ar	† 5 55	☩4 05	¶5 00
	Boston, via Portsmouth ar	† 9 10	☩7 15	......
	Boston, via Dover ar	† 9 10	......	¶8 30
	New York, via Worcester ar	♦†7 48	A. M.	A. M.

EASTPORT BRANCH
Eastport to Ayers Junction and Calais

Mls	Nos. of Trains	WEEK DAYS †446	†448	†460	†450	SUNDAYS §704	§708
	STATIONS	A. M.	A. M.	A. M.	P. M.	A. M.	P. M.
	Lubec, Steamer lv	†6 15	†9 00	†11 00	†5 15	......	......
	Campobello, Steamer	6 30	8 15	10 15	4 45	......	......
0	**Eastport** lv	†7 30	†10 00	†12 10	†6 20	§9 40	§6 10
5	Pleasant Point	f7 42	f10 11	f12 24	f6 31	f9 51	f6 21
7	Perry	7 49	10 18	12 33	6 38	9 57	6 28
13	Pembroke	8 02	10 31	12 49	6 51	10 11	6 41
16	**Ayers Junction** ar	†8 10	10 40	†1 00	7 00	10 20	§6 50
	Calais ar	......	†11 30	......	†8 25	§11 05	......

PRINCETON BRANCH
Princeton to Woodland and Calais

Mls	Nos. of Trains	WEEK DAYS †445	†441	†443	SUNDAYS §701	§703
	STATIONS	A. M.	P. M.	P. M.	Night	P. M.
0	**Princeton** lv	......	......	†5 20	§12 05	§5 20
4	Baileyville			f5 33	f12 17	f5 33
12	Woodland	†9 15	†5 20	5 59	12 42	6 00
11	Woodland Junction	9 20	5 24	6 04	12 47	6 05
17	Baring	9 38	5 39	6 25	1 03	6 24
18	**St. Croix Junction**	9 43	5 43	6 36	1 08	6 33
20	Milltown	f9 52	5 47	6 40	1 12	6 37
22	**Calais** ar	†10 05	†5 55	†6 50	§1 20	§6 45

* Daily, Sundays included. † Daily, except Sundays.
§ Sundays only. f Stops on signal or on notice to Conductor.
☩ Daily, except Mondays. ¶ Mondays only.
♦ Saturday night leave Portland 9.40 p. m., arrive New York Sundays 7.52 a. m.

Trains 120-118 Broiler Buffet Sleeping Car Calais, via Portsmouth, to Boston, through coaches Calais to Bangor, and Bangor, via Portsmouth, to Boston.

Trains 422-122-102 Parlor Cars Washington Junction, via Portsmouth, to Boston. Buffet Service Washington Junction to Augusta. Dining Car Augusta, via Portsmouth, to Boston and through coaches Calais to Bangor and Bangor, via Portsmouth, to Boston. B Stops to take passengers.

Richard Dole collection

MAINE CENTRAL RAILROAD

Halifax, St. John and Eastern Maine to Portland, Boston and New York

		WEEK DAYS												SUNDAYS					
	Nos. of Trains		†402	†92			†102				†96	*10	*8			*10			*8
	STATIONS		A. M.	A. M.			P. M.				P. M.	A. M.	A. M.			A. M.			A. M.
	Halifax lv	Atlan	tic Ti	me			‡8 45					*8 00	*8 00			*8 00			*8 00
	St. John	Easte	rn Ti	me			†5 45					*4 45	*5 40			*4 45			*5 40
0	**Vanceboro** ...()lv						†9 45					*7 53	*8 55			*7 53			*8 55
5	Lambert Lake						f9 55						9 05						9 05
13	Tomah						f10 08												
17	Forest						10 17						9 26						9 26
22	Eaton						f10 25						f9 34						f9 34
27	Danforth						10 36					f8 34	9 45			f8 34			9 45
36	Bancroft						f10 52						f10 01						f10 01
39	Wytopitlock						10 59						10 08						10 08
45	Drew........						f11 10						f10 18						f10 18
48	Kingman						11 17						10 25						10 25
56	**Mattawamkeag**			†7 35			11 32				†4 15	*9 20	10 41			*9 20			10 41
59	Winn			7 40			11 37				4 21		10 47						10 47
65	North Lincoln			f7 50							f4 32								
68	Lincoln Centre			7 56							4 41								
70	Lincoln			8 01			11 57				4 48		11 06						11 06
74	South Lincoln			f8 08							f4 57								
79	Enfield			8 18			12 14				5 07		f11 21						f11 21
84	Passadumkeag			8 27			f12 22				5 15		G11 28						G11 28
88	Olamon			8 35			f12 29				5 23		G11 34						G11 34
92	Greenbush			f8 42							f5 29		G11 40						G11 40
96	Costigan			8 50			f12 43				5 37		G11 47						G11 47
101	Milford			9 00							5 46								
102	***Old Town***		†6 10	9 05			12 55				5 50		12 00						12 00
103	Great Works		6 14	9 09							5 54								
106	Webster		6 20	9 15							6 00								
106	Orono		6 22	9 17			1 04				6 02		f12 09						f12 09
107	Basin Mills........		6 25	9 20							6 05								
110	Veazie		6 32	9 27							6 12		G12 17						G12 17
112	Mt. Hope		f6 34	f9 29							f6 14								
114	**Bangor**........ ()		†6 40	†9 35			†1 20				†6 20		*12 25						*12 25
			A. M.	A. M.			P. M.				P. M.	P. M.	Night			P. M.			Night

	Nos. of Trains	†93			*9		†29		†409			*71	*9				*71
	STATIONS	A. M.			A. M.		P. M.		P. M.			A. M.	A. M.				A. M.
136	**Bangor** ....()lv	†7 30					†3 21		†5 30			*3 25					*3 25
138	Mt. Hope	f7 35							f5 35								
139	Veazie	7 38							5 38								
143	Basin Mills	7 45							5 45								
144	Orono	7 48					3 36		5 48			K3 40					K3 40
144	Webster	7 50							5 50								
147	Great Works	7 55							5 56								
148	**Old Town**	8 00					3 45		6 00			3 49					3 49
149	Milford	8 04							6 04								
154	Costigan	8 15							6 14			K3 59					K3 59
158	Greenbush	f8 24							6 22								
162	Olamon	8 35							6 30			K4 10					K4 10
166	Passadumkeag	8 44					K4 12		6 39			K4 17					K4 17
171	Enfield	8 53					4 21		6 48			f4 24					f4 24
176	South Lincoln	f9 01							f6 56								
180	Lincoln	9 10					4 38		7 05			4 40					4 40
182	Lincoln Centre	9 14							7 09								
185	North Lincoln	f9 19							f7 14								
191	Winn	9 30					4 54		7 25			4 57					4 57
194	**Mattawamkeag**	†9 35			*6 05		5 00		†7 30			5 03	*6 05				5 03
202	Kingman						5 17					5 20					5 20
205	Drew						f5 23					f5 26					f5 26
211	Wytopitlock						5 34					5 37					5 37
214	Bancroft						f5 40					f5 43					f5 43
223	Danforth				f6 55		5 58					6 00	f6 55				6 00
228	Eaton						f6 07					f6 10					f6 10
233	Forest						6 17					6 20					6 20
237	Tomah																
245	Lambert Lake						f6 36					f6 41					f6 41
250	**Vanceboro**.......() ar				*7 35		†6 45					*6 50	*7 35				*6 50
	St. John........	Easte	rn Ti	me	*10 40		†10 25					*10 20	*10 40				*10 20
	Halifax ....ar	Atlan	tic Ti	me	*10 20		†8 55					*10 20	*10 20				*10 20
		A. M.			P. M.		A. M.		P. M.			P. M.	P. M.				P. M.

* Daily, Sundays included.

† Daily, except Sundays.

✠ Daily, except Mondays.

§ Sundays only.

() Restaurant.

△ Sundays leave New York at 7.30 p. m., arrive Portland 6.00 a. m. Mondays.

G Stops to leave passengers.

K Stops to take passengers for east of Mattawamkeag and leave passengers from Bangor and points west.

M Stops Saturday nights only.

T Stops to take passengers holding tickets, not mileage, for points east of Freeport.

f Stops on signal or on notice to Conductor.

▬▬ Train goes no farther.

Train No. 11. Parlor Car and Coaches Boston, via Portsmouth, to Bangor and Mt. Desert Ferry. Dining Car Boston, via Portsmouth, to Augusta.

Train No. 25. Buffet Parlor Car and Coaches Boston, via Dover, to Rockland and Bangor.

Train No. 29. Parlor Car Boston, via Dover, to Kineo Station, Mt. Desert Ferry and St. John. Buffet service east of Bangor. Dining Car Boston, via Dover, to Bangor. First and Second Class Coaches Boston, via Dover, to St. John.

Train No. 71. Sleeping Cars Boston, via Portsmouth, to Caribou, except Saturdays, and St. John and Halifax daily, and to Bangor Saturdays only. First and Second Class Coaches Boston, via Portsmouth, to St. John.

Train No. 127. Sleeping Cars Boston, via Portsmouth, to Greenville, Rockland, and Mt. Desert Ferry daily. Broiler Buffet Sleeping Car Boston, via Portsmouth, to Calais, daily. Coaches Boston, via Portsmouth, to Mt. Desert Ferry.

Train No. 153. Sleeping Cars daily, New York to Kineo Station, Bangor, and Mt. Desert Ferry. Dining Car Portland to Bangor. Buffet Smoker New York to Bangor for Pullman passengers only.

Train No. 711. Buffet Parlor Car and Coaches Boston, via Portsmouth, to Bangor and Mt. Desert Ferry, Sundays only.

GRAND TRUNK RAILWAY

MAIN LINE—MONTREAL to PORTLAND 1895

Miles		6 Exp.	2 Exp.	16 Mix'd		20 Mix'd	22 Mix'd	4 Exps.
147.83	Island Pond ♠ .... lve		†1 20	†8 00		†5 00	†12 15	†6 00
152.07	East Brighton			ƒ8 17		ƒ5 13		ƒ6 08
155.25	Wenlock			8 30		ƒ5 25		ƒ6 15
162.77	North Stratford 93		1 45	8 57		5 50	1 15	6 29
167.78	Mc. C.R.R. Crossing			9 15		ƒ6 02		ƒ6 36
170.92	Stratford Hollow			9 26		6 15	ƒ1 51	6 45
175.16	Groveton 42		2 06	9 40		6 45	2 11	6 53
180.93	Stark			ƒ10 01		ƒ7 06	ƒ2 36	7 03
183.00	Percy		2 19	10 10		7 15	2 45	7 08
185.78	Crystal			ƒ10 20		ƒ7 25		ƒ7 13
188.00	West Milan		ƒ2 28	10 29		ƒ7 35	ƒ3 09	7 17
193.72	Copperville			ƒ10 50		ƒ7 57	ƒ3 35	7 28
199.42	Berlin, N.H 6		2 48	11 13		8 20	4 00	7 40
205.85	Gorham ♠ 40 .... arr			11 40		8 45	4 30	7 55
	Gorham ♠ 40 .... lve	†5 00	3 00	12 30			Connects with No. 6 Express.	8 00
211.51	Shelburne	ƒ5 11	ƒ3 08	12 48				8 13
217.24	Gilead	5 21	ƒ3 19	1 09				8 29
223.30	West Bethel	5 33		1 29				8 43
227.24	Bethel 7	5 40	3 35	1 41				8 52
231.99	Locke's Mills	5 49		1 57				9 03
235.53	Bryant's Pond 12	5 55	3 47	2 09				9 12
241.67	West Paris	6 06	3 58	2 29				9 27
250.05	South Paris	6 25	4 10	2 56				9 46
251.55	Norway .... arr	6 32	4 22	3 05				9 57
	(*See page* 17) .... lve	6 15	4 00	2 45				9 35
256.49	Oxford	6 38		3 19				10 02
260.79	P. & R. F. Crossing	6 46						10 12
261.06	Mechanic Falls 88	6 47	4 26	3 35				10 13
265.37	Empire Road	6 55		3 50				10 23
267.56	Lewiston Jct .... arr	7 00	4 36	3 56				10 27
273.06	Lewiston (*See pge.* 17) .. arr	7 24	4 54	4 54				10 47
	Continued on page 17.)	A.M.	P.M.	P.M.	A.M.	P.M.	A.M.	A.M.

Miles.	STATIONS.	6 Exps.	2 Exps.	16 Mix'd	8 Exps.	10 Exps	4 Exps.
	LEAVE	A.M.	P.M.	P.M.	P.M.	P.M.	A.M.
273.06	Lewiston	†7 00	†4 18	†2 30	†2 00	†4 00	†10 12
267.56	Lewiston Jct .... lve	7 22	4 36	3 56	2 12	4 12	10 27
269.78	Danville Jct 29	7 27	4 40	4 50	2 17	4 17	10 33
274.63	New Gloucester	7 39		5 15	2 30	4 27	10 45
278.84	Pownal	7 50		5 35	2 36	4 35	10 55
281.99	North Yarmouth	7 55		5 55	2 41	4 41	11 02
285.15	Yarmouth Jct 146	8 00	5 01	6 10	2 46	4 47	11 10
286.01	Yarmouth	8 02	ƒ5 03	6 15	2 48	4 49	11 12
288.41	Cumberland	8 06		6 28	2 52	4 54	11 18
291.79	Falmouth	8 11		6 45	2 57	5 00	11 27
295.57	Deering	ƒ8 18			ƒ3 03	ƒ5 08	ƒ11 37
296.06	Port. & Roch. Jct. 108	8 20	5 20		3 05	5 10	11 40
297.25	Portland (G.T.S.) 107 arr	†8 25	†5 25	7 20	†3 10	†5 15	†11 45
	via P. & R. R. R.	A.M.	P.M.				
296.06	Port. & Roch. Jct. lve	†8 25	†5 42		†3 10	†5 42	†11 45
298.49	Portland (Union Stn) arr	8 35	5 55		3 20	5 55	11 55
	Via B. & M. R. R.						
298.49	Portland Union Stn) .. lve	†9 00	†6 00			6 00	†12 30
413.49	Boston (East Div.) .. arr	12 55	9 25			9 25	4 10
298.49	Portland (Union Stn) lve	†8 40	†6 05		†3 30	†6 05	†12 20
310.49	Old Orchard Beach .... arr	9 07	6 26		3 55	6 26	12 47
413.49	Boston (West Div.)	12 55	9 25		7 30	9 31	4 14
	ARRIVE	P.M.	P.M.	P.M.	P.M.	P.M.	P.M.

No. 2. Day Express.—*Pullman Buffet Parlor Car* **Montreal to Portland**, leaves Montreal daily except Sunday.

No. 4. *Pullman Sleeping Car* **Montreal to Portland** leaves Montreal daily except Sunday.

Coach **Island Pond to Boston** leaves Island Pond daily except Sunday.

NOTE.—For schedule of through car service between Montreal, Levis and I. C. Ry., see page 18. The through Coach to Boston runs via P. & R. Jct. and Union Station, Portland.

LEWISTON BRANCH.

Miles	To LEWISTON	13 Mixd.	7 Pass.	3 Pass.	15 Mix'd	9 Pass.	5 Pass.	17 Mix'd	11 Pass.	19 Mix'd	1 Pass.
	LEAVE	A.M.	A.M.	A.M.	A.M.	P.M.	P.M.	P.M.	P.M.	P.M.	P.M.
0	Lewiston Jct	*6 35	†8 18	†9 50	†10 35	†2 12	†2 55	†4 50	†6 25	†6 35	*9 37
1.78	Littlefield	6 38	ƒ8 21	ƒ9 53	ƒ10 38	ƒ2 15	ƒ2 58	4 53	ƒ6 28	6 38	
5 14	Auburn	6 45	8 28	10 00	10 45	2 22	3 05	5 00	6 35	6 45	9 47
5.50	Lewiston	6 42	8 30	10 02	10 47	2 24	3 07	5 02	6 37	6 47	9 49
	LEAVE										

Miles	FROM LEWISTON	4 Pass.	8 Pass.	18 Mix'd	6 Pass.	10 Pass.	14 Mix'd	12 Pass.	2 Pass.	20 Mix'd	22 Mix'd
	LEAVE	A.M.	A.M.	A.M.	A.M.	P.M.	P.M.	P.M.	P.M.	P.M.	P.M.
0	Lewiston	*6 15	†7 10	†9 25	†10 15	†2 00	†2 30	†4 05	†4 25	†6 05	*9 15
36	Auburn	6 17	7 12	9 27	10 17	2 02	2 32	4 07	4 27	6 07	9 17
3.72	Littlefield	ƒ6 24	ƒ7 19	9 34	ƒ10 24	2 09	ƒ2 39	ƒ4 14	ƒ4 34	6 15	
5.50	Lewiston Jct	6 27	7 22	9 37	10 27	2 12	2 42	4 17	4 37	6 20	9 30
	ARRIVE										

NORWAY BRANCH

Miles	TO NORWAY	4 Pass.	6 Pass.	8 Pass.	10 Pass.	12 Pass.	2 Pass.	14 Mix'd	18 Mix'd
	LEAVE	A.M.	A.M.	A.M.	P.M.	P.M.	P.M.	P.M.	P.M.
0	South Paris	*5 59	†9 50	†10 20	†2 50	†3 40	†4 14	†7 25	†10 15
1.50	Norway .... arr	6 04	9 55	10 25	2 55	3 45	4 20	7 30	10 20

Miles	FROM NORWAY.	15 Mix'd	3 Pass.	5 Pass.	11 Mix'd	7 Pass.	9 Pass.	13 Mix'd	1 Pass.
		A.M.	A.M.	P.M.	P.M.	P.M.	P.M.	P.M.	P.M.
0	Norway .... lve	†9 35	†10 05	†3 24	†7 05	*5 45	†2 35	†4 00	*10 00
1.50	South Paris	9 40	10 10	3 29	7 10	5 50	2 40	4 05	10 05
	ARRIVE								

* Daily. ƒ Flag Station. † Except Sunday. ***Eastern Standard Time.***

Canadian Pacific
July 1, 1937

Halifax, Saint John and Montreal

A.M. (via Canadian National and Canadian Pacific) P.M.

117	41	39	Miles	Canadian Pacific Ry.		40	42	104	118
	*7 10	†9 50	84.4	Lv McAdam, N.B. .... Ar	"	†3 52	‡9 00	§8 35	
	7 25	10.05	90.3	Ar Vanceboro, Me. 12 *Atlantic* Lv	AT	†3 40	‡8 45	§8 20	
	6 35	†9 10	90.3	Lv Vanceboro, Me. *Eastern* Ar	ET	†2 35	‡7 10	§7 10	
	8 17	10 40	146.4	Lv Mattawamkeag .... Ar	"	1 14	5.28	5.28	
	*9.25	†11 53	189.5	Ar Brownville Junc Lv	"	†12.11	‡4 20	§4.20	
†9.30	*9.35	¶12.03	189.5	Lv Brownville Junc .... Ar	"	†12.03	*4.10		†3.15
ƒ10 00			198.0	Barnard	"				ƒ2.51
10 24	u10.15		207.2	Onawa	"	b11.35			2.25
ƒ10 33			210.7	Bodfish	"				ƒ2.14
ƒ10 50			216.0	Morkill	"				ƒ2.02
				Bangor & Aroostook R.R.					
†6 50			0.0	Lv Bangor .... Ar	"				†6.22
†10 05			90.7	Ar Greenville Lv	"				†3.05
				Canadian Pacific Ry.					
†11 20	*10 48	1.22	222.9	Greenville	"	11 07	3 09		†1.12
ƒ11 35			227.7	Squaw Brook	"				ƒ1.02
11 50	u11 09		233.7	Moosehead	"	b10.51			12 49
ƒ12 01			238.5	Somerset	"				ƒ12.39
12 06			241.2	Tarratine	"				12 31
ƒ12 22			245.2	Brassua	"				ƒ12 22
ƒ12 34			249.9	Mackamp	"				ƒ12 11
12 44			254.6	Long Pond	"				12 01
ƒ12 55			259.0	Blair	"				ƒ11 50
1 20	11 53	2.44	263.1	Jackman	"	10.09	2.11		11 35
ƒ1 26			266.4	Attean Landing	"				ƒ11 20
ƒ1 30			269.2	Attean	"				ƒ11 17
ƒ1 43			274.2	Boston Ranch	"				ƒ10 58
2 30	12.15	3.13	275.8	Holeb	"	9.47	1.50		10 55
ƒ2 43			281.9	Keough	"				ƒ10 09
ƒ2 53			284.4	Skinner	"	ƒ9.29			ƒ10 02
ƒ3 05			287.2	Lowelltown, Me.	"				ƒ9.54
ƒ3 22		ƒ3.45	291.4	Boundary, Que	"	ƒ9.17			ƒ9.46
ƒ3 33			296.5	Trudell	"				ƒ9.26
ƒ3 45			300.5	Ditchfield	"				ƒ9.16
†4 00	*1.15	¶4.20	306.6	Ar MEGANTIC 23 Lv	"	†8 45	*12 50		ǂ9.00
39	41	39				40	42		204
ρ4 30	*1 25	¶4 30	306.6	Lv MEGANTIC 23 .... Ar	"	‡8 35	*12 40		ǂ6 45
7 05	3 30	7 05	375.1	Ar Sherbrooke 23 Lv	"	6 05	10 15		4.05
ρ10 30	*6 50	¶10 30	481.7	Ar MONTREAL ‖ 23 Lv	ET	‡2 45	*7 00		ǂ12.30
A.M.	A.M.	A.M.		Windsor Station		P.M.	P.M.		P.M.

PRESQUE ISLE, AROOSTOOK

186	Miles	TABLE 15-A Atlantic Time	185
A.M.			P.M.
†9.30	0.0	Lv Presque Isle, Me. .. Ar	†5.30
ƒ9.45	2.9	Daggett	ƒ5 03
ƒ9.55	3.5	Guiou	ƒ5 00
ƒ10 10	6.4	Parkhurst	ƒ4.50
ƒ10 20	8.3	Campbell	ƒ4 42
ƒ10 25	9.4	Roberts	ƒ4 38
ƒ10 35	11.4	McGraw	ƒ4 32
11 00	14.5	Caribou	4 20
ƒ11.12	18.2	Hurd	ƒ4 04
ƒ11 17	19.3	East Lyndon	ƒ3 59
ƒ11 22	20.3	Maines	ƒ3 55
ƒ11 27	21.3	Goodwin	ƒ3 50
ƒ11 30	21.7	Maynard	ƒ3.47
ƒ11 38	24.0	Stebbins	ƒ3.40
ƒ11.41	25.0	Hopkins	ƒ3.35
12.50	26.5	Fort Fairfield, Me.	3.30
ƒ1.05	31.0	Tinker, N.B	ƒ2.42
†1.15	34.0	Ar Aroostook 15 Lv	†2.30
P.M.			P.M.

PLASTER ROCK, PERTH JCT.

184	Miles	TABLE 15-B Atlantic Time	183
A.M.			P.M.
†11 00	0.0	Lv Plaster Rock ..... Ar	†4.50
ƒ11.05	1.7	Wapske	ƒ4 35
ƒ11.15	4.7	Three Brooks	ƒ4 22
ƒ11.20	6.1	Reed's Island	ƒ4 18
ƒ11.25	7.8	Beveridge	ƒ4 13
ƒ11.30	8.8	Odell River	ƒ4.09
ƒ11.42	12.3	Arthurette	ƒ3.58
ƒ11.45	13.1	Licford	ƒ3.54
ƒ11.50	13.9	Red Rapids	ƒ3.50
ƒ12.01	16.3	Hillside	ƒ3 40
ƒ12.10	18.0	Currie	ƒ3.35
ƒ12.22	20.4	Rowena	ƒ3.27
ƒ12.37	23.5	Tobique Narrows	ƒ3 15
ƒ12.42	25.2	Millicete	ƒ3 08
†12.50	27.5	Ar Perth Junc 15 Lv	†3 00
P.M.			P.M.

HOULTON. WOODSTOCK

Until Sept. 15, railway tickets to Houlton via Debec will be accepted for passage via Woodstock and Raymond Transfer.

		Operated by Raymond Transfer Until Sept. 15. Atlantic Time		
P.M.	A.M.		P.M.	P.M.
†3.30	†10.20	Lv Houlton .... Ar	†12.10	†5.25
3.55	10.45	Richmond Corner	11.50	5.05
†4.20	†11.10	Ar Woodstock Lv	†11.30	†4.45
P.M.	A.M.		A.M.	P.M.

DEBEC JCT., HOULTON

READ DOWN			Miles	TABLE 15C Effective Sept. 16 Atlantic Time	READ UP			
	173	171			172	174		
Rail Service In effect Sept. 16.	P.M.	A.M.			A.M.	P.M.	See Bus Service Above	
	†5.15	†11.05	0.0	Lv Debec Jct. 15 .... Ar	†10.25	†4.40		
	ƒ5.20	ƒ11.10	1.9	Elmwood	ƒ10.20	ƒ4.35		
	ƒ5.25	ƒ11.15	3.5	Green Road	ƒ10.15	ƒ4.30		
	†5.40	†11.30	8.0	Ar Houlton Lv	†10.00	†4.15		
	P.M.	A.M.			A.M.	P.M.		

EXPLANATION OF SIGNS THIS PAGE

* Daily. † Daily ex. Sun. ‡ Daily ex. Sat. § Sun. only. b Stops to detrain from east of Saint John. ƒ Stops on signal. ρ Stops to detrain from east of Saint John, also entrain for west of McAdam. j Tues., Thur., Sat. ǂ Sat. only. r Mon., Wed., Fri. ss Stops on signal Tues. and Thurs. for revenue passrs. u Stops on signal to detrain passengers from points beyond McAdam. y Stops on signal Wed. for revenue passengers.

C.B. Cobb collection

TRAINS BETWEEN BOSTON AND PORTLAND AND INTERMEDIATE POINTS.

FROM BOSTON.—SUNDAYS. June, 1909

Train Nos. STATIONS.	8	275	705	707	709	711	713	489	715	15	717	719	721
	A.M.	A.M.	A.M.	A.M.	A.M.	A.M.	A.M.	N'ON	P.M.	P.M.	P.M.	P.M.	P.M.
BOSTON Lv	6.00	Will not run after Sept. 5.	8.00	9.15	9.30	10.30	11.30	12.00	12.30	1.15	1.30	2.15	3.00
East Somerville			8.06		9.36		11.36		12.36		1.36		3.06
Wellington					9.39		11.39		12.39		1.39		3.09
Edgeworth			8.11		9.42				12.42		1.42		3.12
Malden	6.10		8.14		9.45	10.40	11.43		12.45		1.45	2.25	3.15
Oak Grove					9.47		11.45		12.47		1.47		3.17
Fells					f9.48				f12.48				f3.18
Wyoming			8.18		9.50	10.44	11.48		12.50		1.50	2.29	3.20
Melrose	6.15		8.20		9.52	10.46	11.50		12.52		1.52	2.31	3.22
Melrose Highl'ds	6.17		8.22		9.54	10.49	11.52		12.54		1.54	2.34	3.25
Greenwood					9.57		11.55		12.57		1.57		3.28
Wakefield Jct	6.22				10.00		11.58		1.00		2.00	2.38	3.31
Wakefield	6.24		8.28		10.02	10.54	12.00	12.18	1.02		2.02	2.40	3.33
Reading	6.29		8.33		10.07	10.58	12.05	12.23	1.07		2.07	2.45	3.38
Reading Highl'ds					10.10		12.09		1.11		2.11		3.42
No. Wilmington	6.36		8.40		A.M.	f11.06	P.M.	f12.31	P.M.		P.M.	2.52	P.M.
Wilmington Jct	f6.39		f8.43			f11.09						f2.55	
Lowell Junction			8.47					12.38				2.59	
Ballardvale	6.44		8.50			11.14		12.41				3.02	
Andover	6.49		8.55			11.19		12.46				3.07	
South Lawrence	6.58	8.33	9.03	9.55		11.26		12.56		1.57		3.14	
No. Lawrence. Ar	7.01		9.15	9.58		11.32		1.01		1.59		3.18	
No. Lawrence. Lv	6.50	8.28	8.54	9.46		11.20		P.M.		1.48		3.05	
No. Andover...Lv	7.02	8.37	9.07			11.30						3.18	
Ward Hill	f7.08	f8.43	f9.13			f11.36						f3.24	
Bradford	7.12	8.47	9.17			11.40						3.28	
Haverhill	7.15	A.M.	9.20	10.08		11.42				2.11		3.30	
Rosemont			f			A.M.						P.M.	
Atkinson	f7.21		f9.27										
Westville	f7.24		f9.30				No. 765		No. 767		No. 769		No. 773
Plaistow	7.27		f9.32										
Newton Junction	7.32		9.37				P.M.		P.M.		P.M.		P.M.
Powwow River	f7.39		f9.44										
East Kingston	7.42		9.47			No. 763						No. 771	
Exeter	7.50		9.55	10.33					Will not run after Sept. 5	2.36	Will not run after Sept. 5		Will not run after Sept. 5
Newfields	7.57		10.02			A.M.	Will not run after Sept. 5					P.M.	
Rockingham J. Ar	8.00	No. 685	10.05			Will not run after Sept. 5.							
Rockingham J. Lv	8.00		10.05		No. 687			No. 689					
Newmarket	8.04	A.M.	10.10									Will not run after Sept. 5.	
Durham	8.12		10.18		A.M.			P.M.					
Madbury	8.17		10.23										
Dover	8.27	10.37	10.32	11.01	11.13			2.00		3.05			
Rollinsford	8.34	10.44	10.39		11.20			2.06					
Salmon Falls	8.38		10.43										
Cummings	f8.39	Will not run after Sept. 5.	f10.45										
North Berwick	8.49	No. 761	10.55	11.21						3.25			
Wells Beach	9.00			11.33						3.37			
The Elms		A.M.											
Kennebunk	9.08	8.05		11.42		10.55				3.47			
Arundel													
West Biddeford													
Biddeford	9.23	8.21		11.57		11.11	1.45		3.45	4.03	4.55		6.50
Saco	9.26	8.23		12.00		11.13	1.47		3.47	4.07	4.57		6.52
Temple Av Cros'g													
Camp Ground	f9.32	f8.29				f11.20	f1.53		f3.53		f5.03		f6.58
Old Orchard	9.34	8.32		12.08		11.22	1.56		3.56	4.16	5.06	5.25	7.01
Grand Beach													
Pine Point	f9.39	8.37		f12.13		11.27	2.01		4.01	E4.21	5.11	5.30	7.06
Scarboro Beach	f9.43	8.42		f12.18		11.32	2.06		4.06	E4.26	5.16	5.35	7.11
Rigby		f8.46					f2.11		f4.11		f5.21		f7.16
PORTLAND, .. Ar C. Sta.	9.55	8.55		12.30		11.45	2.20		4.20	4.40	5.30	5.50	7.25
	A.M.	A.M.	A.M.	P.M.	A.M.	A.M.	P.M.	P.M.	P.M.	P.M.	P.M.	P.M.	P.M.

Train Nos. STATIONS.	723	725	61	727	21	731	277	733	735	737	739	741	743	745
	P.M.	P.M.	P.M.	P.M.	P.M.	P.M.	P.M.	P.M.	P.M.	P.M.	P.M.	P.M.	P.M.	P.M.
BOSTON Lv	3.30	4.00	5.14	5.20	6.00	6.05	6.30	7.05	7.30	8.15	8.40	9.15	10.15	11.00
East Somerville		4.06		5.26		6.11			7.36	8.21		9.21		11.06
Wellington		4.09		5.29		6.14			7.39			9.24		11.09
Edgeworth		4.12		5.32		6.17			7.42	8.26		9.27		11.12
Malden	3.40	4.15		5.35		6.20	6.40	7.15	7.45	8.29		9.30	10.25	11.15
Oak Grove		4.17		5.37		6.22			7.47	8.31		9.32		11.17
Fells						f6.23				f8.33				
Wyoming	3.44	4.20		5.40		6.25	6.44	7.19	7.50	8.35		9.35	10.29	11.21
Melrose	3.46	4.22		5.42		6.27	6.46	7.21	7.52	8.37		9.37	10.31	11.23
Melrose Highl'ds	3.49	4.25		5.45		6.30	6.49	7.24	7.55	8.40		9.40	10.34	11.26
Greenwood		4.28		5.48		6.33			7.58	8.43		9.43		11.29
Wakefield Jct		4.31				6.36	6.53		8.01	8.46		9.46		11.32
Wakefield	3.54	4.33		5.52		6.38		7.29	8.03	8.48	8.57	9.48	10.40	11.34
Reading	3.59	4.38		5.57		6.43		7.34	8.08	8.53	9.02	9.53	10.45	11.39
Reading Highl'ds		4.42				6.47			8.12	8.56		9.57		11.43
No. Wilmington	f4.06	P.M.		6.05				f7.42	P.M.		9.09		e10.52	
Wilmington Jct	f4.09			f6.08				f7.45						
Lowell Junction	4.13			6.12							9.15			
Ballardvale	4.16			6.15				7.50			9.18		e11.00	
Andover	4.21		5.48	6.20				7.55			9.23		11.04	
South Lawrence	4.28		5.56	6.27	6.40			8.02			9.31		11.11	
No. Lawrence. Ar	4.32		6.06	6.31	6.46			8.05			9.36		11.16	
No. Lawrence. Lv	4.20		5.50	P.M.	6.32			7.54	No. 273		9.23		11.04	
No. Andover...Lv	4.32		6.00					8.06			9.35		11.15	
Ward Hill	f4.38							f8.12	P.M.		e9.41		e11.21	
Bradford	4.42		6.09					8.16	8.35		9.45		11.25	
Haverhill	4.44		6.14		6.54			8.18	8.38		9.47		11.27	
Rosemont	P.M.		f					P.M.	Will not run after Sept. 5					
Atkinson			6.21											
Westville		No. 775	6.24	No. 777										
Plaistow			6.27											
Newton Junction		P.M.	6.32	P.M.										
Powwow River			6.39											
East Kingston			6.42											
Exeter			6.50		7.19			No. 779						
Newfields		Will not run after Sept. 5	6.57	Will not run after Sept. 5										
Rockingham J. Ar			7.00					P.M.						
Rockingham J. Lv	No. 643		7.00											
Newmarket			7.04											
Durham	P.M.		7.12					Will not run after Sept. 5						
Madbury			f7.17											
Dover	5.25		7.26		7.47									
Rollinsford	5.32		7.33											
Salmon Falls			7.37											
Cummings			f7.39											
North Berwick			7.48		8.05									
Wells Beach					8.17									
The Elms														
Kennebunk		7.00		8.05	8.26									
Arundel														
West Biddeford														
Biddeford		7.15		8.20	8.40									
Saco		7.18		8.23	8.42									
Temple Av Cros'g														
Camp Ground				f8.29										
Old Orchard		7.27		8.32	8.50			9.35						
Grand Beach														
Pine Point		7.32		8.37	E8.54			9.40						
Scarboro Beach		7.37		8.42	E8.58			9.45						
Rigby														
PORTLAND, .. Ar C. Sta.		7.50		8.55	9.10			10.00						
	P.M.	P.M.	P.M.	P.M.	P.M.	P.M.	P.M.	P.M.	P.M.	P.M.	P.M.	P.M.	P.M.	P.M.

Both C.B. Cobb collection

dividends were finally paid off in cash.

At the annual meeting in 1925 the directors formally presented their plan for buying the stock of the Hereford Railway in order to rid the Maine Central of the burden of this lease. The Hereford had for many years been a losing proposition, and the operating deficit and part of the fixed charges could be saved by cancelling the lease and abandoning the road. The saving would represent a very substantial return on the money required to buy the stock. The plan was approved by the Maine Central stockholders, and later in the year the Hereford stock was purchased, the lease was cancelled, and the road was abandoned.

Chapter Fourteen

Rails Fan out through Aroostook County

The importance of railroad communication with the Aroostook country had been appreciated from the beginning of railroad development in Maine. The forest and agricultural resources of the St. John valley were the more fully realized on account of the prominence attained by that region in the Northeastern Boundary controversy, and during the years when the settlement of that international argument rankled in the minds of Americans communications with northern Maine were considered of military importance. The claim of Maine for redress for the injury done her in surrendering about 5,000,000 acres of her rightful territory was constantly kept before the national government by Maine's representatives, and this was the strongest argument presented in the request for national assistance for the building of the European & North American.

Richard Dole collection

When the European & North American received from the State the land grant which made possible the construction of the railroad, it was generally understood that that company practically agreed to build a branch line into Aroostook County; and, indeed, as the land grant was made as a military measure for the defense of the northeastern frontier, there could have been little excuse for state aid unless such an understanding had existed. But the urgency for a military railroad became less after the Civil War, and the completion of the line to Vanceboro as part of the route to St. John and Halifax was then considered of primary importance. A survey was made of a route from Moluncus north into Aroostook, which survey indicates that the European & North American management was not entirely unmindful of its obligation. But before any definite plans were made, the panic of 1873 made railroad financing practicably impossible; and during the period of distress which followed the panic the European & North American Railway Company failed.

Ex-Bangor & Piscataquis 4 "Hamlin", built in 1869 by the Portland Co., is viewed at Milo Jct. in 1908. *470 Railroad Club collection*

Although the European & North American never built a branch line into Aroostook County, the people of Aroostook did secure railroad communication with Bangor by means of that line. The railroad lines in New Brunswick were gradually extended northward, and by the time the European & North American was opened, the New Brunswick & Canada Railway had been built from St. Stephen to Woodstock, crossing the European & North American (New Brunswick Company) at McAdam Junction. The Aroostook & St. Andrews Branch Railroad, which later became the New Brunswick & Canada, opened in 1862 from Debec Junction on the State Line 3 miles to Houlton. Originally 5 feet 6 inch gauge, it was changed to 4 feet 8½ inches in 1879. The Houlton Branch Railroad was opened in 1870, connecting with the New Brunswick & Canada Railway. The New Brunswick Railway, originally three foot gauge, was opened between Edmundston and Woodstock in 1878; and the Aroostook River Railroad, built from a connection with the New Brunswick Railway, was opened to Caribou in 1876 and to Presque Isle in 1881. The New Brunswick Railway leased both the Aroostook River and Houlton Branch Railroads in 1882. The New Brunswick Railway changed ownership in 1880, and soon afterwards this company leased the New Brunswick & Canada Railway and the St. John & Maine. All of these roads became part of the Canadian Pacific system when that company leased the New Brunswick Railway in 1890.

Bangor & Aroostook 4-4-0 212 was built by Manchester in 1873. It is seen at Derby in July 1932. *Ron Johnson collection*

Class P 0-6-0 325, built by Alco-Manchester in 1908, sits at Derby in 1932. *Ron Johnson collection*

Freshly painted 4-6-0 90 shows off its trim lines at Derby in 1936 after an overhaul. *Ron Johnson collection*

For more than twenty years after 1871 the only railroad outlets from Aroostook County were over Canadian railroads. At intervals during this period the agitation for a railroad line within Maine was renewed; but because the proponents of an independent railroad were not railroad men, and because patriotic motives were not supported by economic necessity, these movements secured no definite result. But when the line of the Canadian Pacific across Maine was secured, and that company had leased the New Brunswick Railway and controlled lines, the prospect of economic domination of Aroostook by a foreign railroad aroused a public sentiment which only required a leader in order to accomplish great things.

Franklin W. Cram of Bangor was general manager of the New Brunswick Railway from 1885 to 1890, and during this period had been in close touch with the people of Aroostook. A man of compelling personality, with a vision which admitted no impossibilities, with long experience in railroad operation, and with firm faith in the future of Aroostook, Mr. Cram possessed the necessary qualifications for leadership in such an undertaking. Consequently, when he presented to the leading citizens of Aroostook a definite plan for creating the railroad which they desired, he received at once their enthusiastic support. Closely associated with Mr. Cram was Albert A. Burleigh, who devoted his time and effort to consolidating the sentiment in Aroostook in support of Mr. Cram's program. To these two men is due in large measure the credit for creating the Bangor & Aroostook Railroad.

The Bangor & Aroostook Railroad was chartered in 1891. The first board of directors was composed of Albert A. Burleigh, Charles A. Gibson, Hiram H. Fogg, Frederick H. Appleton and Charles F. Bragg. Mr. Burleigh was president, and Mr. Cram was general manager. The charter granted to the company contained a covenant of the state that railroads parallel within fifteen miles should not be built for twenty years, later changed to thirty years. Also, the state agreed to repay to the railroad company 95% of its state taxes for twenty years. The County of Aroostook subscribed for $728,000 par value preferred stock, and its financial interest was represented in the management by three directors elected by the Aroostook legislative delegation. $519,000 par value additional preferred stock was sold to the public. The original subscriptions for common stock totalled $1,050,000, of which $1,040,000 was acquired by the Aroostook Construction Company for cash and in payments under the original construction contract.

The Aroostook Construction Company was formed in 1891 for the purpose of building the Bangor & Aroostook Railroad, and during the following twenty years did build practically all of the mileage now owned by the railroad company. There was nothing unusual about this method of financing

On a crisp March day in 1949 a southbound freight accelerates out of Millinocket with F3 505 A and B along with 4-8-2 101 providing the muscle. *470 Railroad Club collection*

BL2 52 and GP7 67 handle a northbound tank car train out of Searsport heading for Northern Maine Jct. in September 1977. *Ron Johnson*

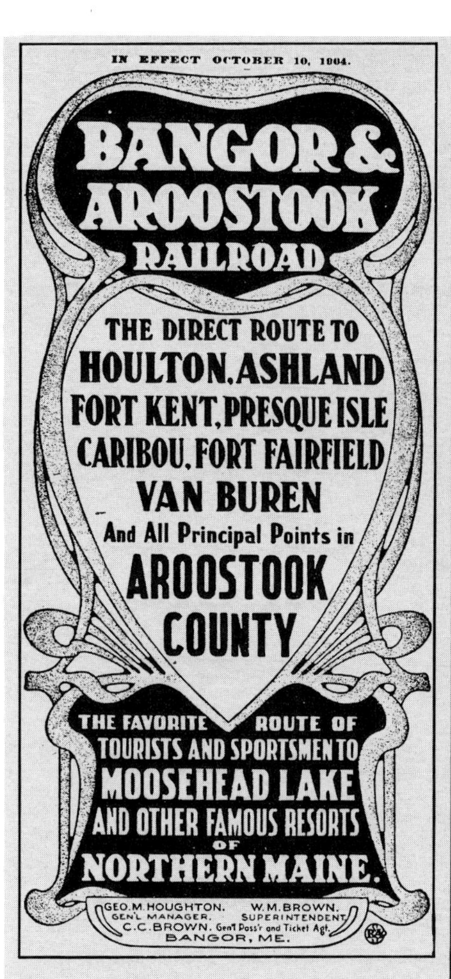

IN EFFECT OCTOBER 10, 1904.
BANGOR & AROOSTOOK RAILROAD
THE DIRECT ROUTE TO
HOULTON, ASHLAND
FORT KENT, PRESQUE ISLE
CARIBOU, FORT FAIRFIELD
VAN BUREN
And All Principal Points in
AROOSTOOK COUNTY
THE FAVORITE ROUTE OF
TOURISTS AND SPORTSMEN TO
MOOSEHEAD LAKE
AND OTHER FAMOUS RESORTS
OF
NORTHERN MAINE.
GEO. M. HOUGHTON, GEN'L MANAGER.
W. M. BROWN, SUPERINTENDENT.
C. C. BROWN, Gen'l Pass'r and Ticket Agt.
BANGOR, ME.

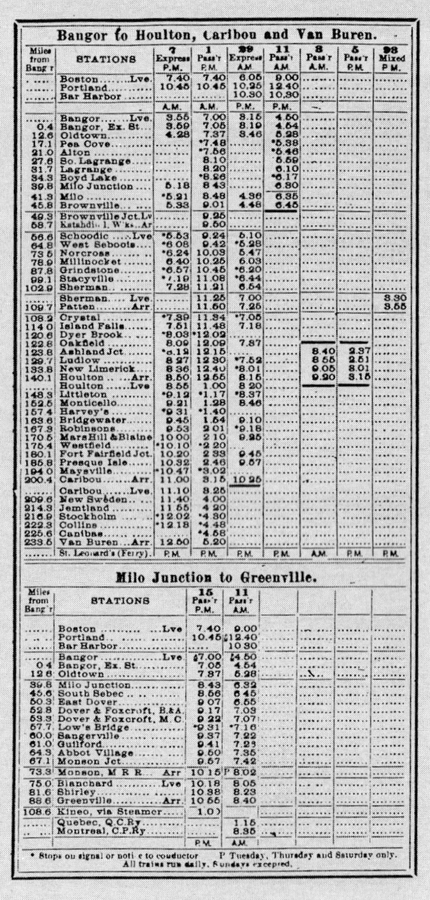

Bangor to Houlton, Caribou and Van Buren.

Miles from Bang'r	STATIONS	7 Express P.M.	1 Pass'r P.M.	29 Express A.M.	11 Pass'r A.M.	8 Pass'r A.M.	5 Pass'r P.M.	98 Mixed P.M.
......	Boston.......Lve.	7.40	7.40	6.05	9.00			
......	Portland........	10.45	10.45	10.25	12.40			
......	Bar Harbor			10.30	10.30			
		A.M.	A.M.	P.M.	P.M.			
......	Bangor.......Lve.	3.55	7.00	8.15	4.50			
0.4	Bangor, Ex. St..	3.59	7.05	8.19	4.54			
12.6	Oldtown.........	4.28	7.37	8.46	5.28			
17.1	Pea Cove........		*7.48		*5.38			
21.0	Alton		*7.56		*5.46			
27.6	So. Lagrange....		8.10		5.59			
31.7	Lagrange		8.20		6.10			
34.3	Boyd Lake		*8.26		*6.17			
39.8	Milo Junction	5.18	8.43		6.30			
41.3	Milo	*5.21	8.48	4.36	6.35			
45.8	Brownville... ...	5.33	9.01	4.48	6.45			
49.3	Brownville Jct.Lv		9.25					
58.7	Katahdin I. W'ks..Ar		9.50					
56.6	Schoodic .....Lve	*5.53	9.24	5.10				
64.8	West Seboois....	*6.08	9.42	*5.28				
73.5	Norcross	*6.24	10.03	5.47				
78.9	Millinocket	6.40	10.25	6.03				
87.8	Grindstone.......	*6.57	10.45	*6.20				
99.1	Stacyville	*7.19	11.08	*6.44				
102.9	Sherman..	7.28	11.21	6.54				
......	Sherman. ... Lve.		11.25	7.00				3.30
109.7	Patten........Arr		11.50	7.25				3.55
108.2	Crystal	*7.39	11.34	*7.05				
114.0	Island Falls......	7.51	11.48	7.18				
120.6	Dyer Brook..	*8.03	*12.02					
122.8	Oakfield	8.09	12.09	7.37				
123.8	Ashland Jct......	*8.12	12.15			8.40	2.37	
129.7	Ludlow	8.27	12.30	*7.52		8.55	2.51	
133.8	New Limerick....	8.36	12.40	*8.01		9.05	3.01	
140.1	Houlton .. ...Arr.	8.50	12.55	8.15		9.20	3.15	
......	Houlton ......Lve	8.55	1.00	8.20				
148.3	Littleton	*9.12	*1.17	*8.37				
152.5	Monticello.......	9.21	1.28	8.46				
157.4	Harvey's	*9.31	*1.40					
163.6	Bridgewater......	9.45	1.54	9.10				
167.3	Robinsons	9.53	2.01	*9.18				
170.5	MarsHill & Blaine	10.00	2.10	9.25				
175.4	Westfield	*10.10	*2.20					
180.1	Fort Fairfield Jct.	10.20	2.33	9.45				
185.8	Presque Isle......	10.32	2.46	9.57				
194.0	Maysville........	*10.47	*3.02					
200.4	Caribou......Arr.	11.00	3.15	10.25				
......	Caribou......Lve.	11.10	3.25					
209.6	New Sweden.. ...	11.40	4.00					
214.3	Jemtland	11.55	4.20					
216.9	Stockholm	*12.02	*4.30					
222.3	Collins	*12.18	*4.48					
225.6	Canibas.....		*4.58					
233.5	Van Buren ..Arr.	12.50	5.20					
......	St. Leonard's (Ferry).	P.M.	P.M.	P.M.	P.M.	A.M.	P.M.	P.M.

Milo Junction to Greenville.

Miles from Bang'r	STATIONS	15 Pass'r P.M.	11 Pass'r A.M.
......	Boston ....Lve	7.40	9.00
......	Portland..	10.45	‡12.40
......	Bar Harbor..............		10.30
......	Bangor ....Lve	‡7.00	‡4.50
0.4	Bangor, Ex. St	7.05	4.54
12.6	Oldtown	7.37	5.28
39.8	Milo Junction...........	8.43	6.32
45.6	South Sebec	8.56	6.45
50.3	East Dover	9.07	6.55
52.8	Dover & Foxcroft, B.&A.	9.17	7.03
53.3	Dover & Foxcroft, M.C.	9.22	7.07
57.7	Low's Bridge...........	*9.31	*7.16
60.0	Sangerville	9.37	7.22
61.0	Guilford..........	9.41	7.25
64.3	Abbot Village	9.50	7.35
67.1	Monson Jct.............	9.57	7.42
73.3	Monson, M R R.. Arr	10.15	P 8.02
75.0	Blanchard ....Lve	10.18	8.05
81.6	Shirley..........	10.38	8.23
88.6	Greenville...........Arr.	10.55	8.40
108.6	Kineo, via Steamer.....	1.00	
......	Quebec, Q.C.Ry.........		1.15
......	Montreal, C.P.Ry........		8.35
		P.M.	A.M.

* Stops on signal or notice to conductor. P Tuesday, Thursday and Saturday only. All trains run daily, Sundays excepted.

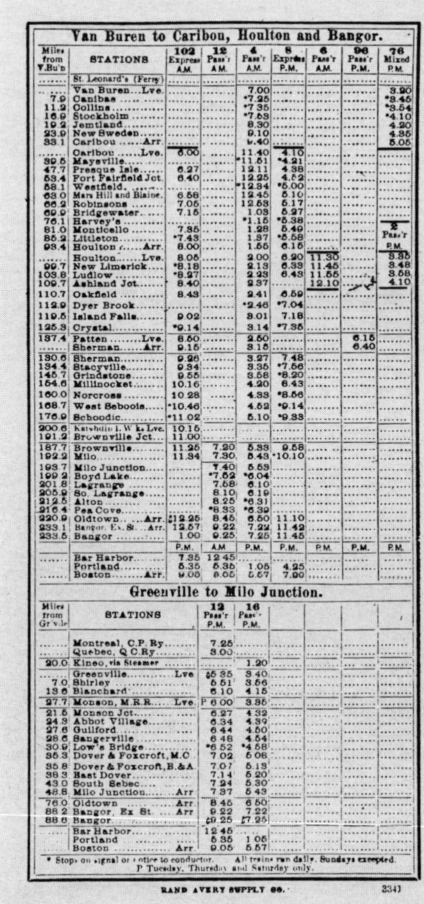

Van Buren to Caribou, Houlton and Bangor.

Miles from V.Bu'n	STATIONS	102 Express A.M.	12 Pass'r A.M.	4 Pass'r A.M.	8 Express P.M.	6 Pass'r A.M.	96 Pass'r P.M.	76 Mixed P.M.
......	St. Leonard's (Ferry)							
......	Van Buren...Lve.			7.00				3.20
7.9	Canibas			*7.25				*3.45
11.2	Collins..........			*7.35				*3.54
16.9	Stockholm			*7.53				*4.10
19.2	Jemtland.........			8.30				4.20
23.9	New Sweden......			9.10				4.35
33.1	Caribou ......Arr.			[illegible].40				5.05
......	Caribou ......Lve.	6.00		11.40	4.10			
39.5	Maysville.........			*11.51	*4.21			
47.7	Presque Isle......	6.27		12.11	4.38			
53.4	Fort Fairfield Jct.	6.40		12.25	4.52			
58.1	Westfield.			*12.34	*5.00			
63.0	Mars Hill and Blaine.	6.58		12.45	5.10			
66.2	Robinsons	7.05		12.53	5.17			
69.9	Bridgewater.....	7.15		1.03	5.27			
76.1	Harvey's			*1.15	*5.38			
81.0	Monticello	7.35		1.28	5.49			2 Pass'r
85.2	Littleton.........	*7.43		1.37	*5.58			
93.4	Houlton ......Arr.	8.00		1.55	6.15			P.M.
......	Houlton.......Lve.	8.05		2.00	6.20	11.30		3.35
99.7	New Limerick....	*8.18		2.13	6.33	11.45		3.48
103.8	Ludlow	*8.27		2.23	6.43	11.55		3.58
109.7	Ashland Jct......	8.40		2.37		12.10		4.10
110.7	Oakfield	8.43		2.41	6.59			
112.9	Dyer Brook......			*2.46	*7.04			
119.5	Island Falls......	9.02		3.01	7.18			
125.3	Crystal..........	*9.14		3.14	*7.35			
137.4	Patten ....Lve.	8.50		2.50			6.15	
......	Sherman......Arr.	9.15		3.15			6.40	
130.6	Sherman..........	9.26		3.27	7.48			
134.4	Stacyville........	9.34		3.35	*7.56			
145.7	Grindstone.......	9.55		3.58	*8.20			
154.6	Millinocket......	10.16		4.20	8.43			
160.0	Norcross	10.28		4.33	*8.56			
168.7	West Seboois.....	*10.46		4.52	*9.14			
176.9	Schoodic.........	*11.02		5.10	*9.33			
200.6	Katahdin I. W'ks. Lve.	10.15						
191.2	Brownville Jct...	11.00						
187.7	Brownville.......	11.25	7.20	5.33	9.58			
192.2	Milo.............	11.34	7.30	5.43	*10.10			
193.7	Milo Junction.....		7.40	5.53				
199.2	Boyd Lake........		*7.52	*6.04				
201.8	Lagrange		7.58	6.10				
205.9	So. Lagrange.....		8.10	6.19				
212.5	Alton		8.25	*6.31				
216.4	Pea Cove.........		*8.33	*6.39				
220.9	Oldtown.. ...Arr.	‡12.25	8.45	6.50	11.10			
233.1	Bangor, Ex. St. ..Arr.	12.57	9.22	7.22	11.42			
233.5	Bangor	1.00	9.25	7.25	11.45			
		P.M.	A.M.	P.M.	P.M.	P.M.	P.M.	P.M.
......	Bar Harbor......	7.35	12.45					
......	Portland.........	5.35	5.35	1.05	4.25			
......	Boston.......Arr.	9.05	8.05	5.57	7.20			

Greenville to Milo Junction.

Miles from Gr'vile	STATIONS	12 Pass'r P.M.	16 Pass'r P.M.
......	Montreal, C.P. Ry........	7.25	
......	Quebec, Q C.Ry.........	3.00	
20.0	Kineo, via Steamer		1.20
......	Greenville..........Lve	‡5.35	3.40
7.0	Shirley	5.51	3.56
13.6	Blanchard	6.10	4.15
27.7	Monson, M.R.R.....Lve	P 6.00	3.35
21.5	Monson Jct..........	6.27	4.32
24.3	Abbot Village..........	6.34	4.39
27.6	Guilford	6.44	4.50
28.6	Sangerville	6.48	4.54
30.9	Low's Bridge..........	*6.52	*4.58
35.3	Dover & Foxcroft, M.C	7.02	5.08
35.8	Dover & Foxcroft, B.&A	7.07	5.13
38.3	East Dover...........	7.14	5.20
43.0	South Sebec....	7.24	5.30
48.8	Milo Junction.......Arr	7.37	5.43
76.0	Oldtown ....Arr	8.45	6.50
88.2	Bangor, Ex St. ...Arr	9.22	7.22
88.6	Bangor	‡9.25	‡7.25
......	Bar Harbor...........	12.45	
......	Portland	5.35	1.05
......	Boston ....Arr	9.05	5.57

* Stops on signal or notice to conductor. All trains run daily, Sundays excepted. P Tuesday, Thursday and Saturday only.

RAND AVERY SUPPLY CO. 3341

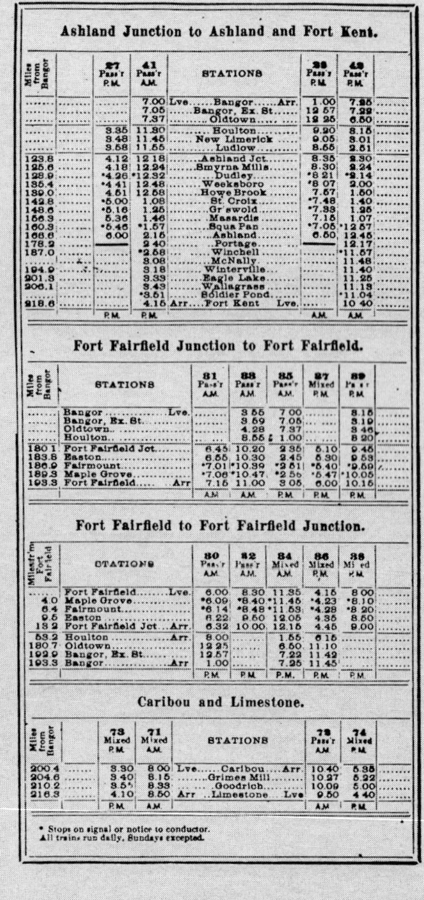

Ashland Junction to Ashland and Fort Kent.

Miles from Bangor		27 Pass'r P.M.	41 Pass'r A.M.	STATIONS	28 Pass'r P.M.	42 Pass'r P.M.	
......	......		7.00	Lve......Bangor......Arr.	1.00	7.25	
......	......		7.05	......Bangor, Ex. St......	12.57	7.22	
......	......		7.37	........Oldtown........	12.25	6.50	
......	......	3.35	11.30	........Houlton........	9.20	3.15	
......	......	3.48	11.45	......New Limerick......	9.05	3.01	
......	......	3.58	11.55	..........Ludlow........	8.55	2.51	
123.8	......	4.12	12.18	........Ashland Jct........	8.35	2.30	
125.6	......	4.18	12.24	........Smyrna Mills........	8.30	2.24	
128.9	......	*4.26	*12.32	..........Dudley..........	*8.21	*2.14	
135.4	......	*4.41	12.48	........Weeksboro........	*8.07	2.00	
139.0	......	4.51	12.58	........Howe Brook........	7.57	1.50	
142.8	......	*5.00	1.08	..........St. Croix..........	*7.48	1.40	
148.6	......	*5.16	1.25	..........Griswold..........	*7.33	1.25	
156.3	......	5.36	1.46	..........Masardis..........	7.15	1.07	
160.3	......	*5.46	*1.57	..........Squa Pan..........	*7.05	*12.57	
166.6	......	6.00	2.15	..........Ashland..........	6.50	12.45	
178.2	......		2.40	..........Portage..........		12.17	
187.0	......		*2.58	..........Winchell..........		*11.57	
......	......		3.08	..........McNally..........		11.48	
194.9	......		3.18	........Winterville........		11.40	
201.3	......		3.33	........Eagle Lake........		11.25	
206.1	......		3.43	........Wallagrass........		11.13	
......	......		*3.51	........Soldier Pond........		*11.04	
218.6	......		4.15	Arr....Fort Kent Lve.		10.40	
		P.M.	P.M.		A.M.	A.M.	

Fort Fairfield Junction to Fort Fairfield.

Miles from Bangor	STATIONS	31 Pass'r A.M.	33 Pass'r A.M.	35 Pass'r A.M.	37 Mixed P.M.	39 Pass'r P.M.	
......	Bangor ....Lve.		3.55	7.00		8.15	
......	Bangor, Ex. St.		3.59	7.05		3.19	
......	Oldtown..		4.28	7.37		3.46	
......	Houlton..		8.55	‡ 1.00		8.20	
180.1	Fort Fairfield Jct........	6.45	10.20	2.35	5.10	9.45	
183.8	Easton.................	6.55	10.30	2.45	5.30	9.53	
186.9	Fairmount..............	*7.01	*10.39	*2.51	*5.40	*9.59	
189.3	Maple Grove............	*7.06	*10.47	*2.56	*5.47	*10.05	
193.3	Fort Fairfield..... Arr	7.15	11.00	3.05	6.00	10.15	
		A.M.	A.M.	P.M.	P.M.	P.M.	

Fort Fairfield to Fort Fairfield Junction.

Miles fr'm Fort Fairfield	STATIONS	30 Pass'r A.M.	32 Pass'r A.M.	34 Mixed A.M.	36 Mixed P.M.	38 Mixed P.M.	
......	Fort Fairfield.......Lve.	6.00	8.30	11.35	4.15	8.00	
4.0	Maple Grove............	*6.09	*8.40	*11.45	*4.23	*8.10	
6.4	Fairmount..............	*6.14	*8.48	*11.53	*4.28	*8.20	
9.5	Easton	6.22	9.50	12.05	4.35	8.50	
13.2	Fort Fairfield Jct ..Arr.	6.32	10.00	12.15	4.45	9.00	
53.2	Houlton ....Arr.	8.00		1.55	6.15		
180.7	Oldtown................	12.25		6.50	11.10		
192.9	Bangor, Ex. St.........	12.57		7.22	11.42		
193.3	Bangor..............Arr	1.00		7.25	11.45		
		P.M.	P.M.	P.M.	P.M.	P.M.	

Caribou and Limestone.

Miles from Bangor		73 Mixed P.M.	71 Mixed A.M.	STATIONS	72 Pass'r A.M.	74 Mixed P.M.	
200.4	......	3.30	8.00	Lve......Caribou....Arr.	10.40	5.35	
204.6	......	3.40	8.15	........Grimes Mill........	10.27	5.22	
210.2	......	3.55	8.33	........Goodrich..........	10.09	5.00	
216.3	......	4.10	8.50	Arr ..Limestone.. Lve	9.50	4.40	
		P.M.	A.M.		A.M.	P.M.	

* Stops on signal or notice to conductor.
All trains run daily, Sundays excepted.

Richard Dole collection

construction, which had been in common use during the period of American railroad development. The Aroostook Construction Company built the railroad with its own money, which was often secured by pledge of the personal credit of its promoters, and received its pay for the construction in the securities of the railroad company. The value of these securities, especially in the early stages of development, was problematical and dependent upon the success of the railroad. In the case of the Aroostook Construction Company there has been for many years a popular misunderstanding of its functions, its financing and its profits which has worked an injustice toward those men who created the Bangor & Aroostook Railroad.

For forty years a railroad into Aroostook had been urgently needed and earnestly desired, but no one could be found to build it. The financial experiences of railroad builders in Maine were not encouraging to the hope that such an undertaking could be financed or that the railroad, when constructed, would pay. Various attempts to secure state and municipal aid had failed. And when the promoters of the Bangor & Aroostook in 1891 came forward with a definite proposition to build this railroad they were welcomed by the legislature with open arms. It was generally admitted that no group of men could be expected to devote their efforts to and risk their fortunes in building a railroad, which would be by far the greatest enterprise ever undertaken in Maine, unless an opportunity was afforded for profit from its successful operation; and it was well understood in the beginning that the reward of the builders would be the common stock of the Bangor & Aroostook Railroad, to be issued at the rate of about $6,000 per mile. The probable future value of this stock no man could predict.

By the time when the Aroostook Construction Company had finished its job in 1912 the personal fortunes of its promoters had been several times in danger, and the construction company was heavily in debt. This latter condition continued until 1924, when the Bangor & Aroostook common stock was sold by the Aroostook Construction Company. The result of this venture in building over 600 miles of railroad was a profit to the original promoters of about six per cent a year on their actual cash investment in the enterprise. This briefly is the story of the Aroostook Construction Company.

As the first step the Bangor & Aroostook leased the Bangor & Piscataquis Railroad, which carried control by lease of the Bangor & Katahdin Iron Works Railroad built in 1881. After the cancellation of its lease to the European & North American, the Bangor & Piscataquis Railroad was for some years operated by its owners with fair success. In 1884 the company had completed an extension from Blanchard to Greenville, which with the Bangor & Katahdin Iron Works road made about 95 miles in operation. The Monson Railroad, a narrow gauge line to

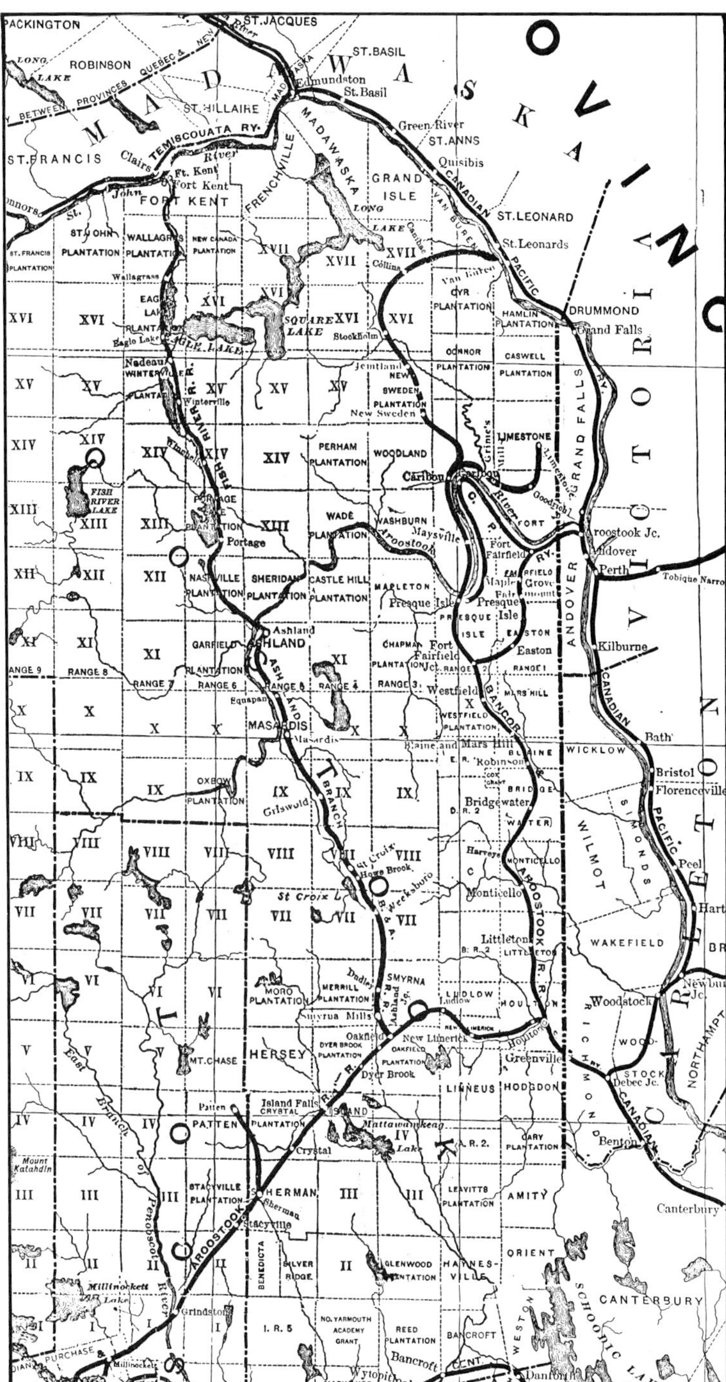

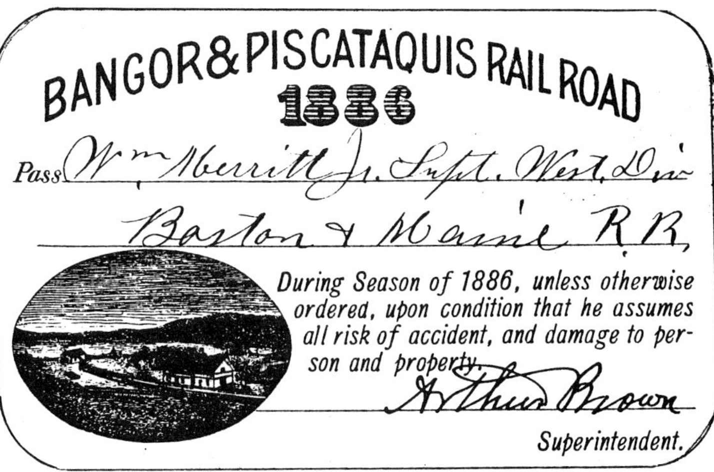
BANGOR & PISCATAQUIS RAIL ROAD
1886
Pass Wm Merritt Jr. Supt. West Div
Boston & Maine R.R.
During Season of 1886, unless otherwise ordered, upon condition that he assumes all risk of accident, and damage to person and property.
Arthur Brown
Superintendent.

Richard Dole collection

Two views of the Monson narrow gauge in the early 1900's at Monson are presented in summer and winter. *Russell Monroe collection*

the slate quarries at Monson, was opened in 1884, and by its connection with the Bangor & Piscataquis furnished a substantial amount of business, often as much as 100 cars of slate a month. In the late eighties, after the Katahdin Iron Works were closed, the Bangor & Piscataquis earnings were not as satisfactory, and the property deteriorated. The lease to the Bangor & Aroostook, executed in 1892, was at a rental which provided for interest charges on its bonds, most of which were held by the City of Bangor, and for the rental of the Bangor & Katahdin Iron Works road. The line from Old Town to Greenville was rebuilt by the Bangor & Aroostook, which later purchased the property outright.

The decision to follow the Bangor & Piscataquis line to Brownville and to build from Brownville to Houlton, rather than to adopt a shorter route north from the Maine Central at some point on the old European & North American road, came from several motives. Mr. Cram believed, and truly as events proved, that the logical development of manufacture of forest products would move nearer to the raw material and that the water power on the upper Penobscot waters, given railroad facilities, would be transmuted into commodities which a railroad could haul. The dominant motive, however, was the desire for economic independence, which could only be secured by reaching tidewater at Bangor; and during the years when the terminus was in Old Town the charter right of an independent line into Bangor was preserved.

Construction was started from Brownville toward Houlton early in 1893 and the road was opened to Houlton on January 1, 1894. The following year saw the road extended to Caribou and Fort Fairfield. In 1895 a branch was built from Ashland Junction to Ashland, and in 1897 another branch, called the Aroostook Northern Railroad, was opened between Caribou and Limestone. The main line was extended to Van Buren in 1899. In the same year, the old original Bangor & Piscataquis bonds maturing, this line was purchased outright from its former owners. The Bangor & Katahdin Iron Works Railroad was purchased a few years later, as was

[LEFT:] **Consolidation 182 is southbound along Eagle Lake on July 3, 1948.** *Robert Baker* [BELOW:] **Ten-Wheeler 93 is ready to depart Greenville on August 9, 1949.** *470 Railroad Club collection*

also the Patten & Sherman Railroad, a short branch line built independently in 1895 and 1896 by Albert A. Burleigh. In 1902 Fish River Railroad was built from Ashland to Fort Kent, and in 1903 this line was sold to the Bangor & Aroostook, it having been built for and as part of that system.

The builders of the Bangor & Aroostook encountered no serious natural obstacles. On the original line there were several tangents from three to five miles in length, and there was one stretch of straight track over thirteen miles long. Although modern improvements have rendered obsolete much of the original construction, the railroad was for its time a well built road, and was so reported by the Maine Railroad Commissioners. The chief difficulty was to find the money. Maine capital, as usual, was indifferent to the opportunity for helpful employment at home, and with the exception of a small amount of preferred stock which was purchased by interested parties practically all of the permanent capital was secured outside of Maine. The construction of the main line from Brownville to Caribou was financed in part by the sale of the first mortgage 5s, due 1943, and by the issue of a second mortgage on the same property. The American Express Company loaned the Company $600,000 at one critical period. In the late nineties the credit of the Bangor & Aroostook was fairly established, and the various extensions were financed with little difficulty.

During the first five years of operation the Bangor & Aroostook earnings showed a steady growth in gross and net. About 1900 the Great Northern Paper Company began its development at Millinocket, and along the west branch of the Penobscot River, and traffic from this source soon became the most important item in the industrial freight business. This new business, together with the traffic afforded by the increasing population and steady agricultural development in Aroostook County, resulted in the gross earnings doubling from 1899 to 1904. The terminal facilities at Old Town were inadequate for handling this volume of traffic, and there were difficulties and delays in moving it through Bangor on the Maine Central, especially on account of the steep grade coming out of the Penobscot valley just west of Bangor.

About this time there appeared in railroad operation a new influence which might properly be called the "Harriman Idea" in honor of its leading exponent. The supporters of this idea advocated the expenditure of money on improvements, such as reduction of grades, reduction of distances, and better terminal facilities. The theory, which had been clearly demonstrated in practice, was that a railroad which was flat and straight and carrying heavy trains at a high rate of speed would produce a substantial increase in net earnings through reductions in unit costs of operation. Most of the mileage added to the Bangor & Aroostook lines after 1904 was built in response to this influence.

The conception of the Northern Maine Seaport Railroad was Franklin W. Cram's. The plan involved the construction of a railroad from South Lagrange south twenty-five miles to a connection with the Maine Central six miles west of Bangor, and from that point down the valley of the Penobscot to a tidewater terminal at Searsport on Penobscot Bay. The important advantages which President Cram expected to gain by building this railroad as planned were the solution of the terminal problem on freight destined for Maine Central and western lines, shortening the haul and the time on through traffic, gaining independence of the Maine Central by introducing the competition of water transportation, and, in consequence of the last, securing a more favorable division of rates on through freight traffic. Incidentally an important advantage was the elimination of a large amount of west bound freight movement on the Bangor grade. Both the railroad and the industries in the territory which it served would be assured of a constant supply of coal, which would eliminate the expense incident to

[ABOVE:] **Mountain 123 at Derby in 1946.** *Forest Bunker*
[BELOW:] **Mountain 103 at Millinocket in 1949.** *470 Railroad Club collection*

[BELOW:] **BAR Train ON-28 (Oakfield-Northern Maine Jct.) nears the top of the grade at Dyer Brook out of Oakfield with the six Geeps in 8th notch. This October, 1984 scene was snapped just a few weeks before Oakfield yard closed for good.** *Ron Johnson*

[RIGHT:] **Train 2 leaves Presque Isle behind Pacific 251 on May 18, 1947.** *Ron Johnson collection* [BELOW:] **A BL2 handles the first trip on the Greenville train with a diesel over Bunker Brook trestle on July 23, 1952.** *470 Railroad Club collection*

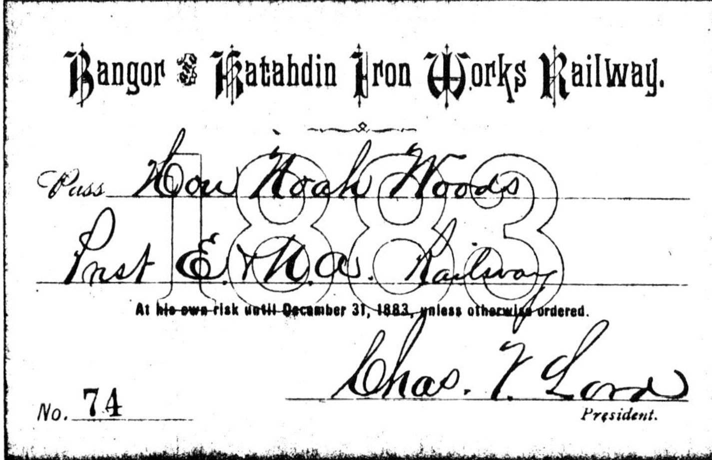

Bangor & Katahdin Iron Works Railway.

Pass Hon Noah Woods

Prest E. & N.A. Railway

1883

At his own risk until December 31, 1883, unless otherwise ordered.

No. 74

Chas. T. Low

President.

Richard Dole collection

getting in all the winter coal supply during the open water months on the Penobscot River. In actual practice all of these expectations were realized.

The Northern Maine Seaport Railroad was built by the Aroostook Construction Company in 1905, and was opened the same year. The property was leased to the Bangor & Aroostook, which owned the stock of the terminal company until the merger in 1919. The terminal company issued $4,743,000 first mortgage five per cent bonds which were guaranteed, principal and interest, by the Bangor & Aroostook. The high cost of construction, approximately $5,250,000, was largely on account of expensive approaches and fills at Northern Maine Junction and the building of wharves, storehouses and other terminal property at Searsport. It was believed that the creation of this tidewater terminal would cause a tremendous increase in real estate values around Searsport, where the citizens had visions of the rapid growth of a great city, but these dreams never came true.

The superficial examination which the general public gives to great undertakings is likely to focus on points of minor importance, and in the case of the Northern Maine Seaport Railroad the prevalent opinion seems to be that it cost a lot of money and was a failure because Searsport never grew in accordance with the predictions made at the time; and that the Aroostook Construction Company was the only party to the undertaking that profited by it. As a matter of fact, while several defects in the plan became apparent in actual operation and the tidewater terminal was disappointing in visible results, the advantages claimed for the terminal from the standpoint of railroad operations were mainly gained; and although the effect cannot be mathematically computed, it appears certain that the net earnings of the Bangor & Aroostook have been substantially increased by reason of the existence of the Northern Maine Seaport Railroad, and that business interests in Northern Maine have gained great

[ABOVE:] **Consolidation 403, built by Alco-Schenectady in 1937 pulls past the new Van Buren brick station being built on September 5, 1947.** *Ron Johnson collection* [BELOW:] **ON-28 pulls into Millinocket on October 10, 1980 with all first generation power including two F3's, a BL2 and GP7.** *Ron Johnson*

advantages by it.

From 1905 to 1912 new construction was almost continuous. The extension of the Great Northern Paper Company development to East Millinocket caused the construction of a branch nine miles long to Medway, which was built as the Schoodic Stream Railway and later merged. The low grade "Medford Cut-Off", twenty-eight miles between Packards and South Lagrange, was completed in 1907. This route, together with the Seaport Terminal line, made possible an increase in the average freight train load from 25 to 30 loaded cars on the old route to 100 loaded cars on the new line. The Washburn Extension, consisting of 55 miles connecting the two northern branches of the road, was completed in 1910. The principal purpose of this extension was to improve the grades for south bound lumber traffic out of Van Buren. When this road was opened, the train load increased over 60 per cent. The St. John Extension, 60 miles along the St. John River from Van Buren through Fort Kent to St. Francis, was also completed in 1910. The same year a survey was made for an Allagash Extension from Seboois, by Chesuncook and Chamberlain Lakes, down the Allagash Valley to St. Francis, but no construction work was ever done on this line. With the completion of these extensions the construction program practically ceased. In 1912 there were 630 miles of railroad in operation, which was approximately the mileage in 1925.

The financing of this contruction caused many changes in capitalization. The common stock remained at $1,050,000 par value until 1904, and was gradually increased to $3,198,300 par value in 1911. The initial dividend was paid at the rate of 3% annually in 1904, and was increased to 4% in 1906, which rate was maintained until 1912. The rate varied from 3% to 4% from 1912 to 1922, and is now 6%. The original preferred stock owned in part by the County of Aroostook was finally retired in 1904. The consolidated and refunding mortgage was created in 1901, securing the 4% bonds which were sold from time to time to acquire the Fish River Railroad, to retire the preferred stock, to finance additions and betterments, and for other purposes. The Medford, Washburn, and St. John Extensions were financed in part by bonds secured by mortgages on these extensions. Considering the capitalization of the company, which at one time was over $24,000,000 in bonds with about $3,200,000 par value stock, it appears remarkable that bonds could have been sold in such amounts at such prices as the records disclose.

It was generally recognized when the Northern Maine Seaport Railroad was built that the Maine Central would share in some of its advantages over the old route through Old Town and Bangor; and recognition of this fact led the Maine Central to assume a portion of the expense incident to the operation of the new facilities. This was known as the Northern Maine Junction Operating Allowance. Under this arrangement the roads continued to exchange traffic, and although the Bangor & Aroostook management accepted the Maine Central allowance under protest that it was insufficient, nevertheless the business relations of the two companies were harmonious. Finally, however, the Maine Central ceased to pay the allowance. Thereupon the Bangor & Aroostook filed with the Interstate Commerce Commission a complaint against the Maine Central pertaining to this allowance and to other matters in dispute. The differences were finally adjusted by negotiation in 1913. Out of this negotiation came the traffic agreement of 1913, which has been remarkably well advertised, considering that so little seems to be known about it.

An important increase in traffic came to the Bangor & Aroostook through the creation of the Van Buren Bridge Company. This company was incorporated in 1913, as a subsidiary of the Bangor & Aroostook, and in 1915 opened a connection with the Canadian Railway lines in New Brunswick by the construction of the international bridge across the St. John River at Van Buren. This new route shortened the railroad haul from Campbellton to Boston by about two hundred miles, and from this line the Bangor & Aroostook received south-bound freight averaging about five hundred cars per month.

During the construction period the financing of the Bangor & Aroostook had been ably managed. Although the capitalization consisted in large part of funded debt, the bonds had been sold at high prices. But in later years the markets in various issues were neglected and prices declined. In 1917 an effort was made to correct the proportion of funded debt, and a new seven per cent preferred stock was created, of which $3,480,000 par value was sold at par to a banking syndicate formed by Brown Bros. & Co. At the same time the outstanding common stock was increased by the sale of $411,400 par value. With the proceeds of sale of these stocks the company paid $2,000,000 of maturing notes and purchased about $2,300,000 par value of the outstanding bonds, principally from the Aroostook Construction Company. The result of this financing was a reduction in funded debt from $25,315,000 in 1916 to $20,912,000 in December, 1917.

The Bangor & Aroostook preferred stock was not offered to the public for sale for several years. Corporation financing was practically suspended during the war. After the war and until the passage of the Transportation Act the railroad situation was so uncertain that only the roads of strongest credit could sell bonds to advantage. The New England railroads were considered almost hopeless from a financial standpoint, and while the Bangor & Aroostook had made a fair record of earnings during the most difficult period, its securities were considered in the common geographical classification with the securities of the New Haven, Boston & Maine, and Maine Central. In 1920 Bangor & Aroostook 4s were selling around 50, the divisional mortgage bonds were quoted between 55 and 65, and the main line bonds sold in the low 70's. Of course this condition was due in part to the abnormally high interest rates then prevailing.

The Transportation Act and the subsequent rate increases which brought hardship and distress to most New England railroads were peculiarly beneficial to the Bangor & Aroostook. The increase of 40% in freight rates and 20% in passenger rates in the Eastern District was the cause of complaints from roads whose revenues from freight traffic were less in percentage of the total revenues than the average in the district. But the Bangor & Aroostook, which secured about 80% of its traffic revenue from freight, was more than proportionately benefited by the new rates, and the net earnings were soon restored to the levels prevailing before the period of federal control. In 1921 the position of the company was unique in New England, for it was the only railroad in New England paying dividends on its common stock.

It was sometime before the favorable factors of the Bangor & Aroostook situation obtained general recognition, and the bonds continued to sell at low prices until 1922, when there appeared a tremendous demand from Massachusetts savings banks for the Bangor & Aroostook bonds, which caused great advances in market prices. Following this improvement in the market standing of the securities the Bangor & Aroostook preferred stock was publicly offered for sale.

In 1924 there was a strong market in railroad stocks, and the shares of prosperous railroads rose to high figures. Taking advantage of the opportunity the Aroostook Construction Company sold its Bangor & Aroostook common stock to Hornblower & Weeks. To facilitate the distribution of the stock

Train 2 with E7 701 is about to stop at the West Seboois station on September 24, 1950. *470 Railroad Club collection*

the par value was changed from $100 to $50, and two shares were issued in place of each old share. The stock was sold to investors throughout the country. The offering was not popular with Maine investors and only a small portion of the stock was purchased by Maine people.

Late in 1925 there occurred an incident which furnishes another demonstration of the perils which lie in public indifference to the ownership of the public service corporations which supply our vital needs. The Bangor & Aroostook stock which had been distributed in 1924 was scattered throughout the country and was not held in strong hands. The stock had not made an impressive record in the market, and there were many holders who were looking for a chance to get out of it. Taking advantage of this condition, a group of western capitalists accumulated a substantial amount of the stock, and by virtue of their position as owners of the largest single block of stock, they attempted to influence the directors to increase the dividend rate. The management had adopted a policy, which was manifestly to the advantage of the public served, to continue to use surplus earnings to improve the condition of the road and the equipment. This sudden demand for increased dividends, coming from a new group of stockholders who had no apparent interest in the Bangor & Aroostook except to make money from speculation in its stock, and characterized by most of the features which ususally indicate a stock-jobbing operation, had no effect upon the directors, who voted to maintain the regular dividend rate.

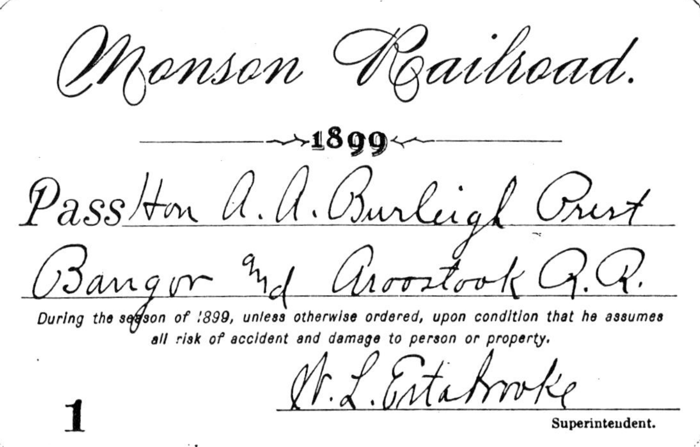

Monson Railroad.

1899

Pass Hon A. A. Burleigh Prest
Bangor and Aroostook R.R.

During the season of 1899, unless otherwise ordered, upon condition that he assumes all risk of accident and damage to person or property.

1 W. L. Estabrooke
Superintendent.

PATTEN & SHERMAN RAILROAD

1898

Pass Mr. Jesse Fry., Asst. G. M.
San Antonio & Gulf R.R.,

Until December 31, 1898, unless otherwise ordered.

No. 1295 Parker P. Burleigh
Vice-President

Both passes Jim McFarlane collection

BL2 54 casts its image in peaceful Cochrane Lake on the way to Houlton on August 2, 1979. *Ron Johnson*

[ABOVE:] **Train 1 with E7 700 passes F3 507 with a local passenger train at Oakfield on April 29, 1950.** [LEFT:] **NW2 803 is in charge of the East Millinocket local, Train 162, at Millinocket on October 20, 1951.** *Both photos 470 Railroad Club collection*

[RIGHT:] **ON-44 with all first generation motive power drops its train at Northern Maine Jct., the terminus, on April 19, 1980. F3 45 backs the train past the former station and coaling tipple.** *Ron Johnson*

Maine Railroad Time Line 1926-1985

1926 — Maine Central ended the lease of the Belfast & Moosehead Lake Railroad on January 1.

The Bangor & Aroostook opened an 800 foot long pier at Searsport on February 1.

On April 26 the Boston & Maine began the passenger train, *Flying Yankee,* from Boston to Portland.

Sandy River & Rangeley Lakes opened the Carrabasset to Bigelow line on June 1.

1927 — Bridgton & Harrison Railway was renamed on March 28 from Bridgton & Saco River.

Maine Central stopped running the Bridgton & Saco River on August 29. On October 10 the first Maine Central train ran over the Carlton Bridge over the Kennebec River at Bath, with ferry service ending there on October 22.

Bangor & Aroostook leased the Katahdin Iron Works branch to Advance Bag & Paper Co. on December 31.

1928 — The Boston & Maine stopped passenger service during 1928 from Portland to Worcester.

The Knox Railroad abandoned passenger service on July 28.

Bangor & Aroostook ran the last train over the Maine Central from Old Town on December 2. The following day service began from Northern Maine Jct. to Bangor.

1929 — The Somerset and Washington County Railway corporations dissolved on March 3.

Kennebec Central stopped operations on July 29.

1930 — Maine Central removed its gas motor car from service on February 2.

1931 — The last passenger train from Eastport to Ayers Jct. ran on April 27. On May 30 Bar Harbor trains ran only as far as Ellsworth.

Sandy River & Rangeley Lakes offered no passenger service after May 31 beyond Phillips.

1932 — The last passenger train from Bangor to Bucksport ran on January 27. On June 27 the last passenger train ran from Newport to Foxcroft. Maine Central began joint operations with the Boston & Maine on September 1. Equipment from both roads was interchanged from Boston to Bangor.

Sandy River & Rangeley Lakes ended service on July 8, 1932.

The Canadian Pacific gained control of the Aroostook Valley on September 13, which had been under the influence of the Bangor & Aroostook. Originally a trolley line, the Aroostook Valley built several branches out of Presque Isle to Caribou, Washburn Jct. and village between 1910 and 1913.

1933 — Wiscasset, Waterville & Farmington stopped operations on June 15.

The last passenger train ran from Bingham to Kineo and Woodland to Princeton on July 22. The track from Austin Jct. to Kineo was abandoned on July 19. On September 5 the last passenger train ran from Waterville to Bingham.

1934 — On March 3 the Boston & Maine abandoned freight service from Rochester to Portland.

Maine Central ran the first air conditioned train on June 28 from Boston to Bangor on the *Pine Tree Limited.*

1935 — On April 1 Maine Central and Boston & Maine ran streamliner 6000 from Portland-Bangor and Boston-Portland as the *Flying Yankee.*

The last train on the Sandy River & Rangeley Lakes ran on May 31.

1936 — Maine Central merged the Eastern Maine Shore Line Railway on March 14. It abandoned track from Austin to Kineo due to flood. On October 3 it abandoned track from Oquossoc to Kennebago for the same reason. Maine Central cancelled the lease of Rumford Falls & Rangeley Lakes as the last run was made on March 20.

1937 — Maine Central abandoned from Waukeag to Mt. Desert Ferry on November 29. It bought the Dexter & Piscataquis on December 7.

1938 — Monson abandoned passenger trains in 1938.

Eastern Maine Shore Line Railway Co. was dissolved on June 27.

Crowleys Jct. to Leeds Jct. was abandoned on February 1.

1939 — Maine Central bought the Dexter & Newport on December 27 for $73,000.

Rumford Falls & Rangeley Lakes Railroad Co. was dissolved on November 14.

1940 — Maine Central in conjunction with the New Haven and Boston & Maine ran the train *East Wind* from New York on June 21.

1941 — Dexter & Newport Railroad Co. was dissolved on February 28, along with the Dexter & Piscataquis.

Lime Rock Railroad abandoned tracks around Rockland in 1941.

Bridgton & Harrison stopped running August 1 and sold for scrap on September 13.

1942 — The *East Wind* stopped running on September 20 due to World War II.

1943 — Monson stopped running on June 1.

Maine Central bought the Portland & Ogdensburg Railway on December 28.

1945 — Boston & Maine removed tracks from Rigby to North Berwick (Eastern).

The Portland & Ogdensburg Railway dissolved on July 21.

Aroostook Valley ran its first freight diesels on July 12.

1946 — In September Maine Central merged the Portland & Rumford Falls Railroad and Railways into its system. The *East Wind* summer train was restored on June 21 and stopped on September 22.

Belfast & Moosehead Lake ran its last steam engine on December 14 and began to use 70 ton diesels.

1947 — Maine Central ran its first passenger diesels 705 and 706 on the Portland Division on July 1. Maine Central's connection with the Canadian National at Portland Jct. was discontinued during 1947.

1949 — Sanford & Eastern began running from Springvale to Rochester, N.H. on July 1.

Maine Central ran its last passenger train from Pittsfield to Harmony on April 23.

1952 — Maine Central abandoned track from Rumford Jct. to west of Canton on May 1.

1953 — Maine Central adopted Dartmouth green and orange yellow colors for diesels and freight cars in 1953. In July two way radios were used on main line diesels and caboose for the first time. On November 15 the new Fore River Bridge was opened. Facilities at Skowhegan were abandoned on October 18.

1954 — The last steam hauled passenger train operated from Portland to Bangor on June 13 with locomotive 470.

1955 — Maine Central ran the last Pullman from Boston to Bangor on October 28. On November 17 it bought the European & North American.

1956 — Boston & Maine began piggy-back service on May 1.

1957 — Maine Central began CTC from Pittsfield to Hermon Pond on January 9. It ran the last passenger train from Bangor to Calais on November 25. The final Farmington branch passenger train ran on April 27.

1958 — Maine Central ran its last passenger trains between Portland and St. Johnsbury, Vermont on April 26. It began piggy-back service on November 28.

1959 — Boston & Maine first ran Budd cars to Portland from Boston.

Maine Central ran its last Rockland passenger train on April 4.

1960 — The last passenger train from Vanceboro to Portland ran on September 6.

Boston & Maine ran the last trip of the *State of Maine Express* on October 29.

1961 — Sanford & Eastern discontinued service on April 11.

Portland Union Station was sold on June 20 and razed on July 28 to September 9.

Bangor & Aroostook ran its last passenger train on October 28.

1962 — Canadian National Railways ran its last passenger train from Portland to Montreal on September 1.

1963 — Maine Central's Howland branch was abandoned on September 8. Its mail merchandise train stopped on September 30.

1964 — Bangor Punta Alegre Sugar Corp. replaced Bangor & Aroostook Corp. in 1964. The Derby-Guilford line was also abandoned during the year.

Maine Central stopped handling less than carload freight on April 1. Royal Jct. tower was abandoned on December 28 and operations were moved to Portland.

1965 — Boston & Maine abandoned all passenger service from Boston to Portland on January 3.

1966 — Maine Central stopped hauling livestock on March 15. It abandoned from Hartland to Harmony on June 15.

1970 — Maine Central abandoned from Canton to Gilbertville on August 1.

1971 — Maine Central's line from Skowhegan to Shawmut was abandoned.

1974 — Maine Central sold to Canadian Pacific its line from Mattawamkeag to Vanceboro on March 24 but kept traffic rights.

1975 — Bangor & Aroostook abandoned its Monticello to Bridgewater line on March 24.

1978 — Bangor & Aroostook abandoned from South Lagrange to Packards on October 31.

Maine Central received ICC authorization to abandon its Eastport branch on August 25 with the last trip on November 4.

1979 — Bangor & Aroostook abandoned some of its Van Buren branch.

1980 — Maine Central stockholders voted to merge with United States Filter Corp. for $14 million on December 10. On December 15 Ashland Oil Co. bought controlling stock of U.S. Filter Corp.

Bangor & Aroostook built a new office at Northern Maine Jct. for maintenance of way and mechanical departments with a restaurant.

1981 — In June, Timothy Mellon of Guilford Industries bought the Maine Central from Ashland Oil Co.

In 1981, effective January 1, 1982 the State of Maine removed regulations of railroads and motor carriers.

1982 — On August 10 the Boston & Maine first ran engines from Mechanicville, N.Y. to Bangor.

1983 — Guilford Industries bought the Boston & Maine for $24,250,000 on June 30.

Maine Central ended freight trains from Rigby to St. Johnsbury, Vt. on September 2. Interchange for the Canadian Pacific became Mattawamkeag.

1984 — Bangor & Aroostook began *Aroostook Express* daily piggy-back service hauling potatoes from Presque Isle to New Haven, Connecticut. Service lasted only a short time because of not enough interest by shippers.

Bangor & Aroostook closed its terminal at Oakfield on October 15 and moved the mechanical and operating departments to Millinocket.

1985 — Maine Central announced its intent to abandon its Bangor to Calais, Brunswick to Rockland and Steep Falls to Fryeburg lines.

The Lewiston Lower local hustles out of Rigby Yard in April, 1984 with U18B 404 leading in Guilford colors. *Ron Johnson*

[LEFT:] **What a lash-up! BASE (Bangor-Selkirk) pulls west out of Rigby in August 1985 with ex-D&H, now MEC U23B 287, ex-LV, now D&H C420 409, D&H GP38-2 7420 and ex-D&H, now MEC U23B 290.** *Ron Johnson*

[ABOVE:] **BAED (Bangor-East Deerfield) hauls into Rigby in January 1985 with B&M GP40-2 352, D&H GP38-2 7325, B&M GP38-2 209 and MEC GP7 565 while 581 switches the yard.** [LEFT:] **BASE is westbound at Carmel in February 1984 with U18B 402, GP7 577 and GP7 569 doing the honors.** *Both photos Ron Johnson*

Memorable Maine Rail Moments

[ABOVE:] **GT 2-8-2 3445 blasts out of Danville Jct. on a frosty October 29, 1955.** *470 Railroad Club collection* [RIGHT:] **470 Railroad Club's last excursion on the GT because of high equipment costs crosses Back Cove trestle out of Portland bound for Gorham, N.H. with two CV GP9's and an RS11 on Sunday, September 29, 1980.** *Ron Johnson*

Maine had its own cog railway for a time. The Green Mountain Railway began operating up the face of Cadillac Mountain in Bar Harbor in 1883. The 4 feet 7½ inch gauge line was not successful because people had to boat across Eagle Lake in order to reach the base station. The line ceased operating in 1890 and the equipment was sold to the Mount Washington Cog Railway in New Hampshire. *Both photos Richard Dole collection*

Doubleheaded CP Pacifics chuff past the McAdam, N.B. station on August 15, 1954. Shortly they will cross the border into Maine, heading west. *Robert Baker*

CP rail car 9008 pauses at McAdam, N.B. eastbound on August 15, 1954 after traversing the state of Maine. *Robert Baker*

CP C424 pulls east at Brownville Jct. in October 1984, doing a double take in the still water of the West Branch of the Pleasant River. *Ron Johnson*

[ABOVE:] The "Flying Yankee" stops at Lewiston in 1936 before continuing east on the Back Road to Bangor. *Howard Kirkpatrick* **[LEFT:] Big time MEC steam in the form of 2-10-2 655 pounds through Etna on Train 350 in September 1947.** *470 Railroad Club collection* [OPPOSITE PAGE TOP:] **A westbound passenger train with E7 709 passes under the elms on the Lower Road at Brunswick in the mid 1950's.** *Robert Baker* [OPPOSITE PAGE BOTTOM:] **MEC RB-1 (Rigby-Bangor) with GP38 257 and two GP7's reflect their image in the Presumpscot River at West Falmouth in February 1976.** *Ron Johnson*

709
709
709
MAINE CENTRAL

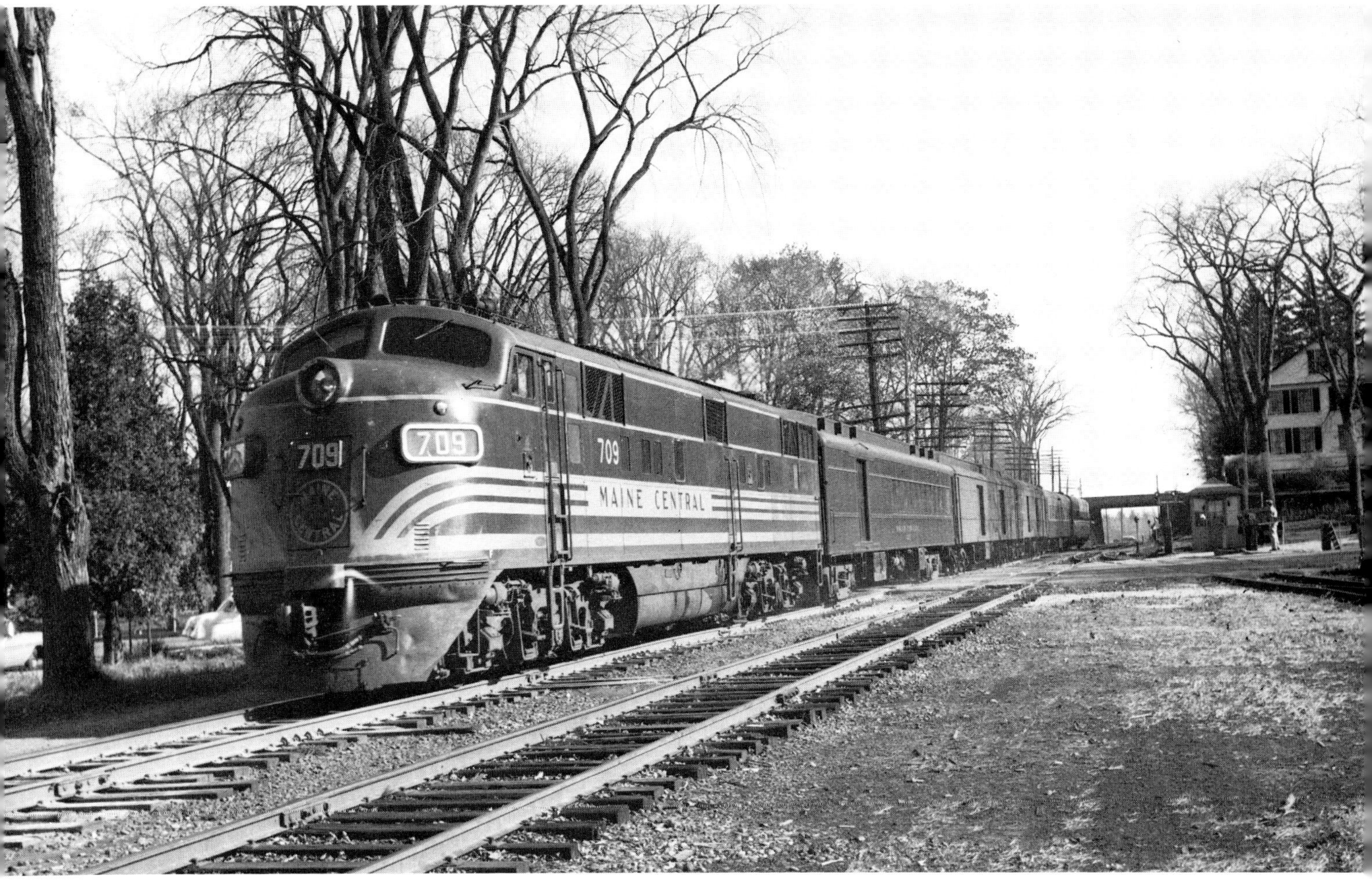

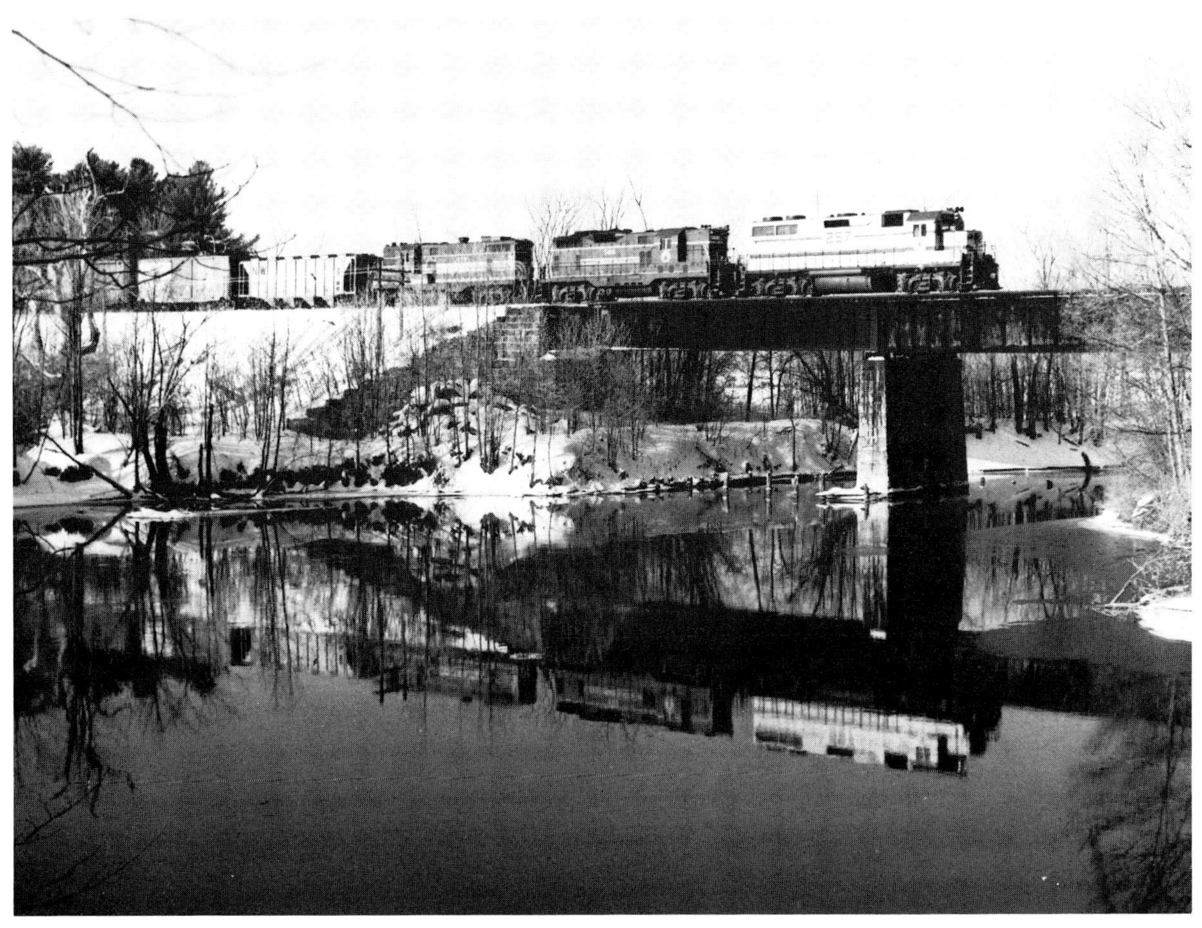

[ABOVE:] **B&M Pacific 3713, now on display at Steamtown, pounds through Kennebunk in 1940 with the "East Wind".** *Russell Monroe collection* [BELOW:] **Two B&M GP18's stretch their train across the Scarboro salt marsh westbound in the winter of 1976.** *Ron Johnson*

B&M N-1 roars through Biddeford with two F3A's and a B on September 1, 1947. *Russell Monroe collection*

Big Berkshire 4000 barks eastbound for Rigby Yard at Rockingham Jct. on August 21, 1940. *Russell Monroe collection*

AVR
11
AVR
12

509

LOOK
LISTEN
STOP
681
MAINE CENTRAL

[OPPOSITE PAGE TOP:] **Two MU'd 44 tonners of the Aroostook Valley switch an industrial park in Presque Isle in 1976.** *Ron Johnson* [OPPOSITE PAGE MIDDLE:] **Two freight trains meet at the Fairgrounds in Lewiston on July 8, 1950. MEC Consolidation 509 is pictured on the left with the conductor waving train orders on the right.** *470 Railroad Club collection* [OPPOSITE PAGE BOTTOM:] **MEC F3 681 and two GP7's roll a freight through Burnham Jct. on August 13, 1954.** [ABOVE:] **Ex-B&M 2-10-2 652 loafs through Brunswick with a westbound freight in June 1942.** [BELOW:] **In a Christmas card scene in January 1957 MEC GP7 577 hauls the eastbound Sunday Rockland train through a fresh wet snow at Cook's Corner in Brunswick.** *All three photos Robert Baker*

[ABOVE:] **B&M Pacific 3712 pulls a MEC wreck train east through Rockingham Jct. on June 8, 1952.** *Howard Moulton* [BELOW:] **Steam returned to Maine in 1976 in the form of the "Freedom Train". Ex-Reading 4-8-4 2101, renumbered 1 is at the head end of the 23 car special at Wells bound for Portland on April 16.** *Russell Monroe*

Portland

[ABOVE:] **Looking like a model railroad is Rigby roundhouse in South Portland from the air in 1951.** *Sullivan Cameracraft collection* [BELOW:] **A nice overall view of Portland Union station and trainshed is captured in this mid 1950's picture with the Rockland train ready to leave on the left.** *470 Railroad Club collection*

Portland Terminal 0-6-0 832 emerges from Rigby enginehouse on October 24, 1949. *Preston Johnson* [BELOW:] **The last active Portland Terminal Alco S1 1101 enters Rigby Yard in South Portland from Yard 8 in January 1984.** *Ron Johnson*

[OPPOSITE PAGE TOP:] **Two scenes of Maine Central steam in full flower are presented. Pacific 468 with B&M Train 168 to Boston steps across the Fore River bridge out of Portland Union Station at River Jct.** [OPPOSITE PAGE BOTTOM:] **MEC Mikado 627 in neat striping and speed lettering hauls Train 398 along the Fore River in Portland on October 29, 1949, nearing Rigby Yard.** *Both photos Preston Johnson*

Waterville

[ABOVE:] **Waterville station was positioned where the Back Road and Lower Road split, the latter in the foreground. In this September 8, 1940 scene MEC bus 604 is boarding for Madison and points north.** *Howard Kirkpatrick* [RIGHT:] **MEC doubleheaded Mikados depart Waterville westbound on March 21, 1946.** *470 Railroad Club collection*

Howard Kirkpatrick climbed the coaling tipple to obtain an overall view of the shops and roundhouse at Waterville in 1940 with the Kennebec River in the background.

[LEFT:] **MEC Mallet, shortly after being received from the B&M in 1912, rides on the turntable at Waterville before being converted to burn coal. Note the oil filler plug on top of the tender.** *Robert Baker collection* [BELOW:] **Standing in a grassy area where the station used to sit, Ron Johnson captures on film the Wood job lifting its train out of Waterville Yard over the Back Road past Pacific 470 on display in the Fall of 1982. This train is bound for the paper mill at Jay on the Rumford branch.**

575

[OPPOSITE PAGE TOP:] **Mikado 630 is serviced at Waterville on September 19, 1939.** *Howard Kirkpatrick* [OPPOSITE PAGE BOTTOM:] **The local for Gardiner trundles across the bridge spanning the Kennebec River out of Waterville over the Lower Road in February 1982.** *Ron Johnson*[ABOVE:] **MEC 0-6-0 177 switches the yard at Waterville in 1941. Note the stock car.** *Howard Kirkpatrick* [BELOW:] **A MEC inspection train accelerates across the Fairfield-Benton trestle eastbound September 26, 1978.** *Ron Johnson*

Bangor

[ABOVE:] **Looking across the Penobscot River one encounters the impressive Bangor Union Station and trainshed in 1956.** *Russell Monroe collection* [BELOW:] **Howard Kirkpatrick captures some Bangor roundhouse banter in September 1938.**

From left to right: MEC F7 686, E7 711 and RS2 552 are grouped at the Bangor fueling facility for a company photograph in 1949. *470 Railroad Club collection*

[LEFT:] **Ex-E&NA 4-4-0, now MEC 86 leaves Bangor for Mattawamkeag during the flood of 1902.** *Ron Johnson collection* [BELOW:] **MEC S2 312 and S4 315 prepare to depart Bangor on the Old Town Turn on April 21, 1979.** *Ron Johnson*

[ABOVE:] Maine Central F7 685 aids ailing Boston & Maine E7 3812 on B&M Train 168 on September 25, 1950. The odd couple are pictured at Portland Union Station. *Preston Johnson* **[BELOW:] "The beginning of the end", so writes photographer Robert Baker. The first day of regularly assigned E7 power on the MEC sees B&M 3802 haul in alongside MEC "Big O" Ten-Wheeler 405 at Brunswick, ME.**

[ABOVE:] **The numbers match the wheel arrangement on this Pacific taking water at Brunswick in October 1940.** *Robert Baker* [BELOW:] **Train W11 with MEC Mikado 604 rattles the windows of the Richmond Station westbound on the Lower Road during the winter of 1950.** *Henry Preble*

253

56
BANGOR AND AROOSTOOK

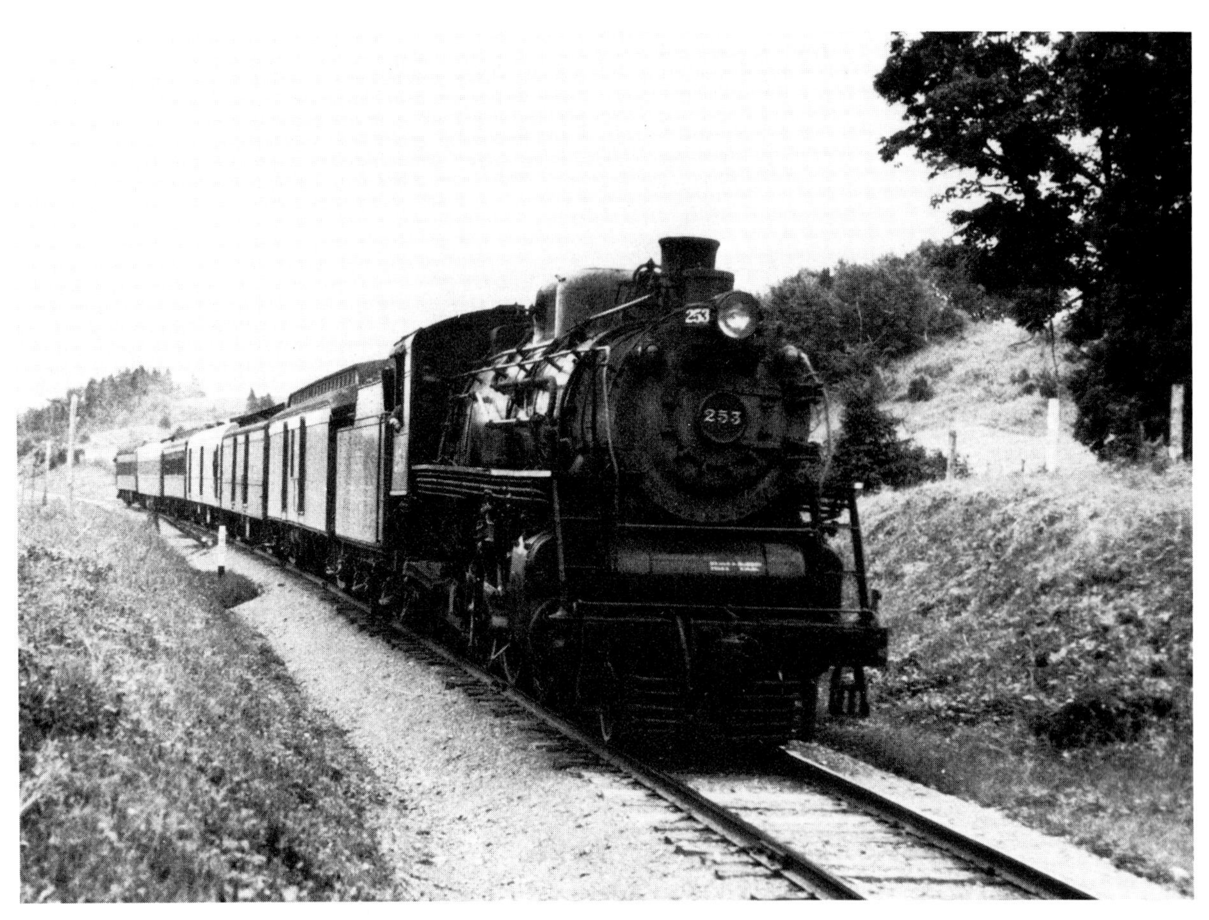

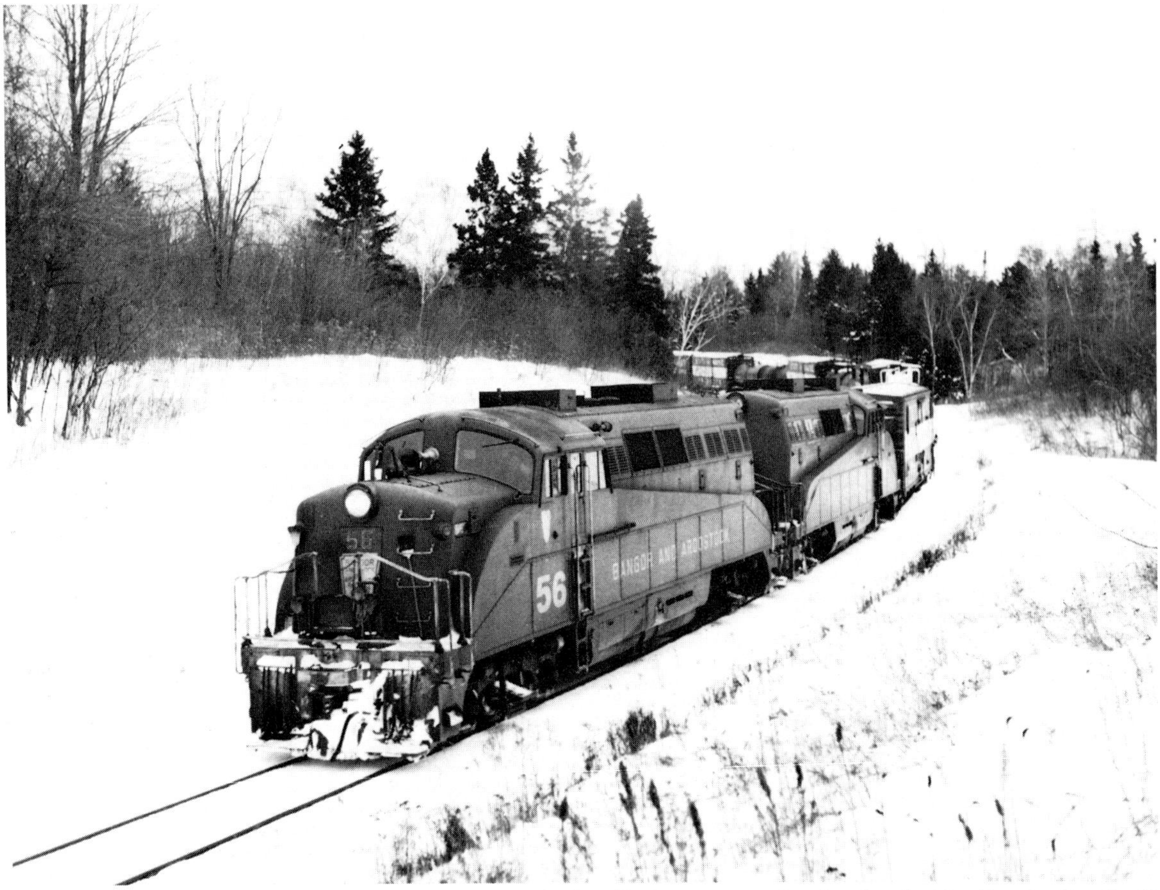

[OPPOSITE PAGE TOP:] **Bangor & Aroostook Pacific 253 handles three baggage cars and three coaches on a passenger train at Milo, in the summer of 1940.** *Robert Baker collection* [OPPOSITE PAGE BOTTOM:] **Back to back BL2's stretch their train around the horseshoe curve out of Searsport on a snowy December 20, 1974.** *Ron Johnson* [ABOVE:] **First generation power accelerates BAR Train ON-44 through Island Falls in September 1976.** *Ron Johnson* [BELOW:] **Belfast & Moosehead Lake 4-6-0 20 on a mixed train nears Belfast as it skirts the edge of the Passagassawakeg River in July 1940.** *470 Railroad Club collection*

[RIGHT:] **Ex-Rock Island U25B's in fresh MEC paint haul a morning westbound train through West Falmouth in December 1982.** *Ron Johnson* [BELOW:] **MEC 2-8-2 630 is in charge of a circus train at Cathance (Ka-dance or Topsham) on July 20, 1947.** *Robert Baker*

[ABOVE:] **MEC through train for Bangor behind 4-6-4 701 lays down the sand while pulling hard out of Brunswick in 1940 with the Rockland train on the left.** [BELOW:] **New in June MEC E7 in experimental paint, with maroon front and yellow stripe and white-aluminum back to match new stainless steel coaches, pauses westbound at Brunswick in the Fall of 1946.** *Both photos Robert Baker*

Bell ringing Pacific 470 struts through Gardiner on the way back to Portland on June 13, 1954, the last passenger run for steam on the MEC. *Carroll Dinsmore*

[ABOVE LEFT:] **The First Train 350 erupts like a volcano through Brunswick with engines 518 and 652 on March 29, 1942.** *Henry Preble* [ABOVE RIGHT:] **MEC DR-2 (Rumford-Rigby) approaches Royal Jct. with a pair of F7's on September 21, 1956.** *470 Railroad Club collection*

Index

Adams, Sprague, 57
Albion, 84
Alna, 48, 84
Anderson, John E., 39
Samuel J., 39
Androscoggin & Kennebec Railroad, 14, 15, 18, 20, 21, 23, 25, 26, 27, 29, 30, 46, 55
Androscoggin Railroad, 25, 26, 41, 53, 55
Anson, 48
Appleton, Frederick H., 98
Moses L., 20, 23
Aroostook Construction Company, 98, 101, 105, 108
Aroostook County, 31, 35, 36
Aroostook Northern Railroad, 102
Aroostook Railroad, 31, 35
Aroostook River Railroad, 97
Aroostook & St. Andrews Branch Railroad, 97
Aroostook Valley Railroad, 111, 112
Ashland, 102, 103
Junction, 102
Ashland Oil Co., 113
Atlantic & Northwest Railroad, 62
Atlantic & St. Lawrence Railroad, 11, 14, 15, 18, 20, 21, 25, 39, 52, 76
Atwood, Leonard, 84
Auburn, 76, 77
Augusta, 15, 18, 20, 22, 23, 24, 29, 48, 50
Ayer, N.C., 50, 57
William M., 75
Ayer's Junction, 111

Back Route, 15
Bancroft, Charles O., 89
Bangor, 5, 6, 8, 11, 15, 20, 21, 22, 23, 29, 31, 35, 36, 41, 45, 47, 50, 52, 55, 56, 57, 74, 102, 111, 132
Bangor & Aroostook Railroad, 62, 74, 98, 101, 102, 103, 104, 105, 107, 108, 109, 111, 112
Bangor & Katahdin Iron Works Railroad, 62, 101, 102, 111
Bangor, Old Town & Milford Railroad, 5
Bangor & Piscataquis Canal and Railroad, 5, 9
Bangor & Piscataquis Railroad, 35, 48, 50, 53, 56, 57, 62, 83, 101, 102
Bangor Punta Alegre Sugar Corp., 113
Bar Harbor, 111, 116
Baring, 67
Bath, 18, 25, 26, 29, 41, 45, 111
Belfast, 6, 46, 47, 48
Belfast & Moosehead Lake Railroad, 46, 47, 53, 111, 112
Belfast & Quebec Railroad, 6, 10
Benjamin, David, 25
Berwick, 36
South, 6, 8, 36
Bethel, 14
Bingham, 75, 111
Blake, Samuel H., 57
Blanchard, 101
Boston & Eastern Mill and Land Company, 6
Boston & Maine Railroad, 6, 8, 36, 38, 53, 58, 59, 60, 83, 84, 89, 96, 111, 112
Boston & Quebec Air Line Railroad, 75
Boston & Worcester Railroad, 5, 9
Bragg, Charles F., 98
Brewer, 57
Bridgton, 84
Bridgewater, 113
Bridgton & Harrison, 111, 112
Bridgton & Saco River Railroad, 84
Bronson, David, 24
Brooks, 47
Brown, John B., 31, 52
Brownville, 60, 102, 103
Brunswick, 15, 18, 25, 26, 27, 41, 113
Buckfield, 76
Buckfield Branch Railroad, 76
Bucksport, 56, 111
Bucksport & Bangor Railroad, 56, 57
Burleigh, Albert A., 98, 103
Buxton, 36

Calais, 67, 113
Calais & Baring Railway, 5, 67
Calais Railway, 5, 67
Cambridge, 48
Camp Ellis, 53
Canaan, 48
Canadian National Railway, 14, 112
Canadian Pacific Railroad, 50, 56, 57, 60, 61, 62, 75, 97, 98, 111
Canton, 76, 112, 113
Caribou, 97, 102, 103
Carrabassett & Canadian Railroad, 75
Carratunk, 20, 48
Chamberlain, George W., 23
China, 84
Chisholm, 76
Chisholm, Hugh J., 76
Churchill, James C. 22
Clapp, A.W.H., 31
Cobbosseecontee Railroad, 74
Coburn, Abner, 23, 52
Connor, William, 23
Corinna, 48
Cram, Franklin W., 98, 102, 104
Crocker, Ira, 22
Crowleys Junction, 112
Cumberland Junction, 52
Cummings, Nathan, 22
Cushman, Benjamin H., 25
Cutter, William, 23

Damariscotta, 41
Danville, 15, 52
Junction, 14
Debec Junction, 97
Deering Junction, 18
Deering, William, 31
Dexter, 46, 48, 60
Dexter & Newport Railroad, 46, 47, 60, 112
Dexter & Piscataquis Railroad, 60, 112
Dover, 46, 50, 60
Dunn, Reuben B., 52
Dwinel, Rufus, 23

Eastern Maine Railway, 57, 111, 112
Eastern Railroad, 6, 7, 8, 53, 54, 58, 96
East Millinocket, 107
Eastport, 67, 111, 113
Ellsworth, 56, 111
European & North American Railway, 5, 21, 22, 31, 35, 36, 50, 53, 56, 57, 62, 67, 97, 101, 102
Eustis Railroad, 83
Evans, George, 15

Fairbanks, H.N., 57
Fairfield, 22, 23, 24, 29, 30, 47, 48
Farmington, 25, 26, 27, 83, 84, 112

Farrar, Samuel, 23
Fish River Railroad, 103, 107
Fobes, Charles, 31
Fogg, Hiram H., 98
Fort Fairfield, 102
Fort Kent, 103, 107
Franklin County, 25
Franklin & Kennebec Railroad, 25
Franklin & Megantic Railroad, 83
Franklin, Somerset & Kennebec Railway, 84
Freeport, 15

Garcelon, Alonzo, 25
Gardiner, 6, 11, 15, 20, 25, 26
Gardiner, Robert Hallowell, 15
Georges Valley Railroad, 46
Gibson, Charles A., 98
Gilbert, Washington, 26
Gilbertville, 113
Glidden, William, 25
Gorham, 36
Grand Trunk Railway, 14, 18, 29, 39, 61
Great Falls & Conway Railroad, 8
Great Falls & South Berwick Branch Railway, 7, 8
Green Mountain Railway, 116
Greene, 25
Greenville, 96, 101, 102
Guilford Industries, 113, 114

Haines, William T., 75
Hall, James, 11
Hallowell, 15
Hamlin, Hannibal, 50, 57
Harmony, 83, 112, 113
Harrison, 84
Hartland, 48, 83, 113
Harwoods Crossing, 41
Hayford, William B. 57
Hereford Railway, 96
Hill, John F., 75
Hollis, 36
Houlton, 31, 62, 97, 102
Houlton Branch Railroad, 97
Howland, 113

International Railway of Maine, 62

Jay, 25
Jewell, Albert J., 46
Jones, John B., 26

Kendall's Mills (See Fairfield), 22
Kennebago, 77, 111
Kennebec Central Railroad, 83, 111
Kennebec & Portland Railroad, 6, 15, 18, 20, 22, 23, 24, 26, 29, 51, 55
Kennebec & Wiscasset Railroad, 48
Kennebunk, 53
Kennebunk & Kennebunkport Railroad, 53
Keyes, Elisha, 25
Kingfield & Dead River Railroad, 83
Kilbourne, William, 25
Kimball, William, 22
Kineo House, 84, 111
Kittery, 53
Knox Railroad, 46, 111
Knox & Lincoln Railroad, 41, 42, 45, 46, 48, 55, 57, 61

Lane, Giddings, 25
Leeds, 26, 27, 41
  Junction, 25, 26, 112
Leeds & Farmington Railroad, 27, 53
Levis & Kennebec Railroad, 50
Lewiston, 11, 15, 18, 25, 26
Lewiston & Auburn Railroad, 14
Lewis, Weston, 75, 83
Lewy's Island Railroad, 67
Libby, H.S., 31
Limerock Railroad, 46, 112
Limestone, 102
Little, Josiah, 11
Livermore Falls, 25, 76
Lockwood, Amos D., 52

Machiasport, 6
Machiasport Railroad, 6
Madison, 48, 74
Madrid Railroad, 83
Maine Central Railroad, 21, 23, 24, 27, 40, 45, 47, 48, 51, 52, 53, 54, 55, 56, 57, 58, 59, 62, 67, 74, 75, 76, 77, 83, 84, 89, 104, 107, 111, 112, 113
Maine, New Hampshire & Massachusetts Railroad, 6
Maine Railways Companies, 89
Maine Shore Line Railroad, 57
Mattawamkeag, 31, 35, 56, 62, 113
Maxcy, Josiah S., 83
McAdam Junction, 97
McDonald, Morris, 89
McLellan, Edward, 23
Mechanic Falls, 14, 76
"Medford Cut-Off", 107
Medway, 107
Mellen, Charles S., 83
Mellon Timothy, 113
Messalonskee & Kennebec Railroad, 50
Milford, 31, 35, 56
Moluncus, 36
Monmouth, 25
Monson, 83, 102
Monson Railroad, 101, 112
Monticello, 113
Moor, Wyman B., 20
Moore, John, 67
Moosehead Lake, 6, 25, 46, 47, 50, 75, 84
Moosehead Lake Railway, 7
Morrill, Joseph, 24
Moses, Oliver, 26, 45
Mt. Desert Ferry, 57, 112

New Brunswick & Canada Railway, 97
New Brunswick Railway, 62, 97, 98
Newcastle, 41
Newport, 46, 48, 111
New York, New Haven & Hartford Railroad, 83, 89
Nobleboro, 41
Norridgewock, 48
North Anson, 75
Northern Maine Junction, 74, 105, 111, 113
Northern Maine Seaport Railroad, 74, 104, 105, 107
Norway Branch Railroad, 14

Oakfield, 113
Oakland, 48, 74
Old Orchard, 53, 54
Old Orchard Junction Railroad, 54
Old Town, 5, 50, 62, 74, 102, 103, 107, 111
Oquossoc, 76, 77, 111
Orchard Beach Railroad, 53
Otis, Ensign, 25
Oxford, 14

Packards, 113
Palmer & Machiasport Railroad, 6
Passadumkeag, 67

Patten, David, 26
George, M., 52
Patten & Sherman Railroad, 103
Peakes, Col. J., 60
Peck, Carson, 84
Penobscot, 56
Penobscot Bay & River Railroad, 45
Penobscot Railroad, 35
Penobscot & Kennebec Railroad, 15, 20, 21, 22, 23, 29, 30, 41, 47, 55
Penobscot & Lake Megantic Railroad, 56, 62
Penobscot, Lincoln & Kennebec Railroad, 41
Penobscot Shore Line Railroad, 61
Penobscot & Union River Railroad, 56
Phillips, 25, 83
Pickard, Thomas, 22
Pickering, George W., 20, 23
Piscataquis County, 5, 50
Pittsfield, 83, 112
Poor, John A., 9, 10, 11, 15, 20, 21, 22, 23, 31, 35, 36, 39, 52
Portland, 6, 8, 10, 11, 14, 15, 18, 21, 29, 31, 36, 38, 39, 60, 61, 76, 77, 125
South, 60
Portland & Kennebec Railroad, 23, 24, 30, 41, 47, 51, 52, 53
Portland & Ogdensburg Railroad, 38, 39, 55, 59, 60, 112
Portland & Oxford Central Railroad, 53, 76
Portland & Rochester Railroad, 36, 39, 55
Portland & Rumford Falls Railroad, 76, 79, 112
Portland & Rumford Falls Railway, 76, 112
Portland & Rutland Railroad, 31
Portland, Rutland, Oswego & Chicago Railway, 31
Portland, Saco & Portsmouth Railroad, 7, 8, 18, 20, 30, 53, 54, 58
Portland Terminal Company, 89
Portland Union Railway Station Company, 84
Preble, William Pitt, 11
Presque Isle, 97
Princeton, 67, 111

Quebec Central Railroad, 50, 75

Randolph, 83
Rangeley Lakes, 76
Rangeley Lakes & Megantic Railroad, 77
Rawson, James F., 52
Reed, Thomas B., 39
Rice, Richard D., 24, 51, 52
Richmond, 18, 41, 45
Ricker Hotel Co., 84
Ricker, John S., 57
Robie, Frederick, 31
Robinson, A.M., 50
Samuel I., 26
Rockland, 41, 45, 46, 84, 112, 113
Royal Junction, 113
Rumford Falls, 25, 76
Junction, 76, 112
Rumford Falls & Buckfield Railroad, 76
Rumford Falls & Rangeley Lakes Railroad, 76, 77, 111, 112

Sam-O-set Hotel, 84
Sandy River Railroad, 83
Sandy River & Rangeley Lakes Railroad, 83, 90, 111
Sanford, 36
Sanford & Eastern, 112
Schoodic Stream Railway, 107
Searsport, 74, 104
Sebasticook & Moosehead Railroad, 83
Seboois, 107
Shaw, Samuel P., 24
Shawmut, 113
Skowhegan, 6, 24, 48, 75, 112, 113
Smith, Benjamin E., 57
Edward, 5
Francis O.J., 20, 22, 23, 76
Samuel, 5
Solon, 75
Somerset Railroad, 48, 50, 53, 74, 75, 76, 83, 84
Somerset & Kennebec Railroad, 20, 22, 23, 24, 29, 48, 51, 53
South LaGrange, 74, 104, 107, 113
South Paris, 14
St. Albans, 48
St. Croix & Penobscot Railroad, 67, 74
St. Francis, 107
St. John & Maine Railway, 57, 62, 97
Stanley, George W., 22
Stetson, Charles, 50, 57
George, 50
Isaiah, 50
Stewart, T.J., 57
Strickland, Samuel P., 20
Sullivan family, 7
Surry, 56

Thomaston, 41
Timetables, 91, 92, 93, 94, 95, 96
Togus, 84
Topsham, 15
Totman, Ezra, 23
Treat, Ezekiel, 25
Tuttle, Lucius, 83

Unity, 6
U.S. Filter Corp., 113

Van Buren, 107, 113
Van Buren Bridge Company, 107
Vanceboro, 35, 36, 62, 112, 113
Veazie, Gen. Samuel, 5
Verrill, Harry M., 89

Wade, Levi C., 61
Wakefield, A.G., 50
Waldoboro, 41
Warren, 41
Washburn, 107
Washburn, Israel, 31
Washington County, 57
Washington County Railroad, 58, 67, 83
Waterville, 15, 18, 21, 22, 23, 29, 41, 46, 52, 48, 84, 111, 128
West, 48, 50
Waukeag, 112
Wellington, 83
Wescott, George P., 38
Westbrook 36
Whitefield, 48
Whitneyville, 6, 7
Whitneyville & Machiasport Railroad, 6
Williams, Reuel, 15, 20, 24
Wilson, Franklin A., 50, 57
Winn, 35
Winslow, 84
Winthrop, 15, 18
Wiscasset, 41, 48, 50, 74, 84
Wiscasset & Kennebec Railroad, 41
Wiscasset & Moosehead Lake Railroad, 48
Wiscasset & Quebec Railroad, 84
Wiscasset, Waterville & Farmington Railway, 84, 111
Wood, Black & Company, 14
Wood, John M., 20, 22, 23
Woods, Noach, 57
Woodland, 111

Yarmouth, 15, 18
Junction, 18
York Harbor & Beach Railway, 53
York & Cumberland Railroad, 18, 36

[LEFT:] **GT Pacific 5283 with Train 17 skips through fresh snow at Bryants Pond on February 22, 1956.** *470 Railroad Club collection*

[ABOVE:] **One of the impressive structures on the Rockland branch is this stone and girder lift bridge at Thomaston spanning the Mill River Branch. MEC GP38 254 is just out of Rockland in April 1978 with general merchandise and cement cars.** *Ron Johnson* [RIGHT:] **MEC 2-10-2 651 sends billowing smoke aloft as it pounds through Greene on April 19, 1942.** *Henry Preble*